Importing Revolution

by
William R. Hawkins

**The American Immigration Control Foundation, Monterey,
Virginia and United States Industrial Council Educational
Foundation, Washington, D.C.**

William R. Hawkins is president of the Hamilton Center for National Strategy. He is a former professor of economics and has published numerous articles in journals of political opinion.

Copies are available from:

American Immigration Control Foundation
PO Box 525
Monterey, VA 24465

The views expressed herein do not necessarily reflect the policies or positions of AICF and USICEF.

Contents

Foreword
by Samuel Francis

In the 1980s, conventional wisdom began to hold that "Marxism is dead everywhere except on American college campuses." Like much that passes for conventional wisdom, the claim was not exactly true, but by the end of the decade, with the overthrow of communist governments in the Soviet Union and Eastern Europe, the American university seemed to stand out as just about the only institution north of Havana and west of Pyongyang where you could easily locate anyone who openly admitted being a Marxist.

On American campuses, Marxism continued to flourish at the same time it was withering away in most other places. The cults of "Political Correctness," "multiculturalism," "Afrocentrism," feminism, "gay and lesbian studies," and similar ideologies and movements often harbored Marxist premises in one form or another, though they combined and tried to buttress those premises with a body of scholarship so shoddy it would have humiliated the original Bolsheviks themselves, not to speak of those dead white males who were responsible for so much tyranny in the modern world, Karl Marx and Frederick Engels.

While most of the cults and movements gained notoriety in the 1980s as they threatened professional standards of serious learning and even the careers of students and teachers who fell afoul of their dogmas, there was another, similar cult that seemed to escape attention. All through the 1970s and 1980s, almost from the time when the Immigration Act of 1965 abolished the "national origins" standard for immigration into the United States, a small band of Marxists and left-leaning radicals was working to exploit the new law and the new masses of immigrants that soon began to arrive in its wake as political weapons against the United States.

Now at last, William R. Hawkins has exposed and documented their work—who they were, how they operated, and (most important) who paid for it. His answers ought to give a lot of Americans pause as they start considering what has been going on while their attentions were directed elsewhere.

The constant theme of Mr. Hawkins in this thoroughly researched monograph is the conjunction of two, seemingly contradictory and hostile forces—the Marxist socialism of the "immigration lobby," which includes not only the political activists among the immigrants themselves but also their army of lawyers and propagandists, and the financial power accumulated by American capitalism that has been stashed away in large tax-exempt foundations.

Specifically, Mr. Hawkins shows how leftists, Marxists, and anti-Americans in the immigration lobby were supported and encouraged by one of the largest and wealthiest philanthropic institutions in the world, the Ford Foundation. Virtually from the beginnings of the political side of the immigration movement, Ford has devoted immense sums to it to assist its legal, "educational," and policy-influencing activities, and at almost every node and juncture of Ford's philanthropy, the recipients have been partisans of the far left.

Thus, Mr. Hawkins shows that MALDEF, the Mexican American Legal Defense and Educational Fund, was established with grants of $2.2 million from the Ford Foundation in 1968 and that Ford awarded more than $5,500,000 to MALDEF from 1983 through 1988. In 1986, Ford trustee Harriet Schaffer Rabb joined the board of MALDEF, thus wedding the two organizations in a marriage that could spawn only more mischievous offspring. If MALDEF were simply a "humanitarian" effort, this level of support might be unremarkable, but the fact is that from its very origins, as Mr. Hawkins also shows, MALDEF's legal work has been under the control of members of the radical-left National Lawyers Guild and like-minded organizations.

Thus, he writes, "MALDEF's principal immigration policy advisor during the 1980s was Linda Wong, also a prominent member of the NLG [National Lawyers Guild] National Immigration Project." Wong was also supportive of the so-called "Sanctuary" movement, which in the early 1980s devoted itself to smuggling illegal aliens into the United States, ostensibly for humanitarian purposes but really for the goal of subverting U.S. anti-communist policies in Central America. Sanctuary itself may originally have been conceived by Guild activists in 1980, and certainly it received their support throughout its history. Here too the money trail leads to the doors of the Ford Foundation, which between 1984 and 1989 gave $2.6 million to organizations involved in Sanctuary activities.

The financial links between Ford, MALDEF, and Sanctuary are merely a few examples of the connections Mr. Hawkins uncovers, and it is impossible to reflect on the pattern he has exposed without thinking of the famous (though probably apocryphal) remark attributed to Lenin to the effect that when the communists got around to hanging the capitalists, the capitalists themselves would sell them the rope. What even Lenin never fully anticipated, perhaps, is that the capitalists would forego the hope of profiting from their own execution and actually donate the rope and endow research toward constructing a better noose. That, in a word, is what the Ford Foundation has done with its money.

What much of Mr. Hawkins's research points toward is the existence for some years of a coordinated strategy on the part of the Marxist left and its cohorts to use immigration as an instrument of national subversion. As he notes, there is a close affinity between what some proponents of large-scale Mexican and Latin American immigration say and what classic Marxist-Leninists have written about American "imperialism," and some of the former have actually worked for the disintegration of the United States as a unified nation-state.

One such activist intones that "today the movement is toward separatism, with the goal of increasing awareness in a small but unified Chicano community that is inner-directed instead of being directed from without. . . . The Chicano people seek self-determination in what were formerly and rightfully their lands, not those of 'Anglo-America.' " Some years ago, surveying similar trends in a monograph for the London-based Institute for the Study of Conflict[1], I suggested the term "demographic warfare" to denote the concept of instigating and exploiting mass population movements from one nation to another (e.g., the Mariel Boatlift of 1980) for the purposes of political and social destabilization, and information discussed here by Mr. Hawkins appears to be consistent with that interpretation of the Mariel phenomenon. If Fidel Castro can understand it, there's no reason others couldn't think of it all by themselves, and indeed, it is not unusual for one or another of the illuminati of immigration to betray such plans in their more unguarded moments.

Destabilization need not be carried out with violence or under the control of hostile foreign powers. Thus, one of the quotations culled by Mr. Hawkins directly illustrates this tactic of ethnic mobilization for political purposes: "If current immigration and birthrates continue, by the year 2000, Latinos will be the largest ethnic group in the United States. Since 85 percent of all Spanish-speaking people are concentrated in nine states and twenty cities that control 193 (or 71 percent) of the electoral votes needed to win the Presidency, they constitute a critical swing vote in future elections."

This sentiment was not expressed by a foe of immigration fearful of the nation being swamped by hordes of Hispanics in alliance with liberal Democrats, but by Sheila Collins, national coordinator of The Rev. Jesse Jackson's Rainbow Coalition, and Mr. Jackson's Operation PUSH also just happened to be well-endowed by the Ford Foundation. In short, the massive immigration into the United States in the last two decades serves the interests of radical political agendas that most Americans find abhorrent, and elements of the extreme left have pushed and supported it for precisely that purpose.

These agendas include not only the actual destabilization and dismemberment of the United States, as evidenced by the remarks quoted above, but also possible terrorist and criminal activities directed toward that end, as well as peaceful (more or less) mobilization of immigrant constituencies for political purposes and Sanctuary's manipulation of immigrants to subvert U.S. foreign policy. But they also include another dimension of cultural subversion, to be implemented through schools, universities, and religious organizations. The advantage of this approach is that it is non-violent and legal and indeed relies to a large extent on American pluralism and liberalism to carry out its goals.

Thus, Jim Corbett, often called the "father of the Sanctuary movement," discussed this strategy explicitly some years ago. "With respect to this kind of strategic advantage," Mr. Corbett said of Sanctuary's ulterior goals, "non-violent insurgency is actually far superior to guerrilla insurgency because it requires no arms supply—just government reaction—in order to maintain momentum and establish the leverage needed for social jujitsu." The concept of "social jujitsu," indeed, is crucial for an understanding of the long-term strategy of the modern left, which no longer depends on bomb-throwing and KGB subsidies as much as it does on Antonio Gramsci's designs for a "long march through the institutions" for the purpose of acquiring "cultural hegemony."

It is precisely by using the institutions of American society against themselves that the left's "social jujitsu" operates to acquire "cultural hegemony," just as real jujitsu works by using the strength, size, and power of an opponent against him. The great advantage that cultural dominance has for whoever obtains it is that it allows them to determine the agenda, to define issues and the terms of public discussion, so that debates are won before they are even engaged. As the ancient Chinese strategist Sun Tzu noted in a famous remark, "To win one hundred victories in one hundred battles is not the acme of skill. To subdue the enemy without fighting is the acme of skill."[2]

Immigration offers a bottomless pit of opportunities for just this kind of cultural subversion because Americans of all political convictions, right and left, find it difficult to discuss immigration apart from slogans about being "a nation of immigrants," taking in the teeming masses, and so forth. As long as these are the terms that frame the immigration debate, it will remain a battle lost before it is even fought, and indeed this is one reason it has not been fought before now. In order to cut through and redefine the terms of the debate, there will have to be some fresh thinking about immigration and its effects on American culture and political life.

There are indeed groups and individuals that are guilty of fresh thinking on the subject—The Rockford Institute's *Chronicles,* the Federation for American Immigration Reform, the American Immigration Control Foundation, the U.S. Business and Industrial Council, experts and authors like Lawrence Auster, Peter Brimelow of *Forbes,* Wayne Lutton, and Mr. Hawkins himself—but the predictable response, from left as well as right, to most of their labors has been to mutter about "xenophobia," "nativism," and "racism." Since these labels usually mean nothing, it is seldom possible to respond to such charges definitively, and indeed the main purpose of making the charges in the first place is to make certain that no debate takes place.

One piece of evidence of the meaningless of such labels comes from a recent opinion survey of attitudes toward immigration among Hispanics conducted by the Latino National Political Survey. Among non-Hispanic whites who are U.S. citizens,

74 percent agreed or strongly agreed with the statement, "There are too many immigrants." Among Mexican-American U.S. citizens, 75 percent agreed or strongly agreed, while 66 percent of Cubans and 79 percent of Puerto Ricans agreed or strongly agreed. Among non-U.S. citizens, 73 percent of Cubans and 84 percent of Mexicans agreed or strongly agreed. The point is that Hispanics themselves are opposed to more immigration, at least as strongly and maybe even more than non-Hispanic whites, so it makes little sense to accuse Hispanics of "racism" toward their own ethnic group.[3]

A debate that has taken place is the one over "multiculturalism" and curricula based on it in schools and universities, and both liberals, like Arthur M. Schlesinger Jr., and conservatives of all kinds have generally agreed on the dangers to serious education it represents. What few have noticed, however, is that multiculturalism is a problem at all only because of the long-term effects of massive immigration from non-Western societies in the last two decades and that the apologists for multiculturalism have themselves insisted on the importance of immigration as a principal reason for the imposition of multiculturalist curricula. Thus, the now-notorious "Curriculum of Inclusion" proposed in 1989 for the New York state school system explicitly invoked the cultural changes in New York life that massive immigration is causing:

> The fact is that in New York the presence of a heterogeneous student body is a statewide condition, not just an urban condition. One half of the counties of New York state have at least one school district with over 10 percent non-European American enrollment; furthermore, over 22 percent of all school districts in the state have over 10 percent non-European American enrollment.

and a similar New York multiculturalist curriculum proposal in 1991, "One Nation, Many Peoples," made much the same argument.

> Since the 1960s, however, a profound reorientation of the self-image of Americans has been under way. Before this time the dominant model of the typical American had been conditioned primarily by the need to shape a unified nation out of a variety of contrasting and often conflicting European immigrant communities. But following the struggles for civil rights, the unprecedented increase in non-European immigration over the last two decades and the increasing recognition of our nation's indigenous heritage, there has been a fundamental change in the image of what a resident of the United States is.
>
> With this change, which necessarily highlights the racial and ethnic pluralism of the nation, previous ideals of assimilation to an Anglo-American model have been put in question and are now slowly and painfully being set aside.

Immigration, in other words, is held to be incompatible with retention of the traditional "Anglo-American" model or identity of the United States, and there is little doubt that this argument is valid. Indeed, the cultural homogeneity of the American people at the time of the adoption of the U.S. Constitution was held by John Jay and other Framers to be an indispensable condition of national political unity. In Federalist No. 2, Jay wrote that

> Providence has been pleased to give this one connected country, to one united people, a people descended from the same ancestors, speaking the same language, professing the same religion, attached to the same principles of government, very similar in their manners and customs, and who, by their joint counsels, arms and efforts, fighting side by side throughout a long and bloody war, have nobly established their general Liberty and Independence.

In so far as the immigration into the United States of culturally disparate peoples removes the cultural unity that is the foundation of national political unity, then, immigration must be seen as a threat to the United States as a coherent and sovereign nation, and since the unity of which Jay wrote and which has pertained ever since has been essentially an Anglo- and Euro-American one, the immigration of large numbers of non-European peoples must be seen as incompatible with the fundamental cultural and political identity of the United States.

Any nation or politically and culturally unified society must define itself in large part through a shared past and a determination to preserve and continue the achievements of its ancestors, and the introduction of large numbers of people who do not have the same ancestors must necessarily dilute its sense of a common past and of national unity. How indeed would it be possible today for Lincoln to speak of ''our forefathers,'' as he did at Gettysburg, without being condemned for ignoring or belittling the contributions of more recent Americans whose forefathers had nothing to do with what the forefathers of Americans in 1863 had accomplished?

Why, indeed, should a West or an America that defines itself exclusively in terms of ''pluralism,'' ''diversity,'' ''tolerance,'' ''the open society,'' and ''equality'' expect masses of immigrants to abandon their native cultures and adopt those of the West or America? Non-Western immigrants may find the affluence of American capitalism, the gratification and entertainment of American pop culture, and the glamour of political power in American mass democracy preferable to those of their own cultures, but why should Americans expect Asians, Africans, and Latin Americans to identify with the deeper symbols, institutions, and achievements of the West, from the wars of the Greeks against the Persians to the conquest of the American Plains or from the Ptolemaic system of astronomy to the Big Bang theory of modern astrophysics?

Since a good deal of Western and American civilization revolves around the political and military conquest or defeat of non-Western enemies, it is hard to see how these triumphs of the West can be retained as positive accomplishments in the midst of a student population composed of large non-Western fragments. There can be little question that the multiculturalists are logically right in drawing from the premise of massive non-Western immigration into the United States the conclusion that traditional Western and American self-images and models must be at least qualified if not abandoned. The proper response to their argument, if Western culture is to be preserved as the main part of the school curriculum, is not to challenge their logic but to challenge the premise—that is, to halt or severely curtail the immigration that is at the root of much of the anti-Western multiculturalist strategy and which provides a never-ending stream of constituents for multiculturalist energies and anti-American agendas.

But in order to curb immigration, it is necessary first to assert the existence, integrity, and legitimacy of the Western and American way of life—to assert, in other words, the legitimacy of a "we" against the demands of a "they." Liberal and neoconservative bleatings about "pluralism" and "diversity" will do nothing to identify a core of Western and American values, habits, and institutions that distinguish us from the non-Western and non-American cultural fragments that suddenly appear at our door demanding that we change the architecture of the whole house. Until Americans, left and right, are more willing to assert their own cultural identity and distinctiveness as a people and a nation, they will be unable to mount any effective or persuasive argument why "our" way of life should prevail over others that are proposed as alternatives or even to claim that "we" have a way of life at all.

What William Hawkins has accomplished in this meticulous study of the political exploitation of immigration and immigrants as well as exploitation of the vulnerabilities of American society by the far left is to show that many of the forces pressing for more immigration, more legal rights for immigrants, and more social services and political power for immigrants are not well disposed to the American way of life in any sense, that in fact they are and have been intent on subverting it and are enemies of it. His study is therefore a critical step in informing Americans that we and our way of life do indeed have enemies, and once we learn that, we may be able someday to get around to figuring out how and why those enemies should be defeated and how and why we the American People should survive and flourish.

ENDNOTES

1. Samuel T. Francis, "Illegal Immigration—A Threat to U.S. Security," *Conflict Studies,* No. 192 (October, 1986), pp. 16–17.

2. Sun Tzu, *The Art of War,* trans. Samuel B. Griffith (Oxford: Oxford University Press, 1963), p. 77.

3. Roberto Suro, "Hispanic Pragmatism Seen in Survey," *New York Times,* December 15, 1992, p. A20.

Chapter One
Americans Decide on Immigration Reform

Neither the overnight visitor, the unfriendly agent of a foreign power, the resident diplomat, nor the illegal entrant, can advance even a colorable constitutional claim to a share in the bounty that a conscientious sovereign makes available to its own citizens and some of its guests.

—U.S. Supreme Court, *Mathews v. Diaz*, 1976 [1]

Immigration is a deeply emotional issue. It has flared up over the past twenty years with unusual acerbity, culminating in two major legislative acts by Congress: the 1986 Immigration Reform and Control Act, and the immigration reform act of 1990. As with most products of the gridlocked 1980s Congress, these bills turned out mostly to be grandiose products of compromise that solved few problems. Perhaps Congress was incapable of grappling with the fundamental questions that lie at the very heart of the debate: What is a citizen of the United States? Who may enter, and for what purpose? And, with what if any responsibilities incurred?

During this most recent round of the debate, one strident voice has risen to advocate the "open borders" approach to immigration policy. In general, open borders allows any person who so pleases to enter the United States. In supporting such a position, the open borders advocates ignore such factors as national origin, employable skills, or level of education in favor of an alleged higher human right to untrammeled migration. Raised against this song are a blended chorus of voices urging variations of some selective policy for admitting immigrants to become naturalized citizens.

Most amazing is how the United States ever became so entangled in this current debate. The issue at first came up in the late 1960s and early 1970s as a police matter, when it was becoming apparent that the Immigration and Naturalization Service (INS) was losing control of our national borders. Nearly fifteen years and five presi-

1

dents later, Congress in 1986 finally acted, but in the process was forced to deal with layers of explosive political questions related to alleged civil rights abuses, both for illegal aliens and for prospective employers. In the course of that action, and in what has transpired since, the debate had deepened into one about the nature and purpose of immigration itself.

This study will examine a few of the key groups engaged in that debate which champion the "open borders" solution to our current policy debates. The involvement in the controversy of many organizations, most notably the Mexican American Legal Defense and Educational Fund (MALDEF), the American Civil Liberties Union, and the National Center for Immigrants' Rights, is widely known. What many are unaware of, however, is that these groups are being bankrolled by some of the largest philanthropies in the country, most notably the Ford Foundation. In addition, much of their legal work is done by lawyer-advocates who moonlight as members of the National Lawyers Guild, an organization far to the left of the American political mainstream.

In addition, while some "open border" advocates truly aim to bring people to America to take advantage of the country's prosperity and standard of living, others harbor a deep antagonism toward the U.S. To them, immigrants are not viewed as "teeming masses" waiting to be lifted to a higher level of existence. They are merely a tool for accomplishing exactly the opposite—destabilizing and eroding America's current residents and their society—all in an effort to further their own self-consciously Marxist ends.

OPEN DOOR, CLOSED DOOR

While neither a history of immigration nor an analysis of enacted legislation, this book must pay some attention to both in order to see the strategy and the agenda motivating some key players in this debate.

America had kept open its doors to Europe with remarkably few barriers for its first century of life, and through those portals at Ellis and Angel Islands flowed tens of millions of new citizens into the near-empty spaces of the continent. America as the "melting pot" may be more ideal than reality, but America as the beckoning hope for the Old World's "teeming hordes" was definitely tangible. Even then, however, the idea of "open borders" was more historical myth than reality, since entry into the world's first new nation was never completely free. Selection, judgment, and requirements faced all those who wished to enter, and many were turned away.

After a century of the open door, a profound shift occurred in public sentiment toward immigration, following the First World War. At that time, a number of restrictions on immigration were erected that have been more constant than changing. Partly this was an aspect of the post-war isolationism that dominated public attitudes during the 1920s, but more than likely it was a response to the closing of the American "frontier" in the West.

While the size of the opening and the warmth of the welcome have shifted during this century, a threshold has been maintained putting constraints on the number of immigrants who could pass. In a still controversial set of decisions, the United States reversed itself on 19th-century immigration policy by accepting a system of quotas that insured a great predominance of Northern European immigrants. What had been a veritable flood became a mere trickle of new citizens from abroad. Immigration quickly sank to levels not seen since the 1830s; during the Great Depression, for the first time in American history, the number of people leaving exceeded the number of those entering.[2]

But following the Second World War, when the U.S. assumed the mantle of world leadership, American policy-makers turned away from those national distinctions that had categorically barred immigrants from entire continents. A wholesale revision of our immigration laws in 1965, the Hart-Celler Act, moved away from the historical standard of national origin, enlarging the ceiling (nearly doubled in size to 290,000 immigrants annually), and divided space equally between the Eastern and Western hemispheres. By declaring immigration available to all peoples, America accepted its present wave of immigration.

Today's migratory pattern differs vastly from any other we have known. During the years 1920 to 1960, Europe accounted for 60 percent of all immigration, South and Central America for 35 percent, and Asia for only 3 percent. But by 1975 these roles had reversed: Europe accounted for only 19 percent, while South and Central American immigrants had grown to 43 percent of the total, with Asia accounting for 34 percent.[3] Today fully 78 percent of new immigrants come from Latin or Asian countries.[4] In consequence entirely new ethnic communities have appeared across the nation. Aside from the refugees from the Indochina War, creating "Little Saigons," streams of Koreans, Thais, East Indians, black Africans, Caribbean Islanders, South Pacific Islanders, and others have appeared in our national midst, establishing their own communities.

While Asia now provides the second largest number of legal immigrants, many of whom like East Indians arrive with graduate degrees, Latin America—the greatest source of immigrants, many of whom are illegal—will have a significant influence on our economy. According to a recent Population Reference Bureau report, Hispanics, 20 million strong (8 percent of the total U.S. population) are the nation's second largest minority after blacks. A heavy birthrate and immigration (both legal and illegal) will increase Hispanic numbers to a share of nearly 30 million, or 11 percent, of the U.S. population by the turn of the century.[5]

Further, immigrants cluster rather than disperse evenly among the populace, just as with other ethnic groups. Most immigrants, especially Hispanics, have settled in the South and West. The number of foreign-born residents in the South grew by 120 percent in the 1970s, and by 97 percent in the West. Three states, California, New York and Texas, now account for more than one-half of all foreign born residents. By contrast, the entire Northeast and Midwest regions increased their number of foreign born by only 10 percent.

The U.S., like all wealthy and free nations, faces huge and growing pressures against its borders from those wanting entry. With regional conflicts rife across the entire globe, the world is awash in refugees more so than any time since 1945. Regional conflicts across the globe have swollen the flood of refugees. Some estimates place the count of displaced persons languishing in refugee camps at 15 million people, ranging from camps in Central America to the Horn of Africa. It is not Third World conflicts that cause all the problem. The new specter haunting Europe especially is the relaxation of political tension as the Iron Curtain rusts and crumbles. There has been an outpouring from former Communist countries unseen since 1945. These new "refugees" seek what others have historically sought, a new and better chance, economic opportunity, and personal or political liberty.

The U.S. received during the 1970s nearly half the world's immigrants.[6] Not since the first wave of immigration at the start of the century have so many foreign born arrived on our shores. While the high water mark had been 1901-09, when over eight million immigrants arrived, the 1980s topped that figure if illegal aliens are counted.

The impact of our new immigrants will be felt for many generations to come. Many who now arrive at our borders possess little employable skills for a highly advanced economy, but are let in anyway. This influx of unskilled laborers could not come at a worse time for the United States. During recent years, it has been apparent that the U.S. is experiencing a wrenching change in its labor market. A seller's market is beginning to emerge with employers desperate for skilled workers to fill jobs. However, these jobs will require skills of more demanding magnitude and more and better education—qualifications that many recent immigrants do not possess.[7]

A "SECOND DOOR"

Swelling the stream of legal and illegal immigration is the parallel policy of accepting refugees. By law "refugees" are those suffering political persecution perhaps even facing death in their homelands, and are therefore allowed almost immediate, unconditional entry into the United States. "Immigrants" are those seeking other rights like economic opportunity, and therefore must use the current means as prescribed by law. After World War II, with the United States assuming world leadership, a frequent recourse to refugee acts offered a haven to displaced peoples, such as those in China, the Baltic region, Yugoslavia, Hungary, Cuba, and Vietnam (all victims of Communist revolutions), as well as to those minorities victimized by Nazi Germany and by nationalist upheavals in the Third World. These refugees were considered allied peoples fleeing the same enemies that menaced the United States itself, and it was thought their addition would strengthen the United States in future conflicts with a common enemy.

This dual approach to immigration law effectively built a "second door" into the United States, with a second line of applicants seeking entry. People in the "regular,'' i.e., immigrant, line could be leapfrogged by those refugees adjudged needful and worthy of special, immediate treatment.

This loophole in immigration laws has been used to move huge numbers of people into the United States. In 1975, following the downfall of the American-supported government of South Vietnam, some 130,000 Indochinese refugees were resettled into the United States, and continuing Communist turmoil and political expulsions led to the eventual acceptance of more than 800,000 additional Indochinese refugees in 1978. In 1980, Fidel Castro in the famed Mariel boat lift ejected 125,000 of his unwanted to the shores of Florida, highlighting the use of immigration as a foreign policy weapon.

Although hundreds and thousands of immigrants took advantage of the refugee exemption to gain access to the United States, this number is only a fraction of the huge masses who have entered the country illegally. Predominantly Hispanic and from the northern reaches of Mexico, this flow of illegal immigration into the American Southwest increased exponentially during the 1960s. In 1965 the apprehensions of illegals by the Immigration and Naturalization Service reached 110,000; by 1971 this number had increased to 420,000; and by 1979 the number of apprehended illegal aliens had climbed to over 1,000,000. Of course, this is only the number of *apprehended* illegals, almost all of whom were deported back to their country of origin. The number of illegal immigrants who managed to evade the law could be four times as high.

EARLY MOVES TOWARDS IMMIGRATION REFORM

In 1971, during the 92nd Congress, House Immigration Subcommittee Chairman Peter Rodino (D-NJ) initiated a long series of hearings on the control of illegal immigration. Representative Rodino's subcommittee reported a bill four years later to prohibit employers from knowingly employing illegal aliens, because in the committee's words, ''the adverse impact of illegal aliens was substantial, and warranted legislation both to protect U.S. labor and the economy, and to assure the orderly entry of immigrants into this country.''

Endorsed by both the Nixon and Ford administrations, and passed twice by the Democratic House of Representatives, the legislation stalled in the Senate at the behest of agricultural growers who benefitted from employing illegals. The Ford administration settled on similar legislation in December, 1976, but it was not completed during the time remaining in Ford's term. In October 1977, the Carter administration introduced an immigration reform package, but the ensuing controversy led it to appoint a bipartisan select commission in 1978 to undertake a comprehensive review of U.S. immigration policy. [8]

The inauguration of President Jimmy Carter in 1977 was greeted with hope by those who wanted to see immigration policy shifted from a concern for the national interest of the United States toward a concern for the civil rights of immigrants; that is, from a "restrictionist" policy to a "protectionist" policy. Hispanic activists pressed their demands on the new president by claiming that it was votes from the Hispanic community that had tipped the balance in Texas, the state that had won the election for Carter.

Carter soon showed that his administration would adopt this policy shift. He first appointed a Mexican-American, Houston politico Leonel J. Castillo, a former Peace Corps worker and civil rights activist, as Commissioner of Immigration. Castillo soon made his new priorities clear when he addressed the graduates of the Border Patrol Academy in June 1977. He said that the border guards were "the front-line soldiers in President Carter's war against human rights violators. Possibly no other government agency has a greater opportunity to demonstrate to the world our concern for human rights than those of us in the immigration service." [9] As Ambassador to Mexico, Carter appointed former Wisconsin Governor Patrick J. Lacey, who had sponsored a liberal law to protect migrant workers, whether legal or illegal, from every form of social and economic exploitation and discrimination. In April 1977 Carter announced that some form of general amnesty for illegal aliens was "mandatory" in order to end their exploitation. [10] This sent a message that immigration was interpreted as a protectionist, instead of an enforcement, problem —that is, preventing illegal entries and enforcing immigration standards had taken a back seat to the legalization and protection of uninspected aliens and their families. [11]

But there were other, more traditional influences at work on the Carter Administration that pulled it away from pro-immigration forces. The President's Secretary of Labor, F. Ray Marshall, a former University of Texas economist, studied the problem of migratory labor both in the American Southwest and in Europe. Approaching the issue from the perspective of what America's labor needs were, Marshall sounded a tone, sympathetic to a position adopted by the AFL-CIO, that policy should protect American workers from foreign and immigrant competition that would lower their incomes, benefits or working conditions.

On August 4, 1977, President Carter submitted to Congress the recommendations of his presidential task force which attempted to please all groups at once. The proposals included:

- A mild employee penalty with a maximum fine of $1,000 per illegal alien *knowingly* hired (in Germany an employer who knowingly hired illegal aliens could be fined up to $20,000 for each worker and spend up to 5 years in jail [12]).

- An increase in funds for the Immigration Service and Border Patrol.

- Full immigration rights for all non-criminal aliens who had taken up permanent residence in the United States before December 31, 1970.

- Protected "guest worker" status to illegal aliens who had entered before December 31, 1976. For a five-year probation period, such workers could freely reside and work in the United States but could not vote, receive welfare or bring in their families. At the end of this period they could reapply for guest status or for full immigrant status.

- A raising of the limit on non-preference legal immigrants from Mexico and Canada from 20,000 to 50,000 per year. The Secretary of Labor could also, from time to time, allow an influx of temporary workers from Mexico for employment in agriculture (the emphasis here was on "temporary," 6 months or less, to avoid their movement to regular industrial or service jobs that would sustain them as permanent residents or put them in competition with native workers[13]).
- Finally, a greater enforcement of labor, safety, wage, health and tax standards on industries and regions with heavy concentrations of immigrants.

THE HESBURGH COMMISSION

However, instead of pulling together a coalition of groups, the Carter proposals upset every interest that wanted more for its own constituency and less compromise with others. Failing on this front, the president resorted to a standard political ploy; he set up in October 1978, a Select Commission on Immigration and Refugee Policy under Rev. Theodore M. Hesburgh, a respected champion of the civil rights movement.

In May 1981, after the departure of President Carter, the Select Commission reported its findings to a joint hearing of the House and Senate Immigration Subcommittees.[14] As had been intended by Congress, the Commission's recommendations represented a moderate consensus on the emotional and complicated subject of immigration. Hesburgh summed up this finding to the joint hearing:

Some among us, often moved by deeply religious values, ask the question, why should immigration be a problem? Why shouldn't people be free to move wherever they want to? We are all one species, all children of one God, and from the beginning of time human beings have been a curious migratory species. Why not let down the barrier of nation-states and permit people to move freely?

The questions almost answer themselves. Immigration is a problem because nearly all peoples believe in nationalism, in nation states in which to maintain the integrity of national ideologies, institutions, and boundaries. We believe this in the United States, too, but not for narrow nationalistic purposes only, but also because we believe that our Nation has become a symbol of the possibilities of freedom and the potentiality for justice in a world which sees little of either. . . The open society does not mean limitless immigration. Quantitative and qualitative limits are perfectly compatible with the concept of the open society.

I would ask that those who sympathize with the aspirations and the plight of illegal aliens. . .to think about the aspirations of Americans whose wages and standards are depressed by their presence, and also to think about those aliens themselves, not the ones who slip into the system and make a decent living while they adjust to a fugitive life in the shadows, but also the ones who are victimized by unscrupulous employers, those who die in the desert, or in the ballast tanks of ships, and the ones who are waiting patiently in line for so many years to come to the United States through the normal legal immigration channels. [15]

A broad range of groups, including the AFL-CIO, the National Association for the Advancement of Colored People, environmental and population-control advocates such as Zero Population Growth and the Federation for American Immigration Reform, and leading immigration scholars testified in basic support of the commission's recommendations.

One of those supportive scholars, Dr. Michael Teitelbaum, was at the time and remained a resident scholar at the Ford Foundation until his departure in 1982. Teitelbaum was the author of an influential 1980 article in *Foreign Affairs* entitled "Right vs. Right: Immigration and Refugee Policy in the United States," reprinted in the Congressional hearing record, in which he said:

> Beyond (and often behind) such deep-seated arguments of principle or ideology are real differences of perceived political or economic advantage and cost among different advocates and interest groups. Some employers see large-scale immigration (and especially continued illegal immigration) as providing an opportunity to increase their profits by 'disciplining' the work force as to wages, hours, conditions and productivity. Most labor leaders, not surprisingly, see the same phenomenon as undercutting the hard-won gains and future prospects of domestic workers. While some ethnic and religious leaders see large flows of immigrants of their own groups as adding to their political influence and economic power, others of the same groups see such flows as threatening the achievements and social advancement of already resident members. [16]

THE OPEN BORDERS LOBBY TAKES SHAPE

Agricultural employers, who benefitted from the availability of low-paid migrant agricultural workers, had killed all previous attempts at reform in the 1970s. They again testified in opposition to the proposed employer sanctions.

However, a new force, consisting of several organizations, appeared on the scene to denounce any realistic effort of immigration control. Instead of stressing pure economic considerations, their arguments stemmed more from the standpoint of human rights for immigrants. Three different groups rose to testify at the hearings.

First, the Mexican-American Legal Defense and Educational Fund (MALDEF), speaking for several other Hispanic organizations, argued that there was no immigration problem, that undocumented workers do not displace American workers. In addition, proposed employer sanctions would only cause employers to discriminate against Hispanic citizens, regardless of their legal status. MALDEF instead recommended that all illegal aliens be immediately legalized, that the limit on Mexican legal immigration be repealed, and that long-term development assistance be provided to Mexico. [17]

Next, the New York Civil Liberties Union also argued MALDEF's claim that proposed employer sanctions would cause employers to discriminate against Hispanic citizens. The New York ACLU also argued that the proposal would enhance the "sweeping power of surveillance by government over individual lives," and "could prove the irreversible last step in the loss of personal privacy. . ." [18] The American Civil Liberties Union testified to the same effect. [19]

Finally, a formal coalition of groups organized in January 1981, to oppose the restrictionist aspects of the Select Commission's findings provided its lengthy criticism of them. This coalition was organized by Rick Swartz of the Alien Rights Law Project of the Lawyers Committee for Civil Rights Under Law, with the assistance of the National Lawyers Guild's National Immigration Project. Other members and groups endorsing the testimony included the American Friends Service Committee, MALDEF, and the Immigration Law Clinic of the Columbia University School of Law. [20]

The coalition provided 13 pages of dense argument, drafted by Amit Pandya of the Institute for Public Representation of Georgetown University Law Center and the Washington, D.C. representative for the National Center for Immigrants' Rights, which attacked employer sanctions as discriminatory and ineffective, criticized improved border enforcement, and urged development assistance for sending countries. [21]

At the same time that this coalition was trashing the Commission's report, however, polls indicated that a broad national consensus had formed which fully backed the findings. A Roper Poll conducted in 1980 found that 91 percent of Americans supported an all-out effort to stop illegal entry into the United States, and 80 percent supported reductions in legal immigration. [22] In June 1981, the new administration under President Ronald Reagan completed its review of the Democratic-established Select Commission, and also endorsed most of the recommendations.

The Commission had warned that failure to control illegal immigration would inevitably turn public opinion against *legal* immigration. In the introduction to the Commission's report Chairman Hesburgh stated bluntly that "U.S. immigration policy is out of control." With strong public support behind an immigration reform effort, and with a bipartisan consensus building behind the effort, it was clearly time to act.

Chapter Two
Ford Foundation Enters The Fray

"Mr. Chairman, the employees of the Immigration and Naturalization Service . . . are frustrated . . . . Give us a law we can enforce; allow us the pride of a job well done."
—Michael G. Hapold, INS Council [1]

During the years 1983 through 1988, the Ford Foundation granted MALDEF more than $5.5 million. [2] Ford Foundation Trustee Harriet Schaffer Rabb joined the MALDEF Board in 1986. [3]

Public policy analysis, especially in an area so politically intricate as immigration, can rarely attribute the turning of events to any one organization's efforts. Still, it is significant that the Ford Foundation has funded with enormous sums of money most of the non-business opponents of immigration reform. Moreover, the Foundation actively solicits other public and private donors to the same end. [4]

Ford is by far the largest foundation in the United States, both in terms of assets and of grants. [5] While many of its grant areas are balanced, at least from the viewpoint of mainstream liberalism, its bankrolling of "open border" advocacy policy is sharply one-sided, and often extremist. At one time the Foundation was particularly active in movements to limit immigration into the United States, [6] often invoking notions of the so-called "tragedy of the commons" to support the right of a sovereign nation, for demographic and economic reasons, to limit its membership. [7] However, under the leadership of new Foundation President Franklin Thomas in 1981, large scale support for world population control was phased out completely. [8] Since then, the philanthropy has only concentrated on those groups advocating the drastic open borders agenda.

Ford played the leading role in founding, and building, what are now the major Hispanic-based organizations. By its own account (in 1984), "The Ford Foundation's interest in the Hispanic community dates back to the sixties, when efforts on behalf of the civil rights of blacks and other minorities first gained prominence in domestic programming. In civil rights, for example, the Foundation helped establish the Mexican-American Legal Defense and Educational Fund [MALDEF] in 1968. In the area of community and economic development, Foundation support in 1968 helped create the National Council of La Raza . . . which has also become an effective voice for Hispanics.''[9]

One published study shows that in 1977/8, the Ford Foundation provided over half (54 percent) of the support for Hispanic-oriented social action. ''The Ford grants were nine times greater in value than the foundation providing the next highest amount,'' Blanca Facundo says in a major study of philanthropic funding of Hispanic movements. ''MALDEF obtained almost one-third of all monies given to Hispanic-controlled agencies.''[10] Another Hispanic study shows that in 1981 and 1982 Ford provided 37.7 percent of all monies for Hispanics, and that MALDEF received 47 percent of all such funds.[11]

Among certain Hispanic leaders, particularly those at MALDEF, there is a desire to make open immigration the civil rights issue of the 1990s. As Dr. Teitelbaum suggested, ''[S]ome Chicano leaders strongly oppose any measures to reduce such immigration. A minority of radical leaders openly refuse to recognize the legitimacy of the U.S.-Mexico border . . . Others favor continued illegal flows in the expectation of enhanced Chicano political power . . . .''[12] As noted earlier, contrary to the endless ruminations of Ford's favored activists nearly every major poll of Hispanic-American opinion shows a strong majority *supporting* employer sanctions and reducing illegal immigration.[13]

Another intellectual constellation influencing the Foundation on matters of immigration policy was well described by Dr. Teitelbaum:

> In recent years, various groups have pushed the case further, contending that the 'right to immigrate' should be accepted as a part of individual human rights, seeking to redefine the term refugee to include 'economic refugees' escaping poverty, or urging a vision of a new world order of open borders.[14]

FORD'S WHITE PAPER

At first the Ford Foundation's interest in immigration matters was humanitarian, not political. Great assistance was given in helping resettle displaced persons after World War II, and further help was provided in helping resettle Indochinese refugees. Not until 1980 did Ford express an institutional interest in immigration policy in a paper drafted by deputy vice president Francis X. Sutton, as Reverend Hesburgh's Select Commission held hearings across the country.[15] Additionally, Ford refused to endorse the moderate views of its resident expert, Michael Teitelbaum, who is widely considered one of the leading immigration scholars in the United States. Not surprisingly, Dr. Teitelbaum's relations with the Foundation quickly soured, and he parted with the Foundation in 1982.[16]

In August 1983, Ford published a crucial working paper called ''Refugees and

Migrants: Problems and Program Responses." [17] This extraordinary paper quickly cleared any remaining confusion about the Foundation's true agenda on immigration policy. Like all documents of this nature, "Refugees and Migrants" is carefully worded in neutral language, as if the Foundation were funding an all-sided exploration of this complex issue. However, on closer reading, and particularly with the benefit of retrospection, the call is made for vast intervention in the arena of immigration and refugee policy—not for conventional humanitarian activity—but to advance the social and political agenda of immigration activists. In general, the publication lays bare an extreme and controversial set of policy assumptions that the Ford Foundation adopted.

The Ford document makes absolutely no distinction whether an immigrant has entered the country legally or illegally; indeed, throughout the paper even the distinction between refugee and migrant is collapsed. "As in past periods of major influx there is a widespread belief that the country is being 'overrun' by aliens, a perception, or misperception, reinforced by government statements that the United States has 'lost control of its borders' "(p.10). This irrational reaction is common to the developed world, according to the paper: "Similar perceptions and reports, reflecting a hostile popular attitude toward refugees and especially toward undocumented aliens, are also prevalent in other countries."(p.11) In short: for one to support the admission of refugees but oppose illegal immigration, as Father Hesburgh proposed, is an inconsistent, even "hostile" position under Ford's analysis.

The only immigration "problem" discernible from Ford's working paper is that the United States fails to admit sufficient immigrants and fails to accord sufficient "rights" to those who do enter, especially illegal aliens. Furthermore, there are no legitimate labor, population, minority, cultural or national security interests in limiting immigration—or if such interests exist, they are purely malicious. The paper believes that the desires and wants of immigrants and potential immigrants are interests that need to be advanced in our society. Conversely, American citizens' support for limiting immigration (confirmed in poll after poll) is an unfounded, misguided "perception," unworthy of Foundation support.

The concerns of the United States and other developed nations about increasing immigration, are founded in "misperceptions." "Racism," "xenophobia," and "fear," are the words Ford chooses to describe those advocating limited immigration (p. 11). Additionally, American laws distinguishing between citizens, legal immigrants, and illegal aliens, for example, are only a benighted pretext for placing unfair restrictions on "refugee and migrant rights."

"Refugees and Migrants" also calls for extension of the same constitutional rights guaranteed to naturalized citizens "to all aliens who have entered the United States, regardless of the legality of their presence" (p.19). Although most observers would agree that fair treatment for illegal aliens is a desirable and even noncontroversial goal, the full extension of the constitutional rights and entitlements to any alien who manages to find his way across the border is a contentious proposition at best. This distinction, however, is completely lost in the board room of the Ford Foundation.

The solution to the immigration "problem" is laid out in a three-part strategy. The first part of the proposed strategy was to fund research and policy analysis "from a community of respected independent scholars" in order to counter "misperceptions" among the general public. Although some of this research might be considered neutral (i.e. actually produced by "independent scholars"), more still was evidently commissioned with the expectation of predetermined conclusions favorable to Ford's position. Not surprisingly there were no research projects that recommended employer sanctions, a strengthened Border Patrol, or any other kind of restriction or reform.

Second, "Refugees and Migrants" suggested funding public education and dissemination of information. "The dissemination of balanced information on refugees and migrants could result in broader public understanding of the need for protections and programs on their behalf"(p. 48). This involves building ethnic coalitions, holding public forums, and informing aliens of "the rights and entitlements available to them—information that governments often fail to provide for fear of attracting too many applicants"(p. 49). Like the research project, many of the organizations funded by the Foundation have well-established positions hostile to immigration control. "Such coalitions enable . . . groups to respond more effectively to statements that incorrectly portray their circumstances and to actions that limit the exercise of their rights"(p. 50).

Third, the report recommended advocacy and litigation in favor of illegal immigrants. It proposed that this would be accomplished primarily through establishing minimum standards of treatment for apprehended illegal aliens and asylum claimants, monitoring proposed or enacted immigration reforms, subjecting the Immigration and Naturalization Service, as well as the entire Executive branch and Congress, to "judicial scrutiny," and expanding international protection norms. This last step has been the most effective for Ford and its allies, producing a firestorm of well-organized litigious red tape that has rendered the 1986 Immigration Control Act a dead letter, and everyday enforcement of border control impractical.

The Foundation's strategy has been straightforward: Carefully target funding for organizations which would undertake to refute any academic or public opinion in favor of restricting immigration. The funded "advocacy" groups would resist passage of immigration reform legislation, restrict the powers of the Immigration and Naturalization Service, seek to enact local ordinances forbidding local government cooperation with INS, work to blur the distinction between illegal immigrant and refugee, and so on. A coordinated attack involving formidable lobbying, media, local government, and scholarly and judicial resources, was launched and continues to this day.

In official documents such as "Refugees and Migrants" the Ford Foundation disguises a position that is fundamentally extreme with ambiguous, obfuscating bureaucratic prose that misleads the public—and perhaps even the trustees. Foundation staff is surely aware that the mainstream view differs from its own, given the excellent work of former Ford program officer Michael S. Teitelbaum. Yet the definitely one-sided "Refugee and Migrants" program is regularly described in legitimizing terms such as "broaden understanding of problems," "clarify the rights of aliens," and "promote balanced discussion of refugee and migrant issues."

Ford Foundation President Franklin Thomas, in a 1984 address to the Cooper Union, conceded that "America is the primary receiver of migrants who seek a permanent home. From every point on the immigration compass, the United States is Magnetic North. And, for every one that makes it here, there are hundreds who are desperately eager to follow. Given the state of the world, the pressures will be toward larger rather than smaller pools of potential migrants." [18] What better argument for a prudent approach to immigration policy? Thomas goes on, with what would seem to the careless listener to be a fair and balanced approach, detailing the concerns of restrictionists and expansionists. Yet the crucial topic of illegal immigration is not *once* mentioned, and careful attention to the text shows that Thomas sides with the expansionists: "Free migration represented a gamble with destiny that America has decisively won . . . . I believe that the new migration will in the long run be a positive force." There is not the slightest hint in the address that the Foundation had decisively intervened politically on one side of the issue; rather, its programs would be directed to assist "newcomers" and promote assimilation.

THE BATTLE JOINED: SIMPSON-MAZZOLI

The Ford Foundation barged into the political fray as a Congressional committee finished digesting the findings of the Reverend Hesburgh's Select Commission on Immigration and Refugee Policy. The product of the committee's labor was the introduction of the Immigration Reform and Control Act on March 17, 1982. The legislation was known generally as the Simpson-Mazzoli bill after its sponsors, Senator Alan K. Simpson, a conservative Republican from Wyoming, and Representative Romano L. Mazzoli, a moderate Democrat from Kentucky. Both men served on the Judiciary Committees of their respective chambers.

The bill, like the Commission report, tried to forge common ground with both sides of the immigration debate. Although it had provisions for strengthening the country's Border Patrol, it also doubled the annual legal immigration ceiling from Mexico and Canada to 40,000 each. Included was an additional provision that either country could fill any unused slots in the other's quota—a benefit to Mexican immigrants, as Canadians moving to the U.S. seldom topped 10,000 a year. Amnesty was also granted to all illegal aliens already in the country prior to January 1, 1980. A fine of up to $10,000 could be levied for each illegal alien knowingly hired by an employer. Although Simpson-Mazzoli was more restrictive than the legislation President Carter had proposed, it still maintained America's position as the world's most open and liberal society on immigration issues.

The bill also contained a guest worker program that placed no limit on the number of temporary workers allowed in the United States. President Reagan had proposed a guest worker program in July 1981, that would have allowed as many as 50,000 workers to stay in the U.S. for as long as nine months to a year. However, the Labor Department could expand the number of guest workers whenever it determined that there was a need for increased labor. This guest worker provision drew fire from left-wing opponents. James D. Cockcroft, a Rutgers professor and Ford Foundation grantee who, writing from a staunchly Marxist perspective, argued that "There is no hint that such a program would do anything other than allow employers—operating through their associations and the Labor Department—to control and regulate the migratory flow in their favor . . . . Nor was there mention of the fact that the Reagan 'guest worker' program would tend to force American workers' wages down in the same way they had been forced down under the bracero program." [19]

The Simpson-Mazzoli bill became the focal point of the immigration debate for the next four years. It encountered many seemingly fatal set-backs over its long road to passage in 1986 and was amended constantly. However, in the end it was still based on its original three key elements: employer sanctions, amnesty and a guest worker program. Every liberal-left organization involved in immigration issues took shots at it. However, the fact that such massive and well-funded lobbying could be overcome to pass a major piece of legislation (even in watered-down form) attested to the strong need felt among the general public, finally reflected in congressional action, that a serious problem existed along the nation's southern border.

THE "OPEN BORDERS" LOBBY ATTACKS

The heaviest criticism of Simpson-Mazzoli was directed at the use of employer sanctions. Opponents usually tried to turn the issue into one of civil rights, claiming that sanctions would require all nonwhite workers, despite their status to prove they were not illegal aliens. Simpson-Mazzoli, however, required employers to obtain proof of citizenship for *all* new hires regardless of appearance, race, sex, or any other characteristic.

Sanction foes also pointed to the thriving underground industry of providing illegals with fake documents. Dr. Kitty Calavita of the University of California-San Diego's Program in United States-Mexican Studies made the dubious claim that employer sanctions would actually lead to the "double criminalization" of illegal workers, the first crime being crossing the border, the second the acquisition and use of bogus papers! [20]

So common was the use of phony Social Security cards and birth certificates that it was claimed that employer sanctions would lead firms to reject any foreign looking (i.e., Hispanic) job applicant for fear that the documents provided by the job-seeker would subsequently prove to be fake, making the employer vulnerable to penalty. Alternatively, it was asserted that an employer could use the threat of arrest and deportation against an illegal worker or applicant in order to pressure him into taking a lower wage, putting in longer hours or submitting to sub-standard working conditions.

The obvious remedy for this problem that supporters of Simpson-Mazzoli pointed out is a national identification card that could not be easily copied. While no ID system is fool-proof, the credit card industry and federal agencies have developed methods to minimize the ability of all but the most sophisticated counterfeiters to copy credit cards. A common national ID would also eliminate the confusion arising from non-common identification such as state driver's licenses, as confusion can only aid the phony document business.

However, since those involved in the "open borders" campaign see themselves as the protectors of those engaged in illegal immigration, they would have nothing to do with a secure system of identification. Herman Baca, a far-left Chicano leader, said they would "lead to an increase in violence and to the creation of an apartheid-type system for Chicanos."[21] Jose Trevino of the League of United Latin American Citizens (LULAC) alleged that "[i]t institutes identification practices comparable to Nazi Germany and South Africa."[22]

Not mentioned is the fact that most nations, including most democracies, have developed ID systems far more comprehensive than that of the United States. But the immigration lobby benefitted by falsely maintaining a link of common interest between the illegal and the innocent (legal alien or naturalized citizen), gaining the support of the innocent against measures aimed at the illegals. Perpetuating this deception was—and still is—a major part of the anti-national identification campaign.

Even measures considered to be favorable to immigrant workers, such as the expansion of the guest worker program and the granting of amnesty, were attacked. The immigrant lobby argued that the increased use of legal guest workers, combined with increased enforcement against the employment of illegal aliens, was actually an anti-union strategy (despite the fact that unions, hemorrhaging membership because of the employment of low-wage illegal aliens, were often the most vocal proponents of immigration reform). "By making it illegal for 'undocumented' immigrant workers to be employed in the first place," argues the Ford-funded James Cockcroft, "the Simpson-Mazzoli bill guillotines the unionizing activities already undertaken by the AFL-CIO and AFW among immigrant Mexican workers. [B]y keeping the door open for a regular and dependable flow of these workers, Simpson-Mazzoli makes it that much easier for employers, in collusion with the Department of Labor. . .to use them as an antiunion, antistrike force in their conflicts with labor."[23]

The difference between guest workers and illegals in the view of Crockcroft and others is that the guest worker program, which is closely regulated by the government, allows the United States to maintain some modicum of control over its borders. The flow of illegals obviously is out of the reach of federal enforcement. On the other hand, guest workers, as temporary residents, cannot be expected to join the "pan-Mexican" movement in the United States or gain political rights and power. Also, the admission and employment of guest workers serves national economic interests, meaning to the Marxist orientation of the activists, "capitalist" interests rather, than the human rights and presumed egalitarian agenda of the immigrants.

The deadlock on the guest worker provision was broken by the adoption of an amendment by Representative Charles Schumer (D-NY). The amendment stated that the Attorney General could grant lawful permanent resident status to any illegals who could prove they had been working in agriculture for at least twenty full days during the year from May 1, 1985 to May 1, 1986. Giving these illegals the right to obtain resident alien status based on past work experience, and thus acquire legal protections and the chance for future naturalization, was meant to appease left-wing immigration reform opponents who opposed a pure guest worker program. It also reduced the fears of farmers in the Southwest that the thousands of illegals they employed each year for seasonal work would make them subject to employer sanctions.

However, the concept of amnesty was rejected as a policy by Ford's analysts because it is based on a supposedly illegitimate philosophical premise, that of national sovereignty. "Amnesty is a process by which criminals or political prisoners are pardoned by the state," says Cockcroft. It should be inapplicable to workers—since when in the United States is it a crime to sell one's labor power cheaply to an employer?"[24] This, however, twists the issue; the crime in contention is not "working," it is entering the country without the permission of the national authorities. And the "punishment" is simply being returned to the country of origin.

MALDEF COMES TO THE FORE

As mentioned earlier in this chapter, the Mexican American Legal Defense and Education Fund jumped to prominence during the debate over immigration reform. At first considered in the press as a "moderate civil rights" organization, MALDEF has since provided a prime example of the radicalization of the immigration debate. [See Chapter Six for a more detailed history of the organization.]

"We seem to be headed for a new kind of McCarthyism in this country, one that might be called Simpsonism, after Senator Alan Simpson of Wyoming," proclaimed John E. Huerta, Associate Counsel of MALDEF at a 1983 immigration conference. "Simpson has no blacks in his community, no undocumented workers, not even Hispanics displacing the white labor force. He has no political base other than a group of white voters in his community who feel threatened, who identify with 'white power' . . ."[25] Huerta was also Vice President of the National Lawyers Guild and Guild delegate to the 1975 founding conference of the Association of American Jurists.[26]

At the very beginning of 1985, Representative Ed Roybal, a liberal Democrat from California, predicted that Simpson-Mazzoli would be defeated in its current form, and introduced an alternative reform bill with these features: employer sanctions, including a powerful private right of action; better enforcement of wage and tax laws; a three-year Agricultural Labor Transition Program; and a moderate legalization program.[27] Roybal had vociferously opposed employer sanctions and the Simpson-Mazzoli bill on the grounds that it would promote discrimination, but believed that only an alternative proposal could defeat it. Rep. Roybal was chairman of the Hispanic Caucus and had long argued for full civil rights and immigrant status for all undocumented aliens. He had personally been the victim of housing discrimination as a young city councilman in Los Angeles in the early 1950s, and was also the only member of the L.A. city council to vote against a 1950 ordinance that required members of the Communist Party to register with the sheriff.[28] Despite Roybal's solid credentials on the left and in the immigrant rights movement, his attempt at realistic compromise was shot down by MALDEF.

Within days of the introduction of the Roybal alternative, MALDEF distributed a political action memo viciously attacking *all* features of his proposal: "Roybal's bill will have a divisive effect among our friends and allies. Organizations which have remained opposed to any form of sanctions may become more isolated. FAIR [the Federation for American Immigration Reform, a public-interest group advocating immigration control] and others can use the public opinion polls to further divide Hispanic leaders and organizations from the Hispanic community."[29]

"INELUCTABLE LOGIC"

Meanwhile, the major Hispanic organizations had generally gone to a posture of compromise rather than confrontation, sometimes as a consequence of change in elected leadership—all except MALDEF, described by the *Christian Science Monitor* as taking a hard-line stand against employer sanctions.[30]

MALDEF refuses to accept the fact that any immigration reform advocates could have legitimate motives, calling them, "groups that use a supposed concern for the poor, the environment and the economy to turn public opinion against dark-skinned immigrants."[31] MALDEF opposes employer sanctions, opposes interior enforcement, and opposes border security. MALDEF says it is *not* "open- border," but does support: expanded family reunification; exempting Mexico from per-country limitations; permanent resident alien status for all illegals here more than one year; temporary resident alien status for all illegals here less than one year (convertible to permanent resident alien status); and expansion of Immigration and Naturalization Service functions aiding aliens. Conversely, sanctions are strongly opposed, claiming they would result in discrimination and scapegoating; the identification card proposal is vehemently denounced, as a basic threat to immigrant liberty.[32]

Independent academics have observed that MALDEF's position, if adopted, would amount to no less than an open border with Mexico: "If the supply of illegals is not closed at the border and inland, and if demand is not diminished at the hiring end, then there is really no way to keep the illegal immigrants out. This is the ineluctable logic of the MALDEF position."[33]

One can understand the dubious logic from the words of Vilma S. Martinez, MALDEF's General Counsel from 1973 to 1983. In a 1983 lecture to the Columbia School of Law, she noted "at [MALDEF's founding] our scarce resources were divided among what we considered to be the major areas of concern to Mexican-

Americans—education, employment and voting. After careful deliberation . . . in April 1977, our Board adopted immigration as a fourth major program area. Our definition of Mexican-American had expanded to encompass not only the citizen, but also the permanent resident alien and the undocumented alien.''[34] Obviously, MALDEF's definition of what comprises an American citizen is considerably out of the mainstream of public opinion.

[Curiously, Martinez's talk was part of a lecture series at Columbia endowed by the Samuel Rubin Foundation, another Ford grantee and a far left educational organization. A number of other organizations, endowed by Ford, helped as well.[35]]

When President Carter proposed in 1977 a ''consensus'' immigration reform plan, Martinez would not stand for it. ''Some of the Washington-based Hispanic leadership were persuaded that this was the best we could do—trade off employer sanctions for a generous amnesty. I am proud to say that the Hispanic organizational leadership stayed together in opposition to the Carter plan. This was not easy. There were varied pressures to support the plan: many within our own communities genuinely believed that illegal aliens were taking 'our' jobs. . .''[36]

MALDEF AND THE GUILD

MALDEF's principal immigration policy advisor in the 1980s, Linda Wong, was also a prominent member of the National Lawyers Guild's National Immigration Project, a confederation led by Peter Schey of the National Center for Immigrant's Rights,[37] a Board Member of the Southern California ACLU,[38] and Chair of the Board of Directors of the Central American Refugee Center (CARECEN) of Los Angeles.[39] Writing in 1982 for the National Lawyers Guild, Wong said that ''the four Hispanic organizations which originally united in their opposition to the Reagan plan—the American G.I. Forum, the National Council of La Raza, the League of United Latin American Citizens, and the Mexican-American Legal Defense and Educational Fund—were split. When the first set of joint hearings were held on April 1st [1982], only LULAC and MALDEF spoke out against the legislation. The G.I. Forum and the Council had been 'bought off' by the legalization proposal and resigned to the inevitability of employer sanctions.''[40]

In attacking Roybal in the 1985 memo, Wong said, ''By adopting arguments advanced by FAIR and the AFL-CIO that undocumented workers displace American workers and present an unfair competitive advantage, [Roybal] gives credibility to nativist elements and undermines our efforts to change the framework of discussion and peoples' perception of the immigration 'problem'.''[41] In another memo Wong accidentally discloses the deliberate relation of the ''sanctuary'' campaign [see Chapter Seven] to the immigrants' rights campaign: ''[T]he number of Salvadorans who have entered the U.S. in the last two years shows the obvious impact that U.S. support for that government has had on the native population. Yet, representatives who oppose U.S. intervention in Central America have not taken a clear position on the immigration issue. While they have not hesitated to speak out against Reagan for his continued support of dictatorships, they also have not been quick to condemn Simpson-Mazzoli. It is this gap which must be closed in the next phase."[42]

During the summer of 1985, Rep. Rodino, by this time Chairman of the Judiciary Committee, introduced another version of Simpson-Mazzoli in the House. In mid-September 1985, the Senate passed its own version that included a 350,000 annual guest worker provision. This provision became the main obstacle to a compromise between the two houses of Congress. In June 1986, Rep. Charles Shumer (D-NY) proposed an additional category for amnesty for undocumented aliens who worked at least twenty days in perishable agriculture between May 1985 and May 1986. This allowed those guest workers to apply for resident status, according to the proposed legislation. Eventually an adequate compromise was reached when the twenty-day period was stretched to 90 days, breaking the deadlock. The House of Representatives passed Rodino's bill on October 9, 1986.

However, when the Senate and House bills were reconciled in joint committee, Schumer's guest worker provision was completely dropped. Both houses adopted the compromise in mid-October and the bill, now known as the Simpson-Mazzoli Immigration Reform and Control Act, was signed into law by President Reagan on November 6, 1986.

At the time, many involved in the immigration controversy thought that the debate was settled with that one stroke of the Presidential pen. They did not realize, however, that the legal war against America's immigration control policy had already geared up, and had already laid the groundwork to cast aside many of the accomplishments of the 1986 Immigration Control and Reform Act. It is a struggle that the "immigrants' rights advocates," and their allies in the National Lawyers Guild and Ford Foundation, have carried to the present day.

Chapter Three
The Radicalization of the Immigration
Debate

"Peter Schey, a Los Angeles attorney originally from South Africa . . . explains, 'This country saw massive antiwar movements. This country saw a massive movement, a grass roots movement, to support the rights of black persons. I do not think North America has ever seen the kind of civil disobedience that is going on with the mass of undocumented persons that are here today. It is the biggest single act of disobedience in the history of North America.' "

—Reporter Sasha G. Lewis, 1979 [1]

The notion of employer sanctions—prohibiting employers from knowingly employing illegal aliens—is common to every country regardless of political or economic systems. Not only does it starve the supply-demand equation that drives so much illegal immigration (thus saving jobs for native-born and naturalized Americans here at home), it is a humane way of keeping aliens from working in the harsh conditions of so-called "sweat shops." [2]

Employer sanctions were first proposed as early as 1949, but were delayed and then defeated in 1954 by powerful agricultural interests. When Representative Peter Rodino and Senator Edward Kennedy, with the backing of the AFL-CIO, reintroduced the notion in the early 1970s, virtually the whole spectrum of public opinion was supportive, with the powerful exception again being agricultural growers and a few employers' associations generally opposed to regulatory burdens. [3]

At that time, the traditional Mexican-American organizations supported employer sanctions, including the United Farm Workers. To this day the majority of Latin Americans are still supportive of sanctions, although the casual observer may have the mistaken impression that this group is vociferously opposed to such measures.

21

However, as we have seen in earlier chapters, American public opinion, especially including that of the Hispanic rank-and-file, is of little interest to the politicized elite manipulating the immigration issue.

This view is summed up well by an approving member of the Mexican-American intelligentsia:

> While at first Chicanos appeared to accept the negative impact of illegals, the reversal of Chicano opinion represents one of the more dramatic instances of the effectiveness of the Chicano left. For the left organized a campaign to expose, on the one hand, the history and invidiousness of the American government's effort to 'blame' the illegals for its own inability to solve crucial economic problems, and to cement, on the other hand, a solidarity between Mexican illegals and Chicanos . . . . The Chicano intelligentsia has largely moved from a colonial analysis of Chicano conditions to a Marxist orientation. [4]

Peter Skerry, a writer critical of the Hispanic-American elite, noted in 1987 that

> much of the [immigration] debate has focused on charges that sanctions on the hiring of illegal aliens will cause employers to discriminate against foreign-looking workers in order to avoid breaking the law. By raising this concern, opponents of immigration restriction have gained the ear of sympathetic liberals, as well as much attention from the media. Their efforts go a long way toward explaining why immigration legislation has been delayed for years and at various points almost killed. . . Opinion polls have shown that a substantial segment, perhaps even a majority, of Mexican-Americans support [employer] sanctions. The credit for impeding and weakening their implementation must in large measure go to Mexican-American legal and political activists.

Skerry also notes that years ago the major Mexican-American groups were run by old-style "machine politicians" who generally reflected community opinion. Now, however, activist organizations like the Mexican American Legal Defense and Education Fund have filled the leadership void. Groups like MALDEF have much stronger ties to corporate and foundation sponsors (like the Ford Foundation) than to the people it claims to represent. Organizations therefore have much more latitude in devising a radical and controversial agenda, one that would never be tolerated by a vast majority of their so-called "constituents." [5]

A MARXIST PERSPECTIVE

A candid explanation for the startling transformation of Chicano elite opinion is offered by liberal activist Estevan Flores in his doctoral dissertation, *Post-Bracero Undocumented Mexican Immigration to the United States and Political Recomposition*, University of Texas at Austin, 1982. Flores specifically and explicitly stresses the political utility of the illegal immigration issue in redirecting activists from conventional ethnic agitation within the democratic and reformist framework, to "internationalist" (i.e., Marxist) perspectives. Flores' central thesis is that "a sector of Chicano Movement activists shifted their political activity to the defense of the Mexican immigrant. For many activists and organizers, the use of a class-based analysis replaced the ideology of cultural nationalism." (p. 201)

"In the early and mid-1960s," according to Flores, "the Chicano movement emerged with many, but at least four *primary* areas of struggle: (1) the land grants; (2) education/bilingual education; (3) defense of the community and (4) farmworker organization." (p. 143) However, "A sector of the politically active Chicanos shifted activity to the organization and defense of undocumented Mexican immigrants." (p. 148) "It was not until [Jorge] Bustamante [legal services coordinator with the Ford-funded Center for Northern Border Studies] provided a use-value analysis of undocumented immigration that a Marxist framework was established." (pp. 151-152)

Flores also points out that one of the first organizers to criticize Immigration and Naturalization Service measures was Bert Corona, a long-time Chicano activist with ties to far-left organizations.[6] In 1968, Corona formed the so-called *Centro de Accion Social Autonoma*, or CASA, for the express goal of organizing and defending undocumented illegal aliens.

Groups like CASA exploited the immigrant issue during the early 1970s to revitalize and redirect the efforts of far left college campus organizations like the Chicano student movements that were in their heyday during the 1960s. Successful at many colleges in Southern California, these same methods were reproduced at other campuses all across the Southwest and Midwest. CASA also complemented its activities with student groups and a small number of church groups that struggled to defend the immigrant worker.

Dr. Gilbert Cardenas was Flores' dissertation supervisor and scholarly collaborator at the University of Texas.[7] His own 1975 account further documents the inception of the trend championed by himself and Flores: "A national movement to organize and to promote the protection and equal treatment of alien workers continues to grow in strength. CASA . . . has emerged as the leading organization behind this movement. The American Civil Liberties Union (ACLU) and the National Lawyers Guild have also been vocal supporters of this latest movement to protect alien workers . . . . In a recent suit, the ACLU and Mexican-American Legal Defense and Educational Fund (MALDEF), with the support of the Immigration Lawyers Association and CASA have charged the INS with indiscriminate and unconstitutional arrests and deportations of persons of Latin or La Raza appearance."[8]

In 1975, the national ACLU and MALDEF had not yet established definitive positions on the illegal immigration issue. However, the two organizations were heavily influenced by staffers with ties to the omnipresent National Lawyers Guild. Ramona Ripston was not only a member of the Guild but was also the head of Southern California ACLU, and took the lead in the litigation against the INS.[9] Bill Steiner, as of 1979 Associate Counsel and Los Angeles Director of MALDEF,[10] was also prominent in the National Lawyers Guild and its National Immigration Project. [11]

The importance of CASA and the National Lawyers Guild in building the illegal-alien struggle is further confirmed by irredentist Chicano scholar Rodolfo Acuna, author of the controversially titled *Occupied America*:

> While mainstream Chicano organizations, labor leaders, and activists had supported the INS in the 1950s, actually encouraging the apprehension of undocumented workers, their attitude took a 180-degree turn in the late 1960s . . . . The person most responsible for changing the antiundocumented worker position was Bert Corona, who organized the Centro de Accion Social Autonoma . . . . CASA changed from a service organization to a vanguard organization with a smaller and more disciplined cadre. After Corona left CASA-HGT, the membership spent more time in Marxist study . . . . The group also became more involved in other activist issues and mass rallies. It went out of the business of servicing workers in obtaining their documents. Its leadership spent additional time and energy lobbying progressive professions and organizations such as the National Lawyers Guild to deal with constitutional issues. [12]

A "CONCRETE RESULTS" POLICY

MALDEF, which had been a conventional civil rights organization, became converted to the defense of illegal immigration by participation in the 1975 anti-INS litigation described by Cardenas above and, according to Vilma Martinez, its leader through the period, by litigation initiated in 1978 on behalf of Texas alien schoolchildren. [13]

The origin of this new conflict was in 1975, when the State of Texas revised its education laws to deny state funds to school districts which admitted illegal-alien children. The Texas litigation (*Plyler v. Doe*) was finally settled by the Supreme Court, which in 1982 declared by a close 5-4 vote the Texas law unconstitutional. As outside scholars put it, "Recognizing that the plight of children denied access to education by the state presented facts to evoke the sympathy of the Court, MALDEF initiated a series of 'test cases' that culminated in *Plyler*. . . and provided MALDEF with a major precedent upon which to build. In fact, since *Plyler* MALDEF has initiated a number of lawsuits challenging discrimination against undocumented aliens in a variety of areas. . ." [14]

This analysis demonstrates the process of MALDEF's conversion to the "concrete results" of agitation in support of illegal immigration. Further, according to Flores, "the class-action strategy of the National Center for Immigrant's Rights (NCIR—Los Angeles) has been extremely beneficial to thousands upon thousands of undocumented immigrants of Mexican and non-Mexican origin alike. Essentially, the NCIR acts as a 'back-up' center providing legal assistance, research and counsel in cases where a class of undocumented immigrants will be affected through litigation. At least, this was the explanation provided by Mr. Peter Schey, Directing Attorney of NCIR, in March of 1979. The importance of ethnicity is clear in all of the above examples, since the organizers, attorneys, law students, are almost all of Mexican origin. Second, these same actors had been active in the Chicano Movement prior to their engaging in the movement to defend and organize the undocumented Mexican.'' (p. 175).

Flores considers the education case which MALDEF had filed in Tyler, Texas of particular significance. "In that case, *Doe v. Plyler* (1978), key actors of Mexican descent offered the necessary legal and social scientific expertise to challenge the [Texas] code successfully [n.b.: the key actors referred to here are Dr. Cardenas and Vilma Martinez, Director of MALDEF].'' (p. 179). Legal service's attorneys viewed the outcome in Tyler I.S.D. as positive. However, attorneys at the Centro Para Inmigrantes in Houston felt that the MALDEF case could be improved and strengthened.

At a meeting in Austin, Texas, two attorneys discussed a three-pronged strategy with two social scientists. All four had been activists in the Chicano movement. The attorneys who began to devise this strategy were Isaias Torres and Jose Medina, both of La Raza Legal Alliance and National Immigration Project of the National Lawyers Guild[15]. The social scientists were Cardenas and Flores. (p. 180) Peter Schey of the National Lawyers Guild and of the National Center for Immigrants' Rights argued the Houston case. (p. 185, p. 198)

In 1975, Antonio Rodriguez took over the leadership of CASA in Los Angeles. A friendly reporter wrote in 1978 that he "has been intent on two goals: continuing agitation against restrictive immigration laws, and infusing Leninist ideology into the movement. Under his leadership, CASA has been molded along political and organizational lines similar to those of disciplined Marxist parties.''[16] Members of the National Immigration Project of the National Lawyers Guild and graduates of the defunct CASA are now prominent throughout the Ford-funded immigration network.

Following the demise of CASA, Antonio Rodriguez moved to the directorship of the Los Angeles Center for Law and Justice.[17] A staff attorney with this same organization was Antonia Hernandez, who became head of MALDEF in 1985. Hernandez was also with the Legal Aid Foundation of Los Angeles (LAFLA) as a directing attorney from 1977 to 1979,[18] in which time the LAFLA first established its "Aliens' Rights Project." The Project was the direct forerunner of the National Center for Immigrant Rights, directed by the National Lawyers Guild's Peter Schey.[19]

In 1983, the American Civil Liberties Union sued the Los Angeles Police Department on behalf of Rodriguez and other plaintiffs for violating illegals' rights. This action prompted the Los Angeles police department to hold a news conference to announce, among other things, that Antonio Rodriguez "was a leader of several Latino groups whose numbers caused racial discord in East Los Angeles, smuggled Mexican Communist Party members responsible for the 1968 riots in Mexico City into California and distributed weapons south of the border.'' Rodriguez responded that he had done nothing illegal and has been convicted of no crimes.[20]

Later on, both Rodriguez and Hernandez were honored for their efforts in the immigrant movement: At the end of 1987 MALDEF presented its national Legal Services Award to Rodriguez.[21] In 1988, the Central American Refugee Center (CARECEN) of Los Angeles, headed by another member of the National Lawyers Guild, conducted an awards dinner for "Antonia Hernandez, executive director of . . . MALDEF, [who] has been a leader in the movement to defend and extend the rights of immigrants and Central American refugees."[22]

Writing in 1985, Antonio Rodriguez observed that

> During the past two years the struggle against the Simpson-Mazzoli bill has been national in character. Demonstrations and conferences have taken place in cities such as Los Angeles, San Francisco, San Diego, San Antonio, Seattle, Chicago, New York and Washington, D.C. The battle has included mass demonstrations, public forums and hearings, conferences, mass letter writings, telegrams, petitions, and lobbying visits to key legislators . . . . The League of United Latin-American Citizens (LULAC) and the Mexican-American Legal Defense and Education [sic] Fund (MALDEF) have carried out extensive lobbying against the bill . . . . Without the support of church elements, civil liberties organizations including the ACLU. . .and the National Committee Against Repressive Legislation (NCARL), the Bill would have probably passed through the 97th Congress in 1982.[23]

[NCARL's top priority for years was to defeat immigration- reform legislation. Its leader and Executive Director Emeritus is Frank Wilkinson of the National Lawyers Guild. In the 1950s, Wilkinson served as a staff member of the (National) Emergency Civil Liberties Committee, assisting in a national effort to abolish the House Committee on Un-American Activities (known as HUAC). The Committee called Wilkinson, who refused to testify about his political affiliations and was imprisoned for contempt (*Wilkinson v. United States*, 365 U.S. 397, U.S. Supreme Court). Upon his release in 1962, Wilkinson joined the National Committee to Abolish HUAC, which later changed its name to the NCARL. Bert Corona is currently a Vice-Chair of NCARL, as is John Shattuck, the ACLU's former representative on legislative and immigration issues in Washington, D.C.[24] Reportedly, the minutes of NCARL's 1984 National Committee meeting state that Shattuck praised the "creative marriage of NCARL and ACLU . . . a marriage of dialogue, strategy and organizing, relentless organizing. . . All of this is substantially the creation of the kind of movement that NCARL stands for and has been for the last quarter-century and which the ACLU, for the past decade, has come to learn is the most effective means of working for civil liberties."[25]]

As for the 1984 defeat of the immigration bill, says Antonio Rodriguez, "Perhaps the major force that contributed to the bill's defeat was the collaborated lobbying efforts by MALDEF, LULAC, Hispanic Caucus, ACLU, Immigrant Rights groups, and organized Latino communities."[26] Public "forums," "education" of Congress members, "coalition-building," begun in 1983 according to Rodriguez, were all planned in the 1983 Ford working paper *Migrants and Refugees* and since carried out in a coordinated fashion, with generous grants straight from the Foundation.

The August 1983 Ford working-paper strategy was refined at The Conference of Immigrant and Refugee Advocacy (CIRA), held in Los Angeles, sponsored and organized by MALDEF. According to MALDEF's Conference call, "Immigration is one of the most critical and controversial issues facing our country today. Civil war, political repression, economic pressures and population explosions have impelled large numbers of people to come to the United States. Unfortunately, these immigrants and refugees are not being welcomed with open arms. Instead they are coming under increasing attack, as was evidenced by 'Operation Jobs' in 1982 and more recently, by the Simpson-Mazzoli immigration bill.

"Many churches, civil rights and community organizations are deeply concerned about the denial of basic rights to these men, women and children. Various groups have been organizing locally and regionally, but the immigration attacks are national. We find an urgent need to develop a nationally-unified strategy for immigrant and refugee advocacy . . . . [27] The conference organizer was none other than Linda Wong, the Director of Immigrants Civil Rights for MALDEF and active member of the National Immigration Project of the National Lawyers Guild. [28]

This extraordinary conference requires some listing of the participants, many of whom soon benefitted from the Ford-funded immigration-policy effort. Listings are paraphrased from the CIRA flier, with comments in parentheses.

KEYNOTE PANEL

THE PAST, PRESENT, AND FUTURE OF U.S. IMMIGRATION POLICY

- *The Mexican Perspective* Dr. Jorge Bustamante, Center for Northern Border Studies, Tijuana, Mexico (Ford-funded)

- *Retrospective on the Simpson-Mazzoli Debate* Antonia Hernandez, Associate Counsel, Mexican-American Legal Defense and Educational Fund, Washington, D.C. (soon to become General Counsel of MALDEF, Ford-funded)

- *The Legacy of the Select Commission* Rose Matsui Ochi, former Commissioner, Select Commission on Immigration and Refugee Policy (one of only two on the Hesburgh Commission to vote against employer sanctions; Ochi's staff delegate to the Select Commission was Bill Ong Hing of the National Immigration Project of the National Lawyers Guild[29])

THE IMPACT OF U.S. FOREIGN AND ECONOMIC RELATIONS ON IMMIGRATION

Moderator: Amit Pandya, Esq., Salvadorean Asylum Project of the ACLU, Washington, D.C. (former D.C. representative of the National Center for Immigrants'

Rights and original member of the National Immigration, Refugee and Citizenship Forum, all three organizations Ford-funded) *Panelists*

- *Central America* Mary Solberg, Coordinator, Central America Concerns, Lutheran Immigration and Refugee Service, New York City (a founder of the national Sanctuary movement, Ford-funded).
- *Haiti* Jean Jacques Honorat, Director, Institute of Haitian Studies, New York.
- *U.S. Communities* Gilbert Cardenas, Assistant Professor of Sociology, University of Texas, Austin (Ford-funded).

POLITICAL ASYLUM AND REFUGEE ISSUES

Moderator: Jorge Gonzalez, Legal Services Coordinator, El Rescate, Los Angeles (El Rescate was organized by the National Center for Immigrants Rights, both Ford-funded). *Panelists*

- *Political Asylum: Law vs. Reality* Peter A. Schey, Executive Director, National Center for Immigrants' Rights, Inc., Los Angeles (The National Center for Immigrants' Rights was organized by the National Immigration Project of the National Lawyers Guild, Ford-funded).
- *The Haitian Refugees* The Rev. Gerard Jean-Juste, Executive Director, Haitian Refugee Center, Inc., Miami (Ford-funded, the Center's major legal work was done by Ira J. Kurzban of the National Immigration Project of the National Lawyers Guild).
- *Central America: No Right to Asylum* Blase Bonpane, Senior Research Fellow, Council on Hemispheric Affairs, Los Angeles (Treasurer of the National Committee Against Repressive Legislation; a west-coast founder of Committee in Solidarity with the People of El Salvador, CISPES).
- *The Church as Sanctuary* The Rev. Philip Zwerling, First Unitarian Church, Los Angeles (sanctuary founder and far-left activist in Los Angeles).

Serving on other panels were:

- *Immigrant Use of Social Services: Bursting the Myths* Leo R. Chavez, Director of Field Research, Center for U.S./Mexican Studies, UC San Diego, La Jolla (Ford-funded).
- *The Debate on Immigration and Unemployment* Estevan Flores, PhD. Sociology, Post Doctorate Fellow, UCLA Chicano Studies Research Center. . .Los Angeles.

The Plenary Session:
Alternative Policies
Moderator: Linda Wong, Esq., MALDEF, Los Angeles (Ford-funded).
Panelists

- Dale Frederick Swartz, President, National Immigration Refugee and Citizenship Forum (Ford-funded).
- Antonia Hernandez, MALDEF, Washington, D.C. (Ford-funded).
- Jose Bracamonte, Asst. Professor of Law, University of Houston Law Center, Houston.

Networking and Resourcing: Futuring the Trends and the Advocacy, A Round Table Discussion

- Moderators:

- The Rev. Hector Lopez, Director of Urban Ministries, Southern California Conference of the United Church of Christ
- Linton Joaquin, Esq., National Lawyers Guild Immigration Committee (Ford-funded).

In 1984, the Ford Foundation published its landmark study *Hispanics: Challenges and Opportunities*. This study declared that "Hispanics until recently have been an 'invisible' minority largely unaffected by affirmative action."[30] It identified a problem that the hefty coffers of the foundation could solve: "Most organizations that can advocate for and serve the Hispanic population are young and fragile, having come into existence only within the past fifteen or twenty years. Their funding, like that of other community-affiliated organizations, has been precarious; nor is the federal support on which many of these organizations have often depended any longer assured."[31] The kinds of federal support to which Ford was referring were "the anti-poverty and community-action programs created in the sixties and seventies. . .[that] might have been a training ground for that new generation."[32] Ford proceeded to grant millions annually to sustain and build these organizations, with an eye towards "leadership development of Hispanics." Yet a leadership reared on foundation grants and a left-wing political agenda could only take the movement in one direction.

GROOMING THE CADRE

The large Hispanic population is bound to produce leaders. The natural pattern would be for these leaders to come from the ranks of successful Hispanic entrepreneurs and professionals. Such a leadership class, like the Hispanic leadership of times past, would tend toward middle-class values, moderate politics, the work ethic and integration. However, this is not the kind of leadership the Ford Foundation and its left-wing clientele want. The elite being so well groomed and financed by Ford is to be indoctrinated with rival values; they are to become radical in outlook and oriented towards social welfare programs rather than private enterprise. "The program will be designed to identify especially promising individuals, and. . .encourage them to pursue leadership roles in political, governmental or other public-service oriented careers. . . . The program will provide experience and exposure to local, state and national affairs."[33] Bred to be political animals, the Ford-sponsored Hispanic elite can be expected to outcompete others for power and thus move the entire community leftward.

It was clear that political power and government support was the preferred agenda for Ford's disciples. To overcome the "disadvantaged" status of the Hispanic community, "additional problems must be overcome. Policy-relevant knowledge of the Hispanic population is largely undeveloped. Low political participation rates, gerrymandering, and other factors have left Hispanics underrepresented as elected and appointed officials at the local, state and federal levels."[34] Clearly the path upward is seen as being through the political spoils system and the voting bloc rather than through productive careers in the private sector and assimilation into the mainstream of the larger society.

The low Hispanic voting rate is of special concern to Ford. "Of critical importance to the issue of Hispanic voting is citizenship" proclaims the working paper, which also notes that one out of three Hispanics in the United States is foreign born. "The failure of these residents to naturalize has serious consequences. It excludes them from political office and from such other societal institutions as the jury system. It reduces the accountability of elected public officials to large segments of the Hispanic community. Hispanics who do not naturalize forfeit their eligibility to certain federal entitlements, such as student aid, and are ineligible for federal employment. Failure to naturalize may delay reunification with family members who would otherwise be entitled to immediate entry to the United States."[35]

Though lip-service is paid to the fact that Hispanics in the U.S. "present distinct social and economic profiles" because they have immigrated from different lands (Mexico, Cuba, Puerto Rico, Central and South America, Spain) the emphasis throughout is on unifying all Hispanics into a single mass movement by playing on their supposed "common cultural background."

The Ford Foundation is not above prescribing a healthy dose of irredentism. In the introduction to its working paper it argues that "the history of Hispanic settlement in this country began before the arrival of the Pilgrims at Plymouth Rock. Hispanics first settled in the New World during the early 16th century; by the 17th century Hispanic culture was firmly established in much of what is now Texas, New Mexico,

Arizona, Colorado, and California. The Spanish-speaking cities of Santa Fe, El Paso and St. Augustine predate the Jamestown colony.'' [36] Although the average American who happens to reside in the Southwest would acknowledge the influence of Hispanic culture on the region, few (if any) would agree that this entitles aliens to entry whenever and wherever they so desire. The Ford Foundation clearly has no interest in such arguments.

Chapter Four
Haitians, Cubans and Iranians

"We can't define a solution to the immigration problem unless you point the finger at imperialism."
—Michael Maggio, National Lawyers Guild, 1979[1]

Rabinowitz, Boudin, Standard, Krinsky and Lieberman is a controversial New York City law firm that is said to have represented the legal interests of the Castro government since the early 1960s. This assertion is documented by filings under the Foreign Agents Registration Act for 1966, 1967 and 1968, which show the law firm as a registered agent for the "Republic of Cuba and its instrumentalities." [The purpose of the Foreign Agents Registration Act was to ensure that the government and people of the United States would be informed of the identity of persons engaging in propaganda activities and other activities on behalf of foreign governments.][2]

Principals in the law firm had close connections with the National Emergency Civil Liberties Committee (NECLC), a far-left organization headquartered in New York City. Leonard Boudin served as the organization's General Counsel, Eric Lieberman and Michael Krinsky were Associate General Counsels, Victor Rabinowitz was on the Executive Committee; and Michael Standard served on the National Council and was also a cooperating attorney with the Center for Constitutional Rights.[3]

In early 1980 the National Council of Churches, the NECLC and the Haitian Refugee Center of Miami brought legal action on behalf of illegal Haitians against the U.S. Attorney General.[4] Attorneys for the Haitian Refugee Center were: Ira J. Kurzban of the NECLC and the National Lawyers Guild, Dale Frederick Swartz (Rick Swartz, later founder and President of the National Immigration Refugee and Citizenship Forum), Peter Schey of the National Lawyers Guild[5], and Vera Weisz of the

32

Haitian Refugee Center, who later joined Schey's National Center for Immigrants' Rights [6], and Timothy Barker, member of the NLG and the National Center for Immigrants' Rights in Los Angeles. [7]

The Haitian case was being tried during the week of April 14-18, 1980, and merited original coverage by the *Washington Post*, which quoted Swartz as saying "my own feeling is that this case has raised serious questions about foreign policy. Haiti is worse than the regimes of Iran and Nicaragua that have been overturned. . .". In the same article, Peter Schey, one of the Haitians' lawyers from the National Center for Immigrants' Rights, said "for the first time, we are asking a federal judge to extend the equal protection provision of the Constitution to asylum policy, and that it be objective and impartial and not given just to people from countries that are enemies of the United States." [8] Schey's words were prophetic.

Coincident with the court hearings, unprecedented numbers of Haitians poured into Florida. *The Washington Post* reported on April 15 that "more than 200 more Haitian refugees arrived on South Florida shores yesterday, swelling the two-day total to near 1,000 and taxing the strength of short-staffed and weary immigration officials. 'This has got to be the grand-daddy of 'em all,' sighed immigration official William Metcalf. 'This has absolutely buried us. There's just no way we can hold this number of people. There isn't a jail in this country big enough to hold all of them.' " [9] But this episode was merely a preview of what would follow.

MARIEL

On April 24, 1980, *The Washington Post* flashed the headline: CUBA SUDDENLY PERMITS MASS EMIGRATION TO THE U.S. "The Cuban government has formally opened the door for a mass exodus to the United States of all Cubans who want to leave here, a number that officials have suggested could reach hundreds of thousands." [10] Thus began the famed "Mariel" boatlift, named after the port on the northern shore of the island from which Cubans were permitted to depart.

Some 130,000 Cubans eventually arrived. It was later disclosed that the CIA warned, in a secret report to the House Intelligence Subcommittee in late January 1980, that the communist regime of Fidel Castro "may again resort to large-scale emigration to reduce discontent caused by Cuba's deteriorating economic situation," and repeated the warning several times between January and March of 1980. [11] Two special Cuban-American agents from the Florida Department of Law Enforcement later testified to Congress about details of the onset of the Mariel boatlift. Although the boats on the American side that were ferrying the Mariel entrants were crucial to the Cuban operation, "attempts to prosecute the guilty were almost impossible. Enough legal research had been done to permit persons to be exempt from the laws as they were written, although they were clearly included by their acts in that the spirit of the law had been broken—the manner of operating was a fraud." [12]

A detailed study of the boatlift prepared for the National Defense University by

U.S. Coast Guard Captain Alex Larzelerl concluded that "Of the many purposes the Exodus served for the Castro government, the most basic perhaps was reduction of population pressures, ameliorating several of Cuba's socioeconomic problems in a relatively brief time. Thousands of housing units quickly became available, and unemployment was reduced . . . . Castro brought about a beneficial demographic adjustment for Cuba." Roughly 50,000 men arrived without families. It was reported that some 20,000 were forced by Cuban officials to leave their families behind. Refugees with family members still in Cuba could be pressured by Cuban intelligence agents or, as Larzelerl suggests, "Pressures generated by the desire for family reunification were fully appreciated by the Castro government as it sowed seeds for future migration opportunities." [13]

Dan James, a specialist on intelligence and covert operations, concluded in a 1981 article that "the 130,000 refugees who flooded into the country from the Cuban port of Mariel in April 1980 were essentially pawns in a plan conceived by Cuban President Fidel Castro and his intelligence service to destabilize the United States while relieving Cuba of 'excess' population it could not support." This so-called "Plan Bravo" was revealed to James in an interview with Genaro Perez, a recent defector from Cuba's General Intelligence Directorate (DGI). "Stirring up racial conflict here is . . . part of 'Plan Bravo,' " said Perez. "[Castro is] going to incite Mexicans, Puerto Ricans and blacks. Especially blacks."

James wrote that Castro preferred to forego 'Plan Bravo' in the future for the inception of a so-called 'Plan Alpha,' the goal of which would be a "normalization" of relationships between Cuba and its northern neighbor. Normalization in this context, however, aimed more at influencing the United States to remove its embargo of the dictatorship, which was over two decades old at the time. But belying this endeavor at peaceful "normalization" was the fact that it was directed by the DGI, Cuba's secret police, operating out of the Cuban Mission to the United Nations in New York City. James said that this campaign hid behind a number of fronts, including the so-called Center for Cuban Studies. According to a 1979 fundraising letter the purpose of the Center is to 'bring the facts of Cuban life' to the American public. The sponsors listed in the letter included many well-known supporters of left-wing causes in America, including Leonard Boudin of the pro-Castro law firm mentioned earlier. James writes of Boudin's daughter: "Kathy was reported, in a declassified FBI 'top secret' document, as hiding out in Cuba that same year; a leader of the extreme-left Weatherman organization, she had gone underground after a March 1970 explosion in an alleged Weatherman 'bomb factory' in New York's Greenwich Village. . ." [14]

In 1983, a Cuban intelligence defector, Mario Estebez Gonzalez, told federal officials that he and about 3,000 other Cuban agents infiltrated into the United States among the Marielitos. [15] According to Estebez' Congressional testimony, the Mariel boatlift was carefully planned as an operation to infiltrate the United States. He said about 40,000 hardened criminals were sent in on the Mariel boatlift, including as many as 7,000 agents of various sorts, and that he himself had smuggled groups of Haitians through Cuba to the United States. According to Estebez, the goal of the various Cuban agents is to create havoc in the event of a conflict between Cuba and the United States. [16]

These allegations are consistent with earlier reports. Syndicated columnist Georgie Anne Geyer wrote in 1982 that "responsible foreign intelligence has reported that Haitians and Jamaicans indoctrinated by Castro have come to the United States with the Haitian boat people for the express purpose of organizing refugees." [17] The *New York Times* reported on a spate of Haitian drownings that drew embarrassing worldwide publicity to the United States: "The 33 Haitians who drowned off the coast of Florida last month had spent nearly four weeks in Cuba, where they received food supplies and other assistance permitting them to continue their journey to the United States . . . Federal agents investigating the case said the Haitians spent 27 days in Cuba, got food supplies there and resumed their voyage with the help of a Cuban vessel. . ." [18] In 1987, after troubles in Haiti following the fall of the Duvalier regime, "the [Haitian] army issued a communique on July 31 claiming that the trouble stemmed from 'provocative acts perpetrated by terrorist elements, who were largely trained in Cuba and posed as 'boat people' to be repatriated to Haiti.' These elements, said the army, had smuggled arms into the country 'in sacks of rice' from Miami." [19]

Also among the refugees from Mariel were "undesirables," criminals and political protestors whom Castro wished removed from Cuba—and whose exit would serve to discredit all other "undesirables" who wished to leave Cuba's "workers paradise." Of the total that eventually made it to south Florida, 1,761 (1.4 percent of the total) were classified by the INS as felons convicted of murder, rape or burglary. Another 23,927 (19.1 percent) were former prisoners convicted of another crime. However, most of this number were either political prisoners or held for offenses that would not have been crimes in the United States, such as dealing in the black market, refusing to join a communist organization or being unemployed. [20]

As of 1987, 3,830 Mariel Cubans were serving sentences in Federal, State and local prisons for crimes committed in the United States. Another 3,806 had completed serving sentences and were being detained pending their return to Cuba as an active threat to society. About 3,000 more were on parole or in half-way houses after serving sentences for crimes in the United States, but were allowed to stay in the United States since they were not considered threatening. [21]

Criminal activity and subversion sometimes overlapped in these cases, particularly with regard to drug trafficking. On November 29, 1981, the Coast Guard seized a speed boat carrying 2,500 pounds of marijuana to Florida. Its operator, Mario Esteves, confessed to being a Cuban intelligence agent who had infiltrated the United States via the boatlift. In his testimony he claimed that there were 300 to 400 agents from the boatlift whose primary mission was to distribute cocaine and marijuana in the United States in order to earn hard currency for Cuba. [22]

A "BILL OF RIGHTS FOR UNDOCUMENTED WORKERS"

From April 28-30, 1980, only a few days after the start of the Cuban boatlift, the first International Conference for the Full Rights of Undocumented Workers was held in Mexico City. According to the official delegate from the National Lawyers Guild, a so-called "Bill of Rights for Undocumented Workers" passed unanimously, as well as "a call for an end to political and economic conditions in the United States and Mexico that cause this situation." Many messages of solidarity were received by the conference, including overtures from the Confederation of Cuban Workers, the Palestinian Liberation Organization, and the Revolutionary Coordinating Committee of El Salvador. The World Federation of Trade Unions [an organization that received strong backing from the Soviet Union] voiced "total and unconditional solidarity with the struggle for full rights for undocumented workers."[23] Mainstream trade unions, however, oppose such open immigration measures as being against the interest of the workers they represent.

A few weeks later Miami was hit with the worst race-inspired violence in its history. When the riot finally died down on May 19, 14 people were dead, 371 were injured and 450 more had been arrested. A once-vibrant community lay in smoldering ashes. The liberal Reverend Jesse Jackson, however, obviously did not sympathize with the victims of such violence. "Usually when it's hot, you can reshape the iron," he said. "I would hope that this riot is instructive—making the black and the poor visible again."[24] The National Lawyers Guild was quick to come out with its own deconstructed history of this event, reporting through its National Immigration Project that "the riots, in which [sic] 20 people were killed and over [sic] 1,100 people arrested, started across the street from the Haitian Refugee Center. Haitians were injured and arrested during the fighting and political asylum for Haitian refugees was a major demand."[25] A Citizens Coalition for Racial Justice was hastily formed to "support the demands of the Black community," comprised of the ACLU, the National Alliance Against Racist and Political Repression (headed by Angela Davis of the Communist Party USA), the Haitian Refugee Center, the Nicaraguan Support Committee, the National Lawyers Guild and the (pro-Castro) Antonio Maceo Brigade.[26]

In early September 1981, over 1,000 Haitians rioted at the Krome North Detention Center outside Miami. These camps were the target of withering criticism among the left: In *The Nation*, Aryeh Neier of Helsinki Watch and Americas Watch characterized detention of Cuban and Haitian illegals as "refugee gulags."[27] Robert L. Bernstein, also associated with Helsinki Watch and Americas Watch, objected in *The New York Times* to the detention of Haitian illegal aliens in Puerto Rico.[28] A highly partisan report in *Guardian* stated after the uprising was "crushed by border patrol and immigration guards, 125 of the refugees labeled as 'ringleaders, troublemakers and malcontents,' were transferred from Miami to a federal prison in upstate New York."[29]

Later that year the New York Civil Liberties Union sued the INS over conditions of detention for the illegals transferred to New York. This was shortly followed by another round of litigation, this time filed by six of the Haitians in the New York facility, who challenged the INS over the detentioning of persons who have filed political asylum claims. Counsel for the Plaintiffs was Harriet Rabb, Ford Foundation Trustee and Co-Director of the Immigration Law Clinic at Columbia School of Law. [30]

Rabb's Columbia Immigration Law Clinic teamed up at this time with the New York Civil Liberties Union and the Lawyers Committee for International Human Rights to coordinate volunteer attorneys in an action to gain political asylum for 68 Haitians. [31] In mid-June 1982, the Justice Department said it would parole detained Haitians who have attorneys and local sponsors. [32] This was not good enough for Harriet Rabb, who shot back in a letter to the editor of *The New York Times*, characterizing the Justice Department action as "a deceitful new gambit . . . cruel and discriminatory." [33] Rabb's co-Director of the Columbia Clinic, Sue Susman, managed to gain the release of four of the detainees in October 1982. [34]

Meanwhile in Miami, according to a news report in *The Washington Post*:

> because of [activist] lawyers, the Haitians who are coming illegally are perhaps being accorded more legal rights than those who obey the law. To force the government to provide due process for the Haitians, the lawyers have raised not only the merits of individual cases, but also virtually every possible legal issue to trap the government in its own bureaucratic tangle . . . "Fighting [the Immigration and Naturalization Service] is like shooting fish in a barrel . . ." said Ira Kurzban, who is leading the lawyers. [35]

This massive litigation on behalf of Haitian aliens culminated in *Louis v. Nelson*, brought in Miami in June, 1981, again by the Haitian Refugee Center and the National Emergency Civil Liberties Committee. [36] Ira J. Kurzban was lead attorney and was frequently advised by Ira Gollobin of the NECLC, the American Committee for the Protection of the Foreign Born, and the National Lawyers Guild. [37] [Gollobin addressed the February 22, 1975 seminar held by the New York chapter of the National Lawyers Guild Immigration Committee on "The Bill of Rights and the Foreign Born" [38]]. The lawsuit challenged the detention of Haitian illegal aliens. [39] On December 31, 1981, Jesse Jackson of Operation PUSH met with Haitians at a detention compound near Miami, which he described as a "concentration camp," and said they were victims of a racist immigration policy. [40]

In June 1982, Federal District Court Judge Eugene Spellman ordered parole of the detained Haitians pending the outcome of their political asylum applications, but the government appealed, which led to some continuing detentions. This was resolved in April, 1983, when the 11th Federal Circuit Appeals Court in Atlanta upheld the plaintiffs and found that detention of Haitians was discriminatory. At a news conference celebrating the victory, Haitian Refugee Center Chief Rev. Gerard Jean-Juste was critical of the question of whether the decision could spur renewed immigration from Haiti and elsewhere. "Where else could we get the protection from the bullets the United States is sending to the criminal governments in the Third World?" Jean-Juste asked. [41]

Later in April 1983, as another testimony of the immigrant lobby's clout, a federal magistrate awarded attorney's fees to the plaintiff's counsel, four of whom said they plan to donate the money to organizations that sponsored the lawsuit: Ira Kurzban, $104,640; Dale Frederick "Rick" Swartz, $39,570; Vera Weisz of the Haitian Refugee Center $12,515; Timothy Barker, National Center for Immigrants' Rights, Los Angeles, $3480. There was a dispute concerning award of $61,667 to Peter Schey, who wished to donate the funds to his new National Center for Immigrants' Rights, Inc. [42]

THE HAITIAN ISSUE TODAY

The Haitian immigrant issue remains a substantial problem. The September 1991 military overthrow of Haiti's elected president, Jean-Bertrand Aristide, led to new and larger flow of refugees to the United States. During the nearly 16 months prior to January 14, 1993, an estimated 40,000 Haitians tried to make it to the United States, primarily by boat. Of these, the Coast Guard returned 30,182 to Haiti. President Bush first ordered summary repatriation in May 1992. As Howard W. French of the *New York Times* wrote of this policy, "the spectacle of hundreds of Haitians being returned to the docks of the capital without even a stop at the United States base at Guantanamo Bay, Cuba, was widely credited with having quickly stunted the exodus." [43]

Leftists, of course, denounced the Bush policy. A July editorial entitled "Let Them Drown" in *The Progressive* flatly stated that "Bush's new policy is largely based on racism . . . . . Haitians are black, they are poor and no matter how dire their situation back home, it is best, politically, to keep them out of the neighborhood." [44] This argument was also made by Randall Robinson, executive director of Trans-Africa, the group that spearheaded the sanctions movement against South Africa. Transafrica has since broadened its purview to include the Caribbean. [45]

Under pressure from black civil rights and pro-immigration groups, Bill Clinton had opposed the Bush policy during the presidential campaign, calling it "callous." However, he quickly saw the wisdom in the Bush policy as the day approached when he would be forced to deal with the problem as President. On January 14, 1993, Clinton announced he would continue the summary repatriation policy, acting on intelligence reports that as many as 200,000 Haitians were prepared to rush to sea as soon as Clinton was sworn in. In the immediate aftermath of Clinton's announcement, President Bush sent reinforcements to the Coast Guard patrols near Haiti.

LAWYERS COMMITTEE FOR INTERNATIONAL HUMAN RIGHTS

Parallel to the favorable ruling in *Louis v. Nelson*, a nationwide campaign to free Haitian detainees was undertaken, directed by Arthur C. Helton of the Lawyers

Committee for International Human Rights' Political Asylum Project. Helton reported to the members of the NLG's National Immigration Project that the Lawyers Committee for International Human Rights had

> prepared practice materials on conditions in Haiti, on how to prepare an asylum application, and on how to conduct a hearing and/or appeal in connection with an asylum claim . . . The Haitian representation effort is one of the most ambitious *pro bono* enterprises ever attempted by the legal community in the United States . . . In addition to the Lawyers Committee, the ABA, and AILA [American Immigration Lawyers Association], [participating] groups include the Association of the Bar of the City of New York [Arthur C. Helton, Chair of Immigration Committee [46]], the Legal Aid Society of the City of New York, the New York Civil Liberties Union, the National Lawyers Guild, the Washington Lawyers Committee for Civil Rights Under Law . . . and the American Civil Liberties Union. [47]

As of 1984, Helton also served on the Advisory Board of the National Lawyers Guild's publicly funded National Center for Immigrants' Rights. [48]

At the end of 1981, an "Emergency Southeast Conference on Immigration Rights and Political Asylum" was held in Miami. The Human Rights Internet reported that "this conference was organized by the Haitian Refugee Center, the Farmworkers' Rights Organization of Florida, Friends of Haitian Refugees, and the National Immigration and Refugee Network. It was endorsed by the American Friends Service Committee, the Central America Refugee Center, the Haitian Refugee Project (Washington, D.C.), the National Lawyers Guild (Miami chapter) and eight other organizations." [49]

Conference rhetoric was hard to distinguish from that of the openly pro-Soviet left. A descriptive leaflet stated that "the new Reagan immigration plan, released in August, 1981, has formalized the U.S. government's intensified assault on the democratic rights of undocumented workers and political refugees . . . . The U.S. foreign policy of uniting with anyone against a perceived Soviet threat has our government denying basic rights, brutalizing, imprisoning, and finally deporting political refugees from right-wing dictatorships in Haiti and El Salvador, while accepting with open arms those leaving 'communist' nations." [50]

A participant in the conference reported in the Marxist- Leninist *Guardian* newspaper not only that Jesse Jackson sent a "message of solidarity," but also that "one of the conference's major accomplishments was the forging of links between the struggle of Haitian refugees and that of Salvadoran refugees. One of the major focuses of the conference was the need to begin a well-coordinated national campaign in defense of Haitian refugees." [51] Within a year, that well-coordinated campaign was in place, at the Lawyers Committee for International Human Rights in New York City.

The Lawyers Committee (along with Rick Swartz's Alien Rights Project) "investigated" alleged abuses at the end of 1978, and then publicly charged "the Immigration and Naturalization Service with due process violations against 8,800 Haitians in Miami." At the same time, the next training session of the Lawyers Committee, conducted by Susan Susman and two others, was held on the topic of "Immigration Law and Practice: Representing an Applicant for Political Asylum."[52] Meanwhile, the National Immigration Project of the National Lawyers Guild reported that its member, "Susan Susman of the N.Y.C. Immigration Project" had commented on proposed asylum regulations, and that a major conference on refugee and asylum law would be held, organized by the National Lawyers Guild, the Lawyers Committee for International Human Rights, and Swartz's Alien Rights Project.[53]

The Lawyers Committee for Human Rights and Helsinki Watch (both, like Americas Watch, are projects funded by the Ford Foundation) in 1986 published *Mother of Exiles: Refugees Imprisoned in America*, a document copiously illustrated with dramatic photographs of alien detention centers.[54] "The new detention policy is designed to mistreat all equally. It applies to all aliens who arrive in the United States and are accused of being inadmissible for lack of valid entry documents under the Immigration and Nationality Act."[55] *Mother of Exiles* acknowledges the contributions of such Ford-funded groups as El Rescate, the National Center for Immigrants' Rights, the Haitian Refugee Center, the American Friend Service Committee, and others.[56]

A director of the Ford Foundation, Aryeh Neier, among his many activities an adjunct professor of law at New York University, led a March 1987 seminar at NYU on "Immigration Reform: Making Rights a Reality for America's Undocumented." The program did not candidly list the affiliations of the participants. Excluding three government officials and one Belgian representative, the program's list is here recited, amended by parentheses:

- Daniel Stein, Immigration Reform Law Institute (restrictionist);
- Tom Stoddard, Lambda Legal Defense Fund;
- Deborah Anker, Harvard Law School (National Lawyers Guild—NLG);
- Peter Schey, National Center for Immigrants' Rights, Inc. (NLG);
- Dan Kesselbrenner, National Immigration Project (NLG);
- Isaias Torres, Houston, Texas (NLG);
- Arthur Helton, Lawyers Committee for Human Rights (NLG);
- Patty Blum, University of California (NLG);
- Lynn Alvarez, El Rescate (NLG);
- Lucas Guttentag, American Civil Liberties Union (NLG);
- Virginia Lamp, U.S. Chamber of Commerce;
- Larry Kleinman, Willamette Valley Immigration Project (NLG);
- Robin Alexander, United Electrical Workers (NLG);
- Bill Tamayo, Asian Law Caucus (NLG).[57]

"SUCCESSFUL FASCISM"

By the 1980s, many liberal activists were recognizing the openly radical nature of the immigrants' lobby. In 1988 *The New Republic* said of Neier's Americas Watch that "there is significant bias and a good amount of intellectual dishonesty. The bias clearly is in favor of the totalitarian left, in terms of minimizing the human rights abuses of the Nicaraguan government and the FMLN and of greatly exaggerating the abuses of the elected government of El Salvador."[58]

Author Susan Sontag likewise shocked the American left by attending a 1982 meeting in support of the Solidarity rebellion in Poland. She said that "Communism is fascism—successful fascism, if you will. What we have called fascism is, rather, the form of tyranny that can be overthrown—that has largely failed . . . . These hard truths mean abandoning many of the complacencies of the left, mean challenging what we have meant for many years by 'radical' and 'progressive.' "[59]

Aryeh Neier replied that "mainstream American anti-Communists have given anti-Communism a terrible name. I find it uncomfortable to associate with their anti-Communism, and while this has not deterred me from frequently and vehemently expressing my own anti-Communist views, it has forced me to exercise care about when and where I do so . . . Mainstream anti-Communism is not concerned with promoting liberty."[60]

However, Neier's so-called "anti-Communism" takes peculiar forms, only one of which is giving cover and comfort to the efforts of the National Lawyers Guild to undermine the nation's borders. His first political post after graduating from Cornell University was as executive secretary of the socialist League for Industrial Democracy (1958-1963). From 1963 to 1971 he worked for the New York Civil Liberties Union, and was a member of the editorial board of the flagship of American radicalism, *The Nation*[61]. He served on the Executive Council of the Committee for Public Justice,[62] founded by Lillian Hellman, a lifelong apologist for Soviet terror.[63]

Neier's intolerance of anti-Soviet views comes through in his vitriolic reply to a 1981 *New York Times Magazine*[64] article outlining the pro-Soviet tilt of the Institute for Policy Studies (IPS), a leftist think tank in Washington, D.C. [The Chair of IPS is Peter Weiss, who is also Vice President of the Center for Constitutional Rights and trustee of the Samuel Rubin Foundation.[65]] In the pages of *The Nation,* Neier took sharp exception to the analysis of Joshua Muravchik, the article's author, and condemned the article without bothering to refute it factually. He also personally denigrated Muravchik, himself a liberal Social Democrat.[66] Can a true anti-communist promote liberty by lending support to a notorious Stalinist fellow-traveller like Hellman, while blasting a Social Democrat for the mere sin of quoting the Leninist views of certain intellectuals? Perhaps that is what Sontag meant by complacency.

In 1984, Neier's Fund for Free Expression, the National Lawyers Guild and the National Emergency Civil Liberties Committee,[67] along with the American Civil Liberties Union and others[68] organized a major campaign on "Free Trade in Ideas." Funded by the Ford Foundation, this ongoing forum advocated repeal of the immigration exclusion of communists and fascists from the United States.[69] In its widely touted publicity the project stresses the exclusion of political *visitors* to the United States. However, the repeal they propose would effectively allow alien adherents of totalitarianism to be admitted ahead of immigrants with prospective allegiance to the Constitution and laws of the United States.

This proposal is a complete reversal of policy for many of the participants. For example, from 1951 to 1977, official ACLU policy stated the organization

> will not oppose the refusal of permanent immigration status to present members of the Communist, Fascist, Falangist, or other totalitarian parties. It is not unreasonable for the government to determine that such persons cannot be attached honestly to the principles of the Constitution of the United States. Since only a limited number of persons may enter the United States each year, it is not unjustifiable to exclude members of these organizations because they are opposed to democratic principles.[70]

The mostly unopposed publicity of the "Free Trade In Ideas" project is based on inexplicable distortions. For example, Neier's Watch Committee and Lawyers Committee consider the exclusion of Italian communist Nino Pasti "the most extreme case." In Neier's literature, Pasti is described merely as a former member of the Italian Senate, stationed at the Pentagon from 1963 through 1966 as a member of the NATO Military Committee, who later became an outspoken critic of the U.S. decision to place cruise and Pershing missiles in Western Europe.[71] As the Marxist-Leninist *Guardian* reported at the time, the U.S. State Department failed to grant a visa to Pasti to appear at a meeting of the U.S. Peace Council in Chicago in 1983.[72] The U.S. Peace Council, however, is the U.S. affiliate and subordinate of the World Peace Council, a pro-communist organization that received funding from the Soviet Union.[73] Pasti is also a member of the affiliated World Peace Council.[74] Also rarely mentioned is the fact that the "Free Trade in Ideas" campaign declares that the U.S. Constitution encompasses abolition of area restrictions against nonimmigrant visitors (such as Cuban diplomats), abolition of the requirement that paid lobbyists of foreign powers register, and abolition of export controls over technical data of military utility.[75]

SEEKING ASYLUM IN THE COURTS

The National Immigration Project of the National Lawyers Guild is responsible for most major litigation on U.S. immigration policy, activity so far-reaching as to defy easy summary. By the Project's own account:

> In the 1980s, important advances are being attempted in such areas as: access to public education; restricting the ability of the INS to conduct unlawful raids; working toward a meaningful right to counsel for noncitizens in the immigration context; challenging re-

strictions on release of aliens pending proceedings; forcing the INS to allocate visa numbers properly and admit aliens eligible for residence; safeguarding the right of Haitian refugees to be allowed political asylum; and guaranteeing lawful treatment of Salvadoran refugees and lawful implementation of the entire asylum system.

The Guild's political purpose in the asylum arena is explicit: "the Reagan Administration cannot, on the one hand, certify that progress in promoting human rights is being made in El Salvador, in order to justify continued military assistance to the junta there, while on the other hand grant political asylum to Salvadorans asserting clear cases of persecution . . ."[76] A 1987 Supreme Court case expanding the category of political asylum, *INS v. Cardoza-Fonseca*, was hailed as a victory by immigration activists, human rights advocates, and the sanctuary movement. Although the National Lawyers Guild took credit for the decision, a number of other organizations submitted *amici curiae* in defense of the litigants:

(Ford Foundation grantees printed in boldface)

- **Office of the United Nations High Commissioner for Refugees**[77]
- **The American Immigration Lawyers Association**[78]
- **The American Civil Liberties Union**[79]
- **Political Asylum Project of the American Civil Liberties Union Fund of the National Capitol Area**[80]
- **Immigrant and Refugee Rights Project, San Francisco Lawyers' Committee for Urban Affairs**[81]
- **Lawyers Committee for [International] Human Rights**[81]
- The American Jewish Committee
- The Anti-Defamation League of B'nai B'rith
- **Indian Law Resource Center**[83]
- New Mexico Governor Toney Anaya
- **International Human Rights Law Group**[84]
- **Washington Lawyers Committee for Civil Rights Under Law**[85]

Other litigation illustrates the nature and extent of the Ford Foundation immigration network. *Committee of Central American Refugees (CRECE) et al. v. Immigration and Naturalization Service et al.* (N.D. Cal., 1985) challenged the INS policy of transferring illegal Salvadorans and Guatemalans apprehended in the San Francisco area to INS detention centers. The action was brought by Mark Silverman, Robert Rubin (National Lawyers Guild[86]) and Ignatius Bau of the Ford-funded San Francisco Lawyers' Committee for Urban Affairs. The District Court denied the plaintiff's motion for preliminary injunction. On appeal, the Bar Association of San Francisco and the Ford-funded Lawyers Committee for Human Rights joined as *amici curiae*. Their counsel was Lucas Guttentag, who has ties to the National Lawyers Guild, the American Civil Liberties Union and the Columbia Law School Immigration Law Clinic, all of which are Ford-funded. [87]

Orantes-Hernandez v. Meese, 541 F. Supp. 351 (C.D. Cal., 1982) was brought by the National Lawyers Guild with the National Center for Immigrants' Rights, Inc., and the Center for Constitutional Rights, alleging that the Immigration and Naturalization Service (INS) systematically mistreated Salvadoran "refugees." [88] The Los Angeles chapter of the National Lawyers Guild reported that "*Orantes* is a nationwide class action on behalf of Salvadorans against the Immigration and Naturalization Service which seeks to make permanent the requirement that Salvadoran nationals be given notice of their right to appeal for political asylum when apprehended by the INS." NLG lawyers representing the plaintiffs included Linton Joaquin, formerly of the National Center for Immigrants' Rights, [89] and now working at the Central American Refugee Center, Los Angeles (CARECEN) [90]; Sandra Pettit of the Ford-funded Legal Aid Foundation of Los Angeles [which shares office space with NCIR [91]]; Mark Rosenbaum of the Ford-funded ACLU; Charles Wheeler of NCIR [92]; and Vera Weisz, also of NCIR and formerly with the Ford-funded Haitian Refugee Center. [93]

The newsweekly *In These Times* covered the trial:

> The massive action . . . is being litigated by the American Civil Liberties Union (ACLU), Los Angeles Legal Aid Foundation and the National Center for Immigrants' Rights. Already running for five months of trial time, the lawsuit has generated 18,000 pages of transcripts, including the testimony of more than 60 Salvadoran witnesses and several human rights advocates, in addition to more than 75 State Department and INS officials . . . In the trial a coalition of immigrants' rights groups is representing all Salvadorans in the United States who have been or will be stopped by the INS. Salvadorans and lawyers have come to testify from New York, Florida, Texas, Arizona, California, and Washington, D.C . . .
>
> Mark Silverman, coordinator of the [Ford-funded] Political Asylum Emergency Representation Project of the San Francisco Lawyers Committee for Urban Affairs, said that because of the project, Central Americans detained in San Francisco receive free, individual representation at every stage of proceedings in immigration court . . . "The attorney general is under no obligation to house aliens only where the availability of counsel is at its height," said the [U.S. government's reply] brief . . . Testifying against the government, an expert on that country's administration of justice said the Salvadoran legal system fell apart long ago. "It's not possible at any level for human-rights victims to look to the legal system for protection," said Michael Posner, executive director of the [Ford-funded] Lawyers Committee for [International] Human Rights in New York. [94]

On April 29, 1988, Federal District Court Judge Kenyon ruled for the plaintiffs, and according to the *Guardian*, issued "a virtual bill of rights for Salvadoran refugees, requiring the INS to inform refugees of their right to apply for political asylum and to assist them with information on legal services.'' In the year-long, non-jury trial, more than 180 witnesses assisted the plaintiffs, ''who dealt a setback to the Reagan Administration's Central American policy.''[95] The Guild's Immigration Project newsletter claimed a ''Sweeping Victory.''[96]

Sandra Pettit, a lead litigator in *Orantes-Hernandez*, relayed the progress of the case and related asylum agitation to the September 1987, conference of the Association of American Jurists, held in Havana, Cuba. Pettit basically summed up the role of the National Lawyers Guild and its allied organizations:

> Progressive lawyers, including lawyers with the National Lawyers Guild, have worked to prevent the deportation of refugees from the United States in a number of ways . . . . National Lawyers Guild attorneys have also urged Congress to adopt legislation that would prevent the deportation of Guatemalans and Salvadorans . . . . National Lawyers Guild attorneys have also challenged INS's application of the standard of proof required for obtaining asylum . . . . Attorneys with the National Lawyers Guild have set up refugee defense offices close to the detention camps [where Cuban illegals were held] to represent refugees . . . . Progressive lawyers have filed additional lawsuits challenging INS enforcement of the Refugee Act of 1980 . . . [such as] *Orantes-Hernandez v. Meese* . . . . This trial also demonstrates how progressive attorneys are able to use the law to expose injustices in the United States' foreign policy. The trial itself was a forum for exposing the human rights situation in El Salvador . . . and the Reagan Administration's complicity . . . . [97]

In an unmistakable echo from the past, the visiting American humanitarians then toured and praised the Cuban penal system—a system that now holds more political prisoners per capita than any other country on earth. Cuban dictator Fidel Castro addressed the closing session of the conference and singled out the American delegation specifically for praise, saying he was ''greatly impressed'' with them.[98]

THE IRANIAN CRISIS

On November 4, 1979, the American embassy in Teheran, Iran was stormed and 52 American hostages taken by a mob of students incited by the fundamentalist government of Ayatollah Khomeini. For the next 444 days Americans watched, humiliated and horrified, as their countrymen were abused and mockingly paraded in front of the international media. Americans suffered through one of the most humiliating periods in their entire history, one which still has an effect over a decade later.

Shortly after the crisis began, the Carter Administration moved to locate and deport Iranian students in the United States, a move prompted both to protect their safety and to eliminate a possible source of terrorist activity within the country. The immigration radicals who were hounding the government about Haitian and Hispanic illegals could not resist the temptation to get involved in this crisis as well. Peter Schey sharply criticized this deportation policy, complaining in a *Los Angeles*

Times column that Carter's order was unconstitutional, illegal, nativist and danger-ous. "Forcing Americans to choose between protecting their Constitution or saving face for the President is unfortunate: A legal victory for the Iranian students may well be viewed by many as a victory for those holding the hostages in Tehran. A legal victory for the President may well establish precedent which will return to haunt other identifiable minority groups in the future." [99] President Carter was not moved by Schey's patriotic appeal; on April 12, 1980, the administration announced that all Iranians would be forced to leave the U.S. when their travel documents expired. [100]

At the end of 1979, the National Lawyers Guild resolved at their convention to fight deportation of the Iranian militants and "send a message of solidarity to the Iranian people by way of Radio Iran." The NLG's resolution stated that ". . .the heroic struggles of the Iranian people have succeeded in crushing the Shah's U.S.-backed regime. The revolution in Iran today is a major defeat for U.S. imperialist policy throughout the world."

Chapter Five
Academics and Independent Scholars

"This year the Foundation continued support for several U.S. groups working to ensure fair and effective implementation of the Immigration Reform and Control Act [Simpson-Mazzoli] of 1986."

—Ford Foundation Annual Report, 1989.

CENTER FOR U.S.-MEXICAN STUDIES

If one wanted to find a research center certifying that all immigration, legal or illegal, is good for America, one need search no further than the Center for U.S.-Mexican Studies at the University of California-San Diego. Shortly after the Center's founding in 1980 its Director, Wayne Cornelius, published an opinion piece in the *San Diego Union* asserting that " 'the problem' [with immigration] is not the migrant himself, but his illegal status in the U.S." Therefore, Cornelius argued, the way to reduce illegal immigration is "to transform as many as possible of today's— and tomorrow's—illegal aliens into legal immigrants, whether they are here as permanent settlers or just temporary workers who cannot or do not want to spend the rest of their lives in the United States." [1]

A glossy 270-page publication issued by the Center in July, 1983, with acknowledgments to the Ford Foundation (which demonstrated an appreciation of Wayne Cornelius' cause by donating $448,000 to the Center in 1984, and $550,000 in 1987 [2]) shows a frenzied output of research, conferences and news briefings—most directed towards the U.S. immigration policy debate. Among the dozens of activities described in the report are special outreach and support to the League of United Latin American Citizens, and to Ford-funded organizations such as MALDEF, Pacific

News Service, National Center for Immigrants' Rights, and the American Friends Service Committee.[3]

Center fellow Leo R. Chavez, then Chairman of the San Diego-based Committee on Immigration's Chicano Federation, adequately fulfilled the Ford mandate of "broad dissemination of scholarly research" with a 1983 opinion piece for the Los Angeles *Herald Examiner* entitled "Immigration Reform: What do Hispanics want?":

> "In the furor over the recent demise of the Simpson- Mazzoli immigration-reform bill in the House of Representatives, one sentiment emerged particularly clearly: U.S. Latinos are to blame for the bill's sudden death . . . . many people in the country are confused about the motives and objectives of Latinos concerning immigration reform . . . . I agree with the critics who, citing public-opinion polls, argue that a majority of Latinos favor reform of the nation's immigration laws. I disagree, however, with the notion that Latino leaders do not represent Latinos in general on this issue."[4]

The opinion polls at issue, however, showed strong Hispanic support for the supposedly controversial employer sanctions, but they did not relate to some vague endorsement of "reform."[5] Nevertheless, Chavez goes on to express support for broad amnesty, open legal immigration, decreases in border enforcement, and opposition to employer sanctions. In 1987 his name was billed on a flyer advertising the Southern California "Breakdown the Border" conference organized by the Revolutionary Communist Party (a Maoist organization, allied internationally with the "Shining Path" guerrillas of Peru).[6]

A letter to the editor in response to Chavez was swift to appear, ironically just as the Ford Foundation publicized its working paper on refugees and migrants:

> "As a whole-hearted American of Mexican descent, and a middle-class working man, maybe you'd like to hear what kind of immigration reform my family and friends, all so-called Hispanics, would like. We would like it if all the illegals would just go home. Mexican-American men and women have lost a foothold to illegals in many areas of employment because they work for much less and will tolerate adverse working conditions, thus lowering standards for all. Just the sheer numbers of them have gobbled up the affordable rentals. Their children add to our already overcrowded neighborhood schools. Spanish-surnamed people do not all think alike: We are individuals, just like everyone else. I resent a handful of professional Latinos speaking for me. The sleek public-relations type Latino 'advocates' have done us more harm than good. . ."[7]

This is the sort of American whose views are permitted no legitimacy in the Ford analysis of the immigration "problem."

THE CENTER FOR NORTHERN BORDER STUDIES

The Mexican scholar with the most militant views on illegal aliens' "right" to immigrate to the United States is perhaps Jorge Bustamante, president since 1982 of the Tijuana Center, only a few miles across the border from Cornelius's San Diego Center. Bert Corona, the old Chicano radical who first made a political issue of illegal aliens, has praised Bustamante's "fine research and documentation" and his struggle against the Mexican ruling class on immigration.[8] The radical views of Bustamante are explicit in a 1976 article: "Undocumented Mexican workers and Chicano workers are forced. . .to compete for the lowest paying jobs," he said. "Many Chicano workers in the Southwest blame undocumented Mexican workers for the oppressive living conditions. . ." However, applying a standard Marxian analysis to the issue, Bustamante objects to limiting illegal immigration as this "prevents the development of solidarity between workers." He concludes that opposition to illegal immigration is fostered by the ruling class to distract the working class from the need for revolutionary change: ". . .the myth has functioned to transfer the responsibility for economic crises to powerless immigrants and has made it possible for those who own the means of production to deflect public attention from needed structural changes in society."[9]

Bustamante and James D. Cockcroft (author of the far-left *Outlaws in the Promised Land*) wrote several articles on the immigration issue for the Mexican press, one version of which was printed in a 1981 issue of *Radical America*: "The growth of illegal immigration is due to the domination of Mexico's economy by U.S.-based transnational corporations. Illegal aliens do not displace American workers, who create their own low-wage niche in the economy. A primary cause of both Carter's and Reagan's policies is the growing organizing activity, including incipient unionization and strikes, among the 'undocumented' workers themselves."[10]

Cockcroft, working in Mexico City with the benefit of a seed grant from the Ford Foundation,[11] developed a more thorough analysis of immigration policy for the journal *Contemporary Marxism*. According to this study, "the U.S. working class can realistically strengthen its position only when it adds to its fight-back strategy a commitment to the defense of the unorganized and the 'undocumented'—as well as to workers' struggles from Southern Africa to Central America and the Caribbean . . . U.S. workers must rally to the expression of solidarity with workers of all types in their common struggle against world capital, which is determined to break labor's spirit and to engulf young workers in renewed regional or world war."[12]

Cockcroft's brief Leninist analysis was expanded to book-length in *Outlaws in the Promised Land: Mexican Immigrant Workers and America's Future*, a peculiar volume worthy of much longer analysis. Suffice to say that Peter Schey states on the jacketcover that "Cockcroft might well reshape the immigration debate in this country," while Herman Baca says "A must for everyone who wants to discuss the immigration issue in an intelligent manner." Cockcroft thanks Ford for funding, and Baca and Bustamante "for their contributions to my own intellectual development."[13]

A 1982 San Diego news conference, cited by Cockcroft in *Outlaws*, further illustrates the close connections among these activist scholars:[14]

"A Mexican authority on immigration and a Chicano civil-rights leader doubled up yesterday to criticize what they called an intensified United States campaign to deny human and legal rights to undocumented Mexican workers. . . Jorge Bustamante, director of the border studies program at El Colegio de Mexico. . .attacked President Reagan's immigration proposals. . . Bustamante appeared. . .with Herman Baca, chairman of the Committee on Chicano Rights, and James D. Cockcroft, a Rutgers University specialist who has co-authored many articles with Bustamante. The joint statement by Bustamante and Baca was arranged by Cockcroft. . ." [15]

Like Leo Chavez in San Diego, Cockcroft was billed on a flyer of the 1987 El Paso version of the "Breakdown the Border" conference. It called for "a conference at the Mexican-U.S. border on the U.S. domination of Mexico and the latest stepped-up repression against Latinos." [16] The tired far-left mantra was clearly discernible in the comments of conference organizers who were quoted in an issue of *Revolutionary Worker*: "Among immigrants, especially from the Latin American countries, the vicious boot of U.S. imperialism is getting ready to stomp down harder. . . Will the oppressed close ranks and oppose the attacks on the immigrants who have a deep hatred and experience in fighting U.S. imperialism and are an important force for revolution?" [17]

In an interview taken just prior to the unexpected passage of the immigration-reform law in November 1986, Bustamante commented that "The United States is the only country in the world where employers are legally permitted to hire those who have violated its own immigration laws. That is in response to the demand for labor by U.S. employers . . . . In the United States. . .undocumented immigration . . .is viewed as a crime-related phenomenon that requires a police-type solution. Therefore, the whole question of undocumented immigration is viewed as a domestic problem requiring unilateral decisions like legislation. Mexico sees out-migration as basically an economic, labor-related phenomenon. We view a bilateral solution as the only rational way to approach the question." [18]

In response to the passage of the new immigration law, Bustamante undertook a public relations offensive in the U.S. According to a newspaper report, "Although Bustamante always insists he is speaking only for himself, many inside and outside Mexico believe the sociologist's sometimes harsh broadsides on U.S. policies reflect official Mexican government thinking. His most recent criticism is about the just-passed U.S. immigration reform law, which he calls 'a unilateral solution to a bilateral problem' . . . . The [Northern Border] college is linked to San Diego academic life with working agreements with the UC San Diego's Center for U.S.-Mexican Studies . . . . Also the college received a $250,000 three-year Ford Foundation grant in 1985. . ." [19] And, had received $130,000 from the Foundation in 1983. [20]

Cornelius and Bustamante continue to invite the interest of the American media in their scholarly declarations. Both opposed the passage of the Simpson-Mazzoli immigration-reform law, and can be fairly described as hostile to its control objectives. The front-page story in a 1988 *New York Times* is called, "Immigration Law is Failing to Cut Flow from Mexico." The reporter begins, "The 1986 immigration law is failing to stem the illegal flow of Mexicans into the United States and may be creating new problems on both sides of the border by distorting traditional immigration patterns, Mexican and American researchers say. Studies by immigration specialists at the College of the Northern Border in Tijuana [Bustamante] and the Center for United States-Mexican Studies at the University of California, San Diego [Cornelius], indicate that the number of Mexicans illegally seeking work in the United States has actually increased in recent months." [21]

BILATERAL COMMISSION ON U.S.-MEXICAN AFFAIRS

At a 1983 news conference Wayne Cornelius of the San Diego Center and Professor Clark W. Reynolds from a similar project at Stanford denounced the Simpson-Mazzoli immigration reform bill. Cornelius gave his usual reasons, while Reynolds said that the legislation would only be effective if it established a bilateral commission to deal with Mexico, in order to "come to grips with a new transnational federal policy." [22] In 1985, Ford established the Inter-University Program on Latino Research, [23] with a grant of $150 million made through Stanford University. The IUPLR was a consortium involving Stanford, Cornelius' San Diego Center, the University of Texas at Austin (whose lead researcher, Gilbert Cardenas endorsed the 1987 "Breakdown the Border" conference [24]), and the Center for Puerto Rican Studies in New York. Another immigration policy activist, Fernando de Necochea, was Chairperson of the MALDEF Board in 1984-1985, and is Assistant Provost and Advisor to the President for Mexican-American Affairs at Stanford University. [25]

Coincident with Bustamante's call for "bilateral" solutions, the Ford Foundation announced in 1986 its establishment, with a grant of $600,000, of a new and private Bilateral Commission on U.S.-Mexican Affairs. Ford reported that, "The commission held its first meeting in October [1986] in Tijuana and San Diego where it heard current and former government officials, Chicano leaders, and prominent citizens speak on immigration and other issues . . . The commission will operate with complete autonomy." [26]

The U.S. director of this ongoing commission is Peter Smith, sometime political science professor at MIT, but also the Simon Bolivar Professor of Latin American Studies at University of California, San Diego. In early 1987, Smith published his views on the new Immigration Reform and Control Act: "If it works—that is if it leads to an appreciable reduction in undocumented immigration to the United States, especially from Mexico—then labor costs for employers will increase and their firms and industries will become less competitive . . . . But there is a reasonable chance that Simpson-Rodino will not work . . . . In this case, one might expect illegal migration to continue at its present pace . . . ." [27]

The "independent" Dr. Smith, regardless of the wide diversity of views on immigration policy among American scholars, preferred the in-bred views of other Ford-supported scholars from the left when commissioning his two main papers. For example, Wayne Cornelius' paper, entitled "U.S. Demand for Migrant Labor," and

Jorge Bustamante's "Policy Options for Mexico," repeated the stance in favor of unlimited immigration from Mexico to the U.S.

In the 1987 Commission meeting, held August 28-29 in San Diego and Tijuana, the lay members of the Ford Commission considered the Cornelius and Bustamante presentations along with those of other Mexican scholars present, who uniformly endorsed the fashionable Mexican government notion that the U.S. is to blame for illegal immigration from Mexico, but should do nothing to stop it. The remaining (American) immigration experts called to inform the Commission consisted of long-time immigration-control opponent Kitty Calavita (who is Cornelius' academic sub-ordinate at his Center for U.S.-Mexican Studies), and Marta Tienda of the Universities of Chicago and Wisconsin-Madison who, again predictably, suggested not only that Mexican immigration is inevitable, but that U.S. resistance to such massive illegality is racist. [28]

COLUMBIA UNIVERSITY

In 1986, the Ford Foundation granted $1,310,000 to Columbia University for the establishment of the first university-wide human rights program. According to Ford;

> Columbia's program will consist of interdisciplinary teaching, research, and work with human and civil rights organizations. . . . Visiting researchers from the United States and abroad have joined Columbia's faculty and students in studying themes ranging from the rights of aliens to human rights and development. The Center . . . has worked with such organizations as the Lawyers Committee for International Human Rights, Helsinki Watch, and Americas Watch. Building on these activities as well as existing teaching and research on U.S. civil rights and refugee issues, Columbia's new program will integrate the study of human rights . . ." [29]

Ford Foundation trustee Harriet Schaffer Rabb, Clinical Professor of Law at Columbia University, served from 1980-86 as Co-Director of the Law School Immigration Clinic. The other Director was Susan Susman, who also served with the National Immigration Project of the National Lawyers Guild (NIP-NLG). [30] Upon its 1980 founding, the "Immigration Law Project" (later renamed "Clinic") was described as "especially concerned with those cases involving political asylum. It is working closely with the Lawyers Committee for International Human Rights." [31]

Today the Columbia Immigration Law Clinic is directed by Lucas Guttentag of the American Civil Liberties Union and the National Immigration Project of the NLG. [32] This transfer of power is not surprising, given the program's close ties with the Lawyers Committee for International Human Rights, a project of former ACLU director Aryeh Neier's Fund for Free Expression. [33]

A while later, the Center for the Study of Human Rights at Columbia University became concerned with government surveillance of political revolutionaries and with illegal aliens, developing a course on "Aliens, Refugees, Migration and Rights." On the "themes for 1982-1983" the organization chose, to coincide with research projects, "human rights and national security and the rights of aliens including refugees. . . " The Center also hosted a conference on the 'problems' of illegal aliens, and planned four additional conferences for the coming year. Included in the schedule was an "International Conference on the Treatment of Aliens."[34]

LIBERTARIANS AND NEOCONSERVATIVES

It is common to place these two groups at the opposite end of the political spectrum from people like Cornelius, Cockcroft and Bustamante. Both libertarians and conservatives (neo- and otherwise) are opponents of Marxism and its various socialist incarnations. However, libertarianism, and to a lesser but still substantial effect, neo-conservatism, are rooted in the same 19th-century classical liberalism to which the American Civil Liberties Union appeals and from which comes much of the philosophical base of the open borders movement (even if distorted by leftists with other agendas to advance). Thus, despite a different set of institutional connections, much of what is said and done by these right-of-center activists is similar to the work of the left-wing groups that are the primary focus of this study.

The leading libertarian scholar on the immigration issue is economist Julian Simon, a professor of business administration at the University of Maryland. Simon does his writing for conservative groups such as the Heritage Foundation, the Hudson Institute, and the *Wall Street Journal*; as well as for "free market" libertarian think tanks like the Cato Institute.

Simon favors high rates of immigration into the United States because he believes it is good for the American economy: "An overall increase in immigration is the best way to boost the crucial stock of talented scientists, inventors, engineers and managers." He is quick to cite the benefits the United States gained from the influx of doctors fleeing Castro's Cuba and scientists fleeing Hitler's Germany, as well as the benefits from other middle-class and professional refugees.

This, however, avoids the real debate that focuses on unskilled Third World immigrants, with limited education and employable skills, who flock across the border illegally. Simon constantly (and perhaps intentionally) confuses the two issues, concluding that all immigrants are of value. "Immigrants, legal and otherwise, may be the United States' biggest asset in maintaining and improving competitiveness," he says.[35]

Simon believes in a pure quantity theory of progress: "A larger population implies a larger amount of knowledge being created all else being equal. This is the straightforward result of there being more people to have more ideas."[36] However, if this quantity approach held as a general theory of human development, the great powers of the world today and throughout most of history would be China and India. Russia would have also been the leader (rather than the laggard) of the Industrial

Revolution in Europe. And England, with a population of only 10 million in 1750, would not have won and ruled India (with a population of 175 million at that same time) for two centuries.

Obviously more than mere numbers are at work in the real world. As Simon Kuznets, the dean of American economists specializing in the process of economic growth, has argued, "No clear association appears to exist . . . between rates of growth of population and of product per capita. . . . Apparently other factors—relative availability of natural resources, timing of the inception of the growth process, or institutional conditions—complicate the effects of population growth." [37]

Simon rejects such logic, particularly where the defense of social and cultural institutions is concerned. "The notion of wanting to keep out immigrants in order to keep our institutions and values is pure prejudice." [38] Those who hold such views are mere "Yahoos." When asked in the same *Forbes* article about the success of Japan given its closed, homogenous society and traditional values, he replied, "How Japan gets along, I don't know."

Simon has also called the emphasis on per capita income "suspect" as a measure of living standards and progress. According to him, this logic implies that in order to advance, a society must "Do away with all lower-income people." Yet it is the function of technology and education to improve productivity so all workers can earn a higher income and thus afford better living conditions. What Simon is attempting to do is dispel any concern for the continued existence of an underclass living in poverty, a class that most immigrants join.

Although Simon likes to argue that immigration has no impact on overall wage levels, he will admit when prodded that immigration produces a short-term decline in market wage levels for both alien and native workers. However, after this short-term downturn, he believes that economic growth will eventually push wage levels back up. [39] Simon's thesis would only hold true if immigration were a one-time phenomenon. However, since each year brings a new wave of immigrants, the downward pressure is never relieved.

Vernon M. Briggs, Jr., Professor of Industrial and Labor Relations at Cornell University, takes this analysis further. "No technologically advanced industrial nation that has 27 million illiterate and another 27-40 million marginally literate adults needs fear a shortage of unskilled workers in its foreseeable future." [40] Noting that one-third of the growth rate of the U.S. labor force since 1965 has been from immigration, he argues that immigration policy must be based on the nation's true economic needs, not decided by political pressure.

> [T]he appropriate role of immigration policy is clear. Immigration policy must be made strictly accountable for its economic consequences. It should be a targeted and flexible policy designed to admit only persons who can fill job vacancies that require significant skills preparation and educational investment. The number annually admitted should be fewer than the number needed. [41]

This last point is important. Labor and capital are substitutes, not only within various industries but in the overall mix of industries in the economy. The availability of a large pool of low-skill, low-wage labor skews the economy in the direction of labor-intensive enterprises. The result is that resources flow towards industries that have low-productivity and thus provide poverty-level incomes to those employed there. Meanwhile, the industries of the future, high-tech, capital-intensive endeavors, have fewer resources available to support their growth—growth that would uplift rather than depress the average living standard of the nation as a whole and provide, long-term, better opportunities for citizens.

"[R]apid workforce growth may slow the upgrading of an economy" writes Michael E. Porter, a professor at the Harvard Business School who served on the President's Commission on Industrial Competitiveness. "With a ready supply of employees, pressures to boost productivity, upgrade skills, and seek more advanced forms of competitive advantage are eased. A similar effect occurs when there is large-scale immigration of unskilled workers . . . Part of lagging productivity growth in American industry may be due to population growth more rapid than that of most nations coupled with a higher rate of immigration of low skilled workers and a greater propensity for women to enter the workforce." [42]

Yet such arguments, rooted as they are in the logic of the market, have little impact on open borders advocates like Julian Simon. Simon's basic philosophy is not rooted in economic analysis. It was laid out nearly 20 years ago in his first major essay on population.

> "The value which I wish to use as a criterion for decisions about population growth is one that I think a great many people subscribe to also. . . . In Biblical terms it is 'Be fruitful and multiply.' . . . .
>
> "Other things being equal, a greater number of people is a good thing, according to this value criterion. Furthermore, this criterion suggests that a society may even be better off with a lower average income if more people are partaking in it—though how much lower is a tricky matter of course. . . . The important point here is that I reject average income by itself as a criterion for judgments about population size. Under some conditions, I accept that it is better to have more people and lower per capita income . . ." [43]

This attitude leads him to conclude that there is no over-population or true poverty anywhere in the world.

> I have seen the misery of India. Intestinal disease and blindness all around. A 14-year-old girl catches bricks on a construction job for 30 cents per day as her baby lies on a burlap sack, covered with flies and crying. . . . And yet I choose to think that all these lives are worth living. And these people think their lives are worth living, or else they would choose to stop living. . . . Hence I will not say that the existence of poor people—either in poor countries or, a fortiori, in the United States—is a sign of overpopulation. [44]

The leading neoconservative spokesman on immigration policy is Ben J. Wattenberg, a senior fellow at the right-of-center American Enterprise Institute in Washington, D.C. Though Wattenberg often quotes Simon, he shows far more sensitivity to political and cultural aspects of immigration. This puts him at odds with Simon as well as with the leftists when it comes to particular policy prescriptions. In language that would terrify an advocate from MALDEF or the Haitian Refugee Center, he says, "There is no ignoring the unsettled feeling many people experience upon walking into a New York City subway or a Los Angeles public school—the feeling of being, as the saying goes, 'in a Third World country'. . . . citizens should not be made to feel like strangers in their own land." [45]

Wattenberg is thus a strong supporter of the assimilation of immigrants within the dominant Anglo-European-Western tradition, in particular the attainment of English-language proficiency. This puts him at odds with the leftists who preach ethnic autonomy or separatism. Wattenberg is opposed to "ethnic populism—one bloc against another, with the national interest perceived as nothing more than an aggregate of group appeals."

However, Wattenberg is still an advocate of higher levels of immigration; he just wants more government control over the process and the objectives than Simon or the leftists would accept. He feared that the impact of the 1986 Simpson-Mazzoli Immigration Reform and Control Act would be to keep immigration at too low a level, given the declining demographic trends of the native American population (what he calls the "birth dearth"). [46] He is particularly concerned that the Western nations and the U.S. in particular will lose military, economic and cultural power if their populations continue to fall relative to societies in Asia or Latin America.

While he does not go as far as Simon to equate power with population, he notes that, "While a large population does not guarantee great power status . . . A nation cannot be a great power unless it has a large population." [47] Advanced technology gives the United States the edge over China's larger population; but with equivalent technology, it is the size of the U.S. population (for working or fighting) that gives it the edge over Japan. Thus there is a concept of balance between population and other factors in Wattenberg's works that is missing in Simon's.

Wattenberg has also endorsed the plan of a colleague at AEI, economist Barry Chiswick. The Chiswick plan would limit immigration based on family ties (the principal basis for legal immigration since national quotas were dropped in 1965) to bonafide spouses, minor children and parents. Beyond that, immigration would be based on refugee status and on a "skills-based system, with points awarded for years of school completed, apprenticeship or vocational training, knowledge of English, high professional status or special educational achievements, and some carefully drawn blueprint of occupational demand in the U.S." [48]

Mexican immigrants, Wattenberg goes on to note, "can make valuable economic contributions—from maids, busboys and gardeners, up the occupational ladder as far as aspiration and ability allow. But they do little to improve immediately the overall competence of the American workforce." However, given that the average

Mexican immigrant has only 7.5 years of schooling, he would not garner many points on the Chiswick scale.

The Immigration Act of 1990 contained a scoring system to allot 141,000 visas per year to those with special skills or doctorates. The bill also allotted 4,800 visas to those immigrants who brought $1 million with them and 2,000 slots for those who brought $500,000. This was enough to obtain Wattenberg's endorsement of the bill. Simon, on the other hand, blasted the bill in the *Wall Street Journal*, claiming that, "Behind the law is some combination of economic ignorance and plain racism. The nativism is as clearly at work here as it is in Britain where Margaret Thatcher makes no bones about restricting immigration so as to 'keep Britain British.' " [49] He particularly felt the bill would mean fewer Hispanics and Asian immigrants.

Simon thus found himself again in the company of the far left. Peter Schey, this time identified as director of the Center for Human Rights and Constitutional Law in Los Angeles, also denounced the 1990 bill, declaring that "the whole implication is that if you're poor and uneducated, America doesn't want you." [50]

In the Immigration Act of 1990 the total yearly quota for legal immigrants was increased from 400,000 to 700,000 (dropping to 650,000 in 1995). Of the 300,000 increase, 141,000 were to be in visas awarded on the basis of skills and talents. Family reunification visas were also increased. Oddly enough, most of the opposition came from Republicans in both houses. Representative Tom Campbell, a liberal Congressman from California's Silicon Valley, offered sharp objection to the investment preference provision endorsed by Wattenberg and Chiswick. "Other countries, we are told, have similar programs. But this is intolerable to me. However beneficial the investment may be, the fact remains that America would, for the first time in its history, be granting statutory preference for citizenship based on wealth." [51]

In fact, the number of people being admitted either on the basis of "wealth" or job skills is very small relative to the total number of visas granted, and accounts for only about half of the allowed increase. Indeed, since family members that accompany a person admitted for their skills are also applied against the special 141,000 quota, it is quite possible that a majority of those admitted under the skills category will not themselves have any qualifying skills. This is why labor economists like Vernon Briggs have concluded that despite the rhetoric, "any fair reading of the new immigration law can only be seen as a retreat from any quest to tailor immigration policy to labor market needs." [52]

Richard Miniter, an editor at *The American Spectator* (which caters to both libertarian and conservative readers), attacked the Wattenberg/Chiswick proposal on the libertarian grounds that "Economic planning, even in the guise of immigration reform, cannot work and should not be tried. . . . So why not advocate free and open borders?" [53]

In answering the libertarians, Wattenberg indicated that not every immigrant is a bonus: "[W]itness the castoffs from Cuba's jails and asylums, the nearly 10,000 aliens now serving time in federal prisons and the 50,000 more who have committed crimes but have been released or sentenced to probation. . . . Deportations of undesirable individuals could be speeded, and careful selection of future citizens is well within national prerogative." [54]

To bolster total immigration within a more controlled system, Wattenberg advocates a new program of 150,000 liberty visas per year for the next ten years to take advantage of the opening of Eastern Europe and other communist governments and 75,000 new visas for "democratic Europe," where there is a backlog of immigrants wanting to come to the United States (mainly from Spain, Greece, Ireland, England and Germany). [55] Such a proposal would undoubtedly be considered "racist" by the left and by many libertarians, and would also be attacked by the left for showing once again the "anti-communist flavor of American immigration law." [56]

However, a larger influx of European immigrants would do much to alleviate the fears of those who predict that a rising tide of Third World immigrants will threaten America's cultural values and political stability. As an editorial in the traditionally conservative *National Review* put it, "We have no obligation to throw a party for the whole world . . . we want new Americans to be good Americans." [57]

National Review moved more strongly towards a restrictionist position in its June 22, 1992 issue with the publication of a lengthy essay by Peter Brimelow calling into question the continued utility of mass immigration. Brimelow is Senior Editor of *Forbes*, the same pro-immigration business journal that has featured Julian Simon. Brimelow is also himself an immigrant (British), yet he argues that America must reduce the inflow of immigrants from Third World areas. He cites that

> [m]any current public policies have an unmistakable tendency to deconstruct the American nation. Apart from official bilingualism and multiculturalism, these policies include: multilingual ballots; defining citizenship so as to include children born here— even the children of illegals; the abandonment of English as a prerequisite for citizenship; the erosion of citizenship as the sole qualification for voting; the extension of welfare and education benefits as a right to illegals and their children; congressional and state legislative apportionment based on legal and illegal populations. [58]

Brimelow also gives the ominous warning that perhaps everyone should heed: "just as the American nation was made with unusual speed, so it is perfectly possible that it could be unmade." [59]

Chapter Six
The Mexican American Legal Defense and Educational Fund

"Of [MALDEF's] annual . . . budget, only about two percent comes from individual donations from the Latino community
—Los Angeles Times (Nuestro Tiempo section)[1]

Hispanic activism was not always a radical pro-foreign movement. Illustrative are the early years of the League of United Latin American Citizens (LULAC). Today LULAC is on the forefront of organizations promoting "immigrant rights," but in the past it offered a responsible Americanist agenda. That agenda by contrast shows how far the current LULAC, MALDEF, and similar groups are out of the mainstream.

LUCAC was organized on February 17, 1929, at a convention in Corpus Christi, Texas, to halt the feuding between several fractious Mexican American groups. The hopes of the convention organizers were to form one large, united body that could represent all Hispanic people and work for their civil rights.

The convention, which was opened with the reading of a prayer by George Washington, succeeded in uniting the factions to form the League of United Latin American Citizens (LULAC). Membership was to be limited to American citizens of Latin extraction. English was to be the official language, although LULAC's code encouraged the retention of Spanish as one of "the two most essential languages." The code also stated:

> Respect your citizenship; honor your country, maintain its traditions in the minds of your children; incorporate yourself in the culture and civilization.
> Love the men of your race, take pride in your origins and keep it immaculate; respect your glorious past and help to vindicate your people.[2]

59

Indeed, according to its constitution, LULAC's goal was "to develop within the members of our race the purest and most perfect type of a true and loyal citizen of the United States."

LULAC was thus primarily a middle-class civil rights organization attempting to end discrimination against Mexican-Americans. The organization specifically warned its members not to associate with groups that stressed Mexican nationalism or Hispanic separatism, as its leaders wished to avoid any charge of being a group of radicals or agitators. Members were encouraged to vote as a full expression of citizenship (although LULAC was careful to avoid any semblance of partisan leaning). LULAC's position also held that knowledge of the English language and American civics was of tantamount importance. As writer Mario T. Garcia noted in his history of Mexican-American organizations, "[LULAC] believed that the 'genius' and 'quality' of Americans had made the United States great and that Mexican-Americans should develop such virtues, including individualism. LULAC maintained that only in the United States could citizens progress and retain their individuality."[3]

From its main base in Texas, LULAC developed chapters in 21 states. It organized protests against discrimination, and segregation in public facilities, but unlike many of today's "civil rights protestors," LULAC rejected all attempts to segregate Mexican-Americans as a nonwhite population. In fact, as Garcia writes, "Mexican-Americans expressed ambivalence about race identity and possessed their own prejudices against blacks. . . . LULACers consistently argued that Mexicans were legally recognized members of the white race and that no legal or physical basis existed for racial discrimination."[4]

In 1954 the first case involving Hispanic civil rights reached the Supreme Court. *Hernandez v. Texas* appealed the murder conviction of a Mexican-American defendant from Jackson County, Texas. At that time Hispanics comprised fourteen percent of the county's population, but no Hispanic had served on a jury during the past 25 years. In a landmark decision Chief Justice Earl Warren ruled "that persons of Mexican descent were a distinct class" entitled to the same equal protection of the 14th Amendment as whites and blacks.

LULAC AND THE ORIGINS OF MALDEF

During the decade of the 1960s, the general escalation of political activity that was carrying along black and college student groups also swept up the Mexican-American organizations. Although the *Hernandez v. Texas* decision a decade earlier had been a great victory for LULAC, there nevertheless was still a general lack of this kind of legal activism. A view developed that the tempered, mainstream approach of LULAC would not achieve as much for Hispanics as, for example, the Legal Defense Fund of the National Association for the Advancement of Colored People had done for blacks.

In 1966, attorney Peter Tijerina, the State Civil Rights Chairman for the LULAC chapter in San Antonio, sent a member of the organization to the Chicago convention of the NAACP's Legal Defense Fund. Tijerina followed up this contact with a trip to New York in the spring of 1967 in search of funding for an appeal of a new Texas case on the grounds that no jurors of Mexican extraction were available. Jack Greenberg, head of NAACP-LDF, set up a meeting with Bill Pincus at the Ford Foundation. Tijerina presented his plan for a five-state organization to do for Hispanics what the NAACP-LDF was doing for blacks. Pincus agreed to arrange seed money until a full-scale proposal could be acted on by the Foundation. The Mexican-American Legal Defense and Educational Fund was born.[5]

In February, 1968, Tijerina announced he was asking the Ford Foundation for $1 million. MALDEF's board met in May 1968 in San Antonio to hear Ford's response. To their surprise, Ford *doubled* the request, giving MALDEF $2.2 million over a five year period to fund civil rights legal services for Mexican-Americans. Of this grant, $250,000 was to go explicitly to scholarships for Hispanic law students.

Peter Tijerina took the position of MALDEF's first executive director when its headquarters were opened in San Antonio. Mario Obledo, the Texas Assistant Attorney General, was persuaded to become MALDEF's General Counsel in 1970. Recent law school graduates and VISTA volunteers added to the staff, and there was even enough support to open a small one-attorney office in Los Angeles. A network of corresponding attorneys who filed suits in MALDEF's name (usually without compensation) was established nationwide, numbering some 150 by the middle of 1969. Cases across the spectrum from job discrimination to police brutality, school desegregation to voting rights, were channeled to MALDEF by LULAC, G.I. Forum and other such groups.

During the late 1960s and early 1970s there were a number of Hispanic protests, strikes and demonstrations around the country. MALDEF worked to protect dissidents from legal action, loss of jobs, or expulsion from school. As MALDEF's own written history states, "the Los Angeles office gave legal advice to hundreds of Chicanos arrested during anti-war marches."[6] The organization also worked on draft counseling and placing of Hispanics on local draft boards. By 1973, many Texas cities had draft boards that were half Hispanic.

Student walkouts were used to gain attention to demands for equal education. MALDEF defended student protesters and filed suits against school systems that did not allow Hispanic students to transfer to Anglo schools, that tried to keep Hispanics in vocational tracks, or that appropriated more funds to Anglo schools than to predominantly Hispanic schools.

Suits to enforce Title VII of the 1965 Civil Rights Act against job discrimination were pushed in California, Texas and New Mexico. In the area of voting rights, MALDEF lawyers charged that annual voter registration requirements kept one million Hispanics ineligible to vote; that property requirements were unfair to working class citizens, and that at-large districts kept Hispanic candidates from winning office.

FORD ENGINEERS LEADERSHIP CHANGES

Several years after MALDEF's founding the Ford Foundation began pressuring the activist organization to relocate its headquarters out of the state of Texas. Ostensibly the problem was that MALDEF was acquiring a "militant" image due to its involvement with demonstrations. In addition, one of the MALDEF staffers made "anti-Gringo" remarks that were picked up by the press. Fearing a backlash, the MALDEF directors thought it wise to move to a more "neutral" locale (preferably New York or Washington, D.C.) rather than risk losing Ford financial support.[7] MALDEF did open an office in Washington, D.C., but not until 1973. Instead, it chose San Francisco in 1970 for its new headquarters. This allowed the organization to stay close to its constituency in California and the Southwest. Scaled-down offices were kept in L.A. and San Antonio.

At this time, however, the Ford Foundation was itself under fire for funding other Chicano groups. In 1967 students at St. Mary's University in San Antonio formed the Mexican-American Youth Organization (MAYO). From this group emerged the radical activists who would lead the Chicano cause in the 1970s, including the formation of La Raza Unida, the hard-line Hispanic political party. As an openly radical left organization, MAYO was too controversial even for the Ford trustees, and found grant money hard to come by. But MAYO's leaders found a way around this by forming the so-called Mexican-American Unity Council (MAUC). Officially MAUC was not involved in politics the way MAYO was, thus enabling it to obtain Ford Foundation grants.[8] But given the nearly identical memberships of both organizations, the distinction was only technical in nature.

One of MAYO's first victories was forming and funding an organization of Chicano parents to remove the "no-Spanish" rule in San Antonio schools. A MAYO leader, Mario Campean then ran for mayor and came close to forcing a run-off election. However, this foray into electoral politics backfired, as it presented a challenge not only to Anglos in the community, but to Democratic Representative Henry B. Gonzalez, who considered himself the political leader of the San Antonio Hispanic community.

Rep. Gonzalez, still in the House and now Chairman of the powerful Banking, Housing and Urban Affairs Committee, has had a long record of working for Hispanic civil rights. He was the first Hispanic state senator in Texas in 110 years when he won a seat in 1956. Five years later he won a special election to a seat in the U.S House representing a district that covers central San Antonio and is better than 60 percent Mexican-American. The first Texan of Mexican descent in the U.S. House, Gonzalez has consistently opposed guest worker programs while supporting low-income housing programs and the minimum wage. But despite these generally liberal positions, he opposed and was vocally critical of Chicano activists at their height of power during the late 1960s and early 1970s, and has accused the leadership of such activist organizations as MALDEF and The National Council of La Raza of advocating "reverse discrimination." Probably most importantly, Gonzalez does not consider himself an "ethnic candidate," and has never campaigned under the banner of minority status.[9]

In 1969 Rep. Gonzalez took to the floor of Congress to denounce MAYO, and used his position on the Banking Committee to help pass a tax reform act that included new restrictions on the ability of foundations to fund activist groups like MAYO/MAUC.[10] Shortly thereafter, Ford withdrew its support from MAYO/MAUC, which then became relatively inactive. Peter Tijerina, himself a graduate of St. Mary's law school, was tarnished by his many personal ties to MAYO members. As part of the Ford-backed restructuring of MALDEF, the posts of executive director and general counsel were combined, and Tijerina was forced out as head of the organization he helped to create. Mario Obledo, a MALDEF staffer, moved into the top spot.[11]

At the same time the Ford Foundation was helping to purge MALDEF's radical image, it was also criticizing the organization behind-the-scenes for spending too much time and effort behaving like a legal aid society dealing with individual cases, rather than concentrating on the development of test cases that could set constitutional precedents. In essence, the Ford Foundation, on the one hand, was criticizing MALDEF's support of radical left political movements (a very public spectacle) while urging it to adopt a more radical position via precedent-setting court cases (an event which normally does not get great exposure in the press).

In 1971 MALDEF opened offices in Denver and in Albuquerque, the latter with the help of the University of New Mexico Law School, the New Mexico Legal Rights Project and the Albuquerque Legal Aid Society. As part of its shift to broader court cases, MALDEF strengthened its ties with NAACP's Legal Defense Fund and the National Organization for Women (NOW) in joint demands that the Federal government do more to enforce fair employment practices. In 1973, MALDEF and the NAACP-LDF joined forces to win a case that integrated the schools in Waco, Texas. These cooperative efforts with more established groups served to raise MALDEF's visibility and pass on valuable experience to its battery of lawyers.

In pressing its first test cases alone before the U.S. Supreme Court, MALDEF came away with an inauspicious one-for-three record. The one victory was in *White v. Regester*, which involved the constitutionality of large election districts. *Logue v. U.S.*, however, failed to convince the court that the U.S. government was liable for the negligence of city jail employees. This ruling was a minor setback compared to the loss in *San Antonio v. Rodriguez*. In that case, MALDEF argued that local school financing meant that areas that were heavily Hispanic had less money spent per student than Anglo localities. Therefore, Hispanics were not receiving equal protection under the dictates of the 14th Amendment. The Court, however, did not find that spending on education was a fundamental right protected by the Constitution, and ruled that the Texas state government did not have to subsidize poor school districts.

In the wake of these losses Mario Obledo resigned. According to an account of the court case in the *Social Science Quarterly*, "MALDEF attempted to implement the Ford Foundation's suggestions through a variety of different strategies. . . . But as its loss in *San Antonio* revealed, MALDEF acted too quickly and did not sufficiently 'prime' the Supreme Court either through frequent appearances as amicus curiae or the use of test cases."[12]

Selected to replace Obledo at the helm of MALDEF was Vilma S. Martinez, a 1967 graduate of Columbia Law School who had worked on the staff of the NAACP's Legal Defense Fund before joining a Wall Street law firm. In addition to expanding MALDEF's funding base, Martinez worked to increase the organization's access to Democratic politicians. In 1976, Governor Jerry Brown appointed her to the University of California Board of Regents, and in 1985 she became chair of the board. She also served on the Advisory Board of Ambassadorial Appointments for President Jimmy Carter. Martinez led MALDEF until 1981, when she resigned to join a major California law firm.[13]

Under Martinez, strategic planning for MALDEF became centered in the San Francisco office. Named as Litigation Director was Sanford Rosen, who was charged with molding a systematic case review process with a primary focus on constitutional test cases. Other directors were also appointed to coordinate specific areas such as employment, education and development. And more attention was paid to women's issues after the formation of the Chicano Rights Project in 1978. Martinez recruited experienced Hispanic civil rights lawyers, many from the NAACP-LDF and from the Federal Equal Employment Opportunity Commission. The use of amicus curiae was increased, including the support of the NAACP-LDF and other black litigants in enforcing the 1964 Voting Rights Act. MALDEF also filed suits against the Federal Office of Civil Rights to force action on Hispanic issues from an agency that was clearly placing most of its energy on black complaints.[14]

MALDEF continued to push desegregation cases in employment areas and schools. In Houston the activists won a landmark ruling that ended the practice of counting Mexican-Americans as white so they could be used to desegregate black schools, leaving other schools with only Anglo students. However, a backlash was growing. "By the mid-1970s MALDEF had a new adversary to deal with: a growing conservatism in the courts," according to MALDEF's own history of the period. "The farsighted civil rights decisions of the Warren Supreme Court were being replaced by decisions that limited protection for minorities. A 1973 Denver decision said that to prove *de jure* segregation, 'intent to discriminate' on the part of the school system had to be shown. This was a difficult blow. . . . Means of proving discrimination continued to narrow and a 1976 U.S. Supreme Court decision requiring a showing of 'intent to discriminate' in an employment suit firmly established the conservative trend."[15]

MALDEF was incredulous at these developments, claiming that charges of "reverse discrimination" and "improving the quality of the student body" were being used "to take away that small lifeline to higher education that was gained for minorities through special admissions programs. . . ." The 1978 Supreme Court decision in *Bakke v. University of California Board of Regents*, which struck down admissions policies based on racial quotas as unconstitutional, was the subject of many talks and testimony by MALDEF advocates. [16] The use of the Law School Admissions Test (LSAT) was also attacked as "culturally biased."

THE BILINGUAL-BICULTURAL CAMPAIGN

Despite these new setbacks, Martinez moved quickly to involve MALDEF in the growing campaign for bilingual-bicultural education. According to the organization's history, "for over a decade, blacks had demanded school integration to gain equal education for their children. Chicanos needed to take the battle one step further. Many children of Mexican origin had been confined to barrios all their lives and spoke mostly Spanish. Placing them in schools where they did not understand the language their teachers were using. . .was tantamount to giving them no education at all. . . . The solution pursued by MALDEF was bilingual-bicultural education." [17] In *Serma v. Portales* (1972) a New Mexico court held that bilingual education was constitutionally required for Mexican-American children. MALDEF also filed (with the Western Center for Law and Poverty) the first case in California charging that textbooks were biased against minorities.

This battle over bilingual (actually multilingual, as other minority groups joined the fray) education was part of a larger struggle over the role of America's schools: Whether they were to help immigrants and minorities assimilate into the general society, or whether they would assist in forming distinct, "separate but equal" communities.

In 1968 President Johnson signed into law the Bilingual Education Act. The act had a modest goal, to recognize that non-English speaking students needed special help and to provide local schools with money to meet that need. Local schools could decide what, if any, programs were needed. However, as with so many other so-called liberally-enlightened pieces of legislation, the bilingual law took off on its own power. In 1970 the Office for Civil Rights informed school districts with more than 5 percent non-English speaking minorities that they had a "responsibility to take affirmative steps to rectify the language deficiency." In 1974 the Supreme Court ruled in *Lau v. Nichols* (a suit originally filed only two months after the Office of Civil Rights memo was issued) that the San Francisco Independent School District violated the constitutional rights of non-English speaking Chinese students by failing to provide them with English language or "other adequate instructional procedures." Public schools therefore had to provide services to students with English language disabilities which would secure them equal access to the instructional program. [18]

MALDEF had supported the Chinese plaintiffs in *Lau* and now joined other groups seeking to amend the Bilingual Education Act. A major change that stemmed from the case was that bilingual education was no longer merely a method for teaching English; it needed to be expanded so that general instruction could be received in languages *other* than English. Bicultural programs were also to be undertaken to meet the need of minority children to understand their heritage. And, of course, federal money was to be available to support these programs with material and personnel. The Office of Civil Rights, also under minority group pressure, convened a task force made up primarily of educators sympathetic to bilingual-bicultural education to formulate "Lau remedies" that would meet federal goals. [19]

In 1977 advocates of assimilation counterattacked with an important study by the independent American Institute for Research that was released by the Department of Education in April. The study examined 38 fourth and fifth year projects. It found that less than 30 percent of students in bilingual programs were actually limited in their English-language skills. Fully 86 percent of these bilingual programs kept students in the special classes long after they were able to move on to regular English-language course work. Most importantly, the study found that bilingual education was not having a "consistently significant" impact on student performance in English language, arts, and mathematics. [20]

The Bilingual Education Act came up for reauthorization in 1978. It was passed, but with a new emphasis on the importance of English. The use of non-English languages was to be de-emphasized in the general instructional program. Assimilationists (mainly Republicans) managed to push the program back toward its original intent—to help immigrants learn English—and away from the multiculturalist goal of preserving immigrants in an autonomous culture outside the American mainstream. However, the battle between these two philosophies still continues on a variety of fronts. As Carey McWilliams, a supporter of multiculturalism, put it, "the borderlands (between Mexico and the United States) have consistently remained the borderland of the two cultures, neither has prevailed *in toto* and neither is likely to win a complete victory over the other. . . . Dynamic factors are involved in the extension of the borderland for experience has shown that Mexican immigrants cannot be kept out of the area." Yet the shift in the attitude of immigrants is shown only a paragraph later in McWilliams' book, although he apparently does not understand it himself. "There are more persons of Italian than of Mexican descent in the United States," he writes, "but no one has suggested that bilingual instruction is a major problem in the education of Italian-Americans." [21]

Political writer Tom Bethell, in a 1979 critique of the multiculturalists that would apply today, said that the movement is composed of "those who never did think that another idea, the United States of America, was a particularly good one to begin with, and that the sooner it is restored to its component 'ethnic' parts the better off we shall all be." [22]

MALDEF TODAY

During its first decade of existence, MALDEF paid little attention to immigration issues; its main concern was to keep Mexican-American citizens from being caught up in federal operations aimed at stopping illegal aliens. But by the time the Congressional struggle took shape over immigration reform [see chapters 1-3], MALDEF had already moved 180-degrees away from the values of the LULAC code, with its emphasis on assimilation as the basis for equal rights and true citizenship. This change in attitude led MALDEF to think about immigration exclusively in terms of ethnicity, rather than nationality. All Hispanics, even if they were not legal residents or citizens, were to have equal rights in the United States (including access to jobs, schools and public services). Immigration simply became another front in the bicultural/multicultural campaign.

Recently, MALDEF has appeared willing to take this argument to its ultimate extreme. To allow non-citizens to vote, Joaquin Avila, a San Francisco Bay area lawyer and consultant to MALDEF, has actually demanded that citizenship be eliminated as a voting requirement. "People who contribute to the economy, culture, who pay taxes, should have the right to vote," he argues.[23] Of course, there is no absolute bar to aliens earning the right to vote. Those who come to the United States legally and who make a permanent commitment to the country by going through the naturalization process can become citizens and then vote. Unfortunately, MALDEF and the other radical left immigration advocates have completely missed this quintessential part of citizenship.

The Mexican-American Legal Defense and Educational Fund's war on the Immigration and Naturalization service continues to this day. In July 1992, MALDEF strongly endorsed an out-of-court settlement with INS agreeing that illegal aliens apprehended while crossing the border not only have to be given a written notice of their rights, but also allowed the right to consult with an attorney. Aliens are to be asked if they are liable for political persecution in their countries of origin; if they say yes, they can apply for asylum—and then must be released into America's interior on their own recognizance! The court case was argued by the omnipresent Peter Schey. In San Diego County, where half of all illegal aliens are apprehended, those who have applied for asylum have, since February 1992, been set free pending the outcome of their application, a process that can take months. In addition, the INS (and thus the American taxpayer) agreed to pay fully $200,000 to cover the plaintiffs' legal fees. Although this settlement is to run "only" for 30 months, it is doubtful it will be abandoned.

The leftward pull of MALDEF has also affected LULAC's political stance. In 1987, LULAC joined MALDEF and other Hispanic groups in opposing the nomination of Anthony Kennedy to the Supreme Court, accusing him of "shocking insensitivity" toward the concerns of racial minorities.[24] This particular claim shows that LULAC has now accepted the status of Hispanics as a non-white minority, a concept it had long rejected. LULAC has also become more active in campaigns to increase immigration and the rights of non-citizen immigrants, another about-face from its previous emphasis on securing equality for U.S. citizens of Mexican ancestry. Jose Velez, past president of LULAC said in 1992 that the Border Patrol is "the enemy of my people and always will be."[25]

MALDEF and LULAC have gained a substantial amount of corporate financial support. American Express, ARCO, Chevron, Dayton Hudson, Du Pont, Exxon, Gannett, General Electric, General Mills, Kroger, Pacific Telesis, Southwestern Bell and U.S. Air have given annual amounts of $10,000 or more to one or both groups.[26] A major contributor to both groups (and to the equally radical National Council of La Raza) has been AT&T. Explaining its motives, the telecommunications giant said "[LULAC and La Raza]. . .promote a fair and humane immigration policy which takes family reunification as its cornerstone. Furthermore, they advocate for effective and humane border control." Another major contributor, IBM, explains its motives with equally vapid verbiage: "We support the National Council of La Raza, MALDEF and similar groups. . .[because they are] concerned with improving opportunities for Hispanics in every aspect of American life."[27]

A more pragmatic motive for such contributions is revealed when one realizes that large numbers of Hispanics are employed by these companies. Money spent to buy the goodwill of activist groups that could stir up trouble in the workforce makes good short-term business sense—even if it promotes policies that pose a long-run danger to the country as a whole.

One company that has reconsidered its support for these radical left organizations is Exxon. Replying to complaints, a spokesman said the company harbored "concern over the quality of LULAC's management," and noted that support for the group was eliminated in 1989.[28]

Unfortunately, few other companies have shown the fortitude to cut the umbilical cord from these radical left advocacy groups. Unbeknownst to a vast majority of their own shareholders, the corporate boards of these companies keep shoveling money in the direction of MALDEF, LULAC, and La Raza. In short, such naive financial help is essential to the immigration advocacy organizations, who use the funds to continue their debilitating campaign against the economic system, the delicate social fabric, and the national sovereignty of the United States—aspects of this country that were paramount in allowing these corporate giants to become as large and as powerful as they are today.

Chapter Seven
The National Lawyers Guild

"We have Nicaragua, soon we have El Salvador, Guatemala, Honduras, Costa Rica and Mexico. One day, tomorrow or 15 years from now, we're going to take 5 to 10 million Mexicans and they're going to have one thing in mind—cross the border, go into Dallas, go into Houston, go into New Mexico, go into San Diego, and each one has imbedded in his mind the idea of killing 10 Americans."
                    —Sandinista Tomas Borge, former Nicaraguan Interior Minister [1]

The National Lawyers Guild (NLG) is a politically oriented—often radical—law group of some 8,000 members and 83 lawyers' chapters nationwide. [2] It ostensibly serves as the major U.S. section of the International Association of Democratic Lawyers, [3] an organization that was repeatedly identified in unclassified CIA and FBI reports published by the House Select Committee on Intelligence as a pro-Soviet front operation.

The Central Intelligence Agency classified the IADL as one of thirteen active Soviet international fronts: ". . . the IADL has been one of the most useful Communist front organizations at the service of the Soviet Communist Party. . . . A front is an organization that appears to be independent but is in fact funded and controlled by the Soviets." [4] In 1950, the House Un-American Activities Committee published a document called "Report on the National Lawyers Guild: Legal Bulwark of the Communist Party." [5] A reporter supportive of today's Guild says that the FBI has collected some three million pages of files on the organization. [6]

The NLG routinely dismisses such characterizations as "red-baiting" and "McCarthyist," and vigorously asserts that it is not a communist front. NLG states that it seeks merely to "maintain the letter and the spirit of the Constitution and Bill of Rights." [7] Marc Van Der Hout, past president of the NLG and leader of the affiliated National Immigration Project, says "The guild still has, in many people's eyes, a reputation of being a communist organization and many people are still afraid to associate with it. It's not true by any means. . . ."[8]

While the organization has various stripes of opinion, the dominant view of the NLG is to the far-left. To get a good idea of the origin and mindset of the National Lawyers Guild, one need proceed no further than the group's 1987 convention where, according to a warm article in the Marxist-Leninist weekly *Frontline*, a "decade-by-decade assessment" of the Guild's first 50 years was discussed:

> Guild founder and current activist Marty Popper began . . . with an analysis that underscored the importance of the struggles against racism and anti-communism in creating the Guild. . . . Popper also recalled the consistent internationalist role the Guild has played over the years. . . . Although the particular role of the Communist Party USA (CPUSA) in initiating the Guild and shaping its activities in the '30s was not highlighted in the presentation, Popper did salute the political diversity that is characteristic of the Guild—from liberals to social democrats to communists—as one of its important strengths.[9]

NLG President Haywood Burns provided a two-page interview to the Communist Party USA on the legacy of the Guild, and also reported on a NLG delegation that went to the former Soviet Union several years ago as the guests of the Association of Soviet Lawyers. Said Burns, "I was particularly impressed with the fervor with which people supported Mr. Gorbachev's efforts and initiatives around peace and the end of the nuclear arms race. . . . I hope that in the not-too-distant future Mr. Gorbachev's views will get a better hearing here in the United States."[10]

THE NATIONAL IMMIGRATION PROJECT

In its newsletter, the National Immigration Project of the National Lawyers Guild describes itself as a "network of lawyers and legal and community workers engaged in the legal and political aspects of immigration law and practice." Its primary duties and functions are "to protect, defend, and extend the rights of documented and undocumented immigrants in the United States." Assigned to carry out these duties are two primary "sub-projects," the Central American Refugee Defense Fund, located in the Boston-based Project Office, and the Visa Denial Project, whose offices are in the New York City National Offices. Furthermore, the newsletter mentions that Guild work covers "a variety of issues, such as significant individual asylum and deportation cases; opposition to border violence; and defense of civil rights and liberties of U.S. citizens and the foreign born. In the legislative arena, we respond to requests for comments on proposed Federal Regulation changes, monitor and provide information on Congressional initiatives, and advocate for progressive immigration reform."[11]

A "Visa Denial Project" was set up under Claudia Slovinsky, chief editor of *Getting In: A Guide to Overcoming the Political Denial of Nonimmigrant Visas* (published in 1985), a veritable how-to of avoiding and otherwise violating U.S. laws. The publication almost hurries to give away any pretensions of political impartiality, saying in the introduction: "Representatives of Third World liberation movements who are combatting U.S.-backed dictatorships around the world are routinely denied access to United States audiences." Slovinsky was in a law partnership with Susan D. Susman, the one-time Co-Director of the Columbia Immigration Law Clinic with Ford Foundation Trustee Harriet Schaffer Rabb, [12] and eventually replaced her on the National Steering Committee of the National Immigration Project. [13]

Begun as an informal panel of Guild members, the National Immigration Project was approved by the NLG's Executive Board in 1972, which established two goals for the incipient group: prevent the deportation of political activists and explore the U.S.-Mexico border crisis. [14] Two years later the NIP was formalized and a National Steering Committee appointed, and official headquarters were opened in Los Angeles. [15]

The activities of the project increased significantly beginning in 1978, following a resolution on immigration policy at the 40th convention:

> The National Lawyers Guild further resolves: 1. To support the movement for full democratic rights for all non-citizens and an end to all deportations and manipulations of the borders carried out in the interests of capitalism; 2. To demand an end to government-sponsored violence, racist harassment and mass deprivation of civil rights carried out under the pretext of enforcing immigration laws; 3. To require the granting of political asylum status to applicants fleeing from repressive governments such as those of Haiti, Mexico, Thailand, Chile and Iran; 4. To eliminate all anti-communist provisions presently included in the immigration act; 5. To encourage local chapters to develop training programs and legal clinics to support mass defense efforts against deportations and for aiding immigrants in obtaining permanent residence status; 6. That the National Lawyers Guild through the National Immigration Project and local chapters, encourages and conducts education around the question of open/closed borders. [16]

The level of activity increased dramatically again in 1980, the year of Haitian litigation, the Mariel boatlift (declared by Castro on April 22), the formation of the transborder unions, the first International Conference for the Full Rights of Undocumented Workers in Mexico City, and the preparation for the FMLN insurgency's January 1981 "final offensive" in El Salvador. After successful establishment of the federally funded National Center for Immigrants Rights in Los Angeles, and after the first international undocumented conference, NIP-NLG headquarters were removed from Los Angeles to Boston in August 1980. [17]

NLG AND THE ORIGINS OF THE SANCTUARY MOVEMENT

In the late 1970s civil war flared up again in the Central American country of Nicaragua, pitting the forces of Anastosio Samoza, the country's leader, with those of the Marxist-leaning Sandinistas. The National Lawyers Guild quickly moved to take the side of the revolutionaries in this bitter struggle. Looking for a means of supporting their new-found allies, the Guild once again chose the tool of immigration policy to shape the white-hot iron of revolutionary discontent. Because of "Somoza's campaign of genocide against the Nicaraguan people," reported Guild member Michael Maggio to his colleagues in the National Immigration Project in 1979, a number of concerned organizations went to the Carter State Department to obtain "extended voluntary departure" (i.e. temporary legal residence) for San- dinista partisans and other Nicaraguans in the United States. [18] This move was suc- cessful, at least temporarily.

As the *Washington Post Magazine* uncovered several years later, however, Maggio "was one of the lawyers representing the Iranian embassy during the hos- tage crisis. And when the Sandinistas of Nicaragua could not wrest control of their embassy from the dictatorship they overthrew, they hired him to negotiate the trans- fer." [19] As the communist insurgency in El Salvador prepared for its "final offen- sive" of January 1981, Maggio tried, but failed, to win legal residence for Salvado- rans illegally in the U.S. The Washington, D.C. lawyer complained in the July 13, 1980, *Los Angeles Times* that the State Department's refusal of "extended voluntary departure" was prompted by political rather than humanitarian concerns. [20]

The first *Immigration Newsletter* published after the Project's move to Boston in 1980 was headlined with a directive from Bob Hilliard, a lawyer with the Guild's National Office who had recently returned from a trip to El Salvador. Instructed Hil- liard:

As the revolution in El Salvador intensifies, we can expect an increase in the number of El Salvadorans who come to this country to escape the repression. In addition, many 'economic' refugees from El Salvador, who may not have been politically active when they entered this country as undocumented workers, have identified themselves with the popular struggle in this country and cannot safely return to their homeland at the present time. It is incumbent upon the National Immigration Project to make the ser- vices of the Guild's immigration lawyers . . . available to the growing movement in solidarity with El Salvador. Given the present conflict in El Salvador, it is likely that any Salvadoran in this country has a colorable claim to political asylum. A systematic approach to Salvadorean political asylum cases . . . is one way to directly challenge U.S. foreign policy in a forum that is highly appropriate for the intervention of NLG legal work. . . . In order for the Guild to effectively respond to this need, it is essential for the work of individual attorneys around the country to be as centralized as possible. . . . Some people within the Guild have expressed doubts about the nature and priority of the Guild's international work. The systematic representation of political asylum claims of Salvadoreans presents a unique opportunity. . . ." [21]

The very partisan genesis of the so-called "sanctuary" movement is a far cry from other, more sanitized histories, which frequently assert that it began in Tucson, Arizona, (two years after Hilliard's declaration) as a spontaneous response of religiously inspired persons to human need. Legal action surrounding an immigration controversy did occur in Tucson, but in 1976, when activists with the radical Manzo Area Council were charged with "transportation of illegal aliens, aiding and abetting aliens to evade inspection, knowingly aiding felons, entering false statements, unlawfully copying citizenship papers and conspiracy."[22] The prosecutor, Assistant U.S. Attorney William D. Vogel commented, "[w]hat we are viewing here is the most invidious of modern revolutionary tactics, namely, the using of the established system of justice for its own destruction."[23] The charges, however, were dropped by the Carter Administration shortly after entering office in 1977. According to the National Lawyers Guild, "as a result of the mass movement that is being built to defend the democratic rights of all undocumented people, the U.S. government has been forced to drop all charges against the Manzo 4."[24]

At the time the Manzo defendants' attorney was the ever busy Peter Schey,[25] later to become one of three principal founders of the sanctuary-associated El Rescate. In fact, the very first sanctuary-associated publicity emanated in January 1982 from "the Manzo Area Council in Tucson and El Rescate ("The Rescue") in Los Angeles, two groups providing legal help to the refugees . . . "[26] The Manzo Area Council was central to planning the sanctuary campaign in the beginning of 1981, according to the only detailed journalistic work on the movement.[27]

Margo Cowan, Director of the Manzo Area Council and one of the 1976 defendants, testified before an early Congressional hearing on immigration reform in 1978. Speaking of illegal Mexican immigrants, Cowan said:

> You know, I think what we are speaking to is a real moral issue. You know, we are talking legislating social policy. . . . There are people in the world that are starving, and there is employment here for those people, and we are not going to keep them out. . . . I am hard-pressed, every day, seeing economic refugees, to do anything but assist those people.[28]

Cowan favored open immigration, and presented "A Bill of Rights for Workers Without Visas" that would guarantee such privileges.[29]

But Democratic Representative Morris K. Udall of Arizona sounded incredulous when he said to said to Cowan, ". . . the right of not being deported once they get here; the right to bring their family, and to be reunited . . . the right to vote, the right to all benefits . . . and so on and so forth . . . you are going to scare the pants off most of the members of Congress with those kinds of proposals."[30]

If Cowan's 1978 "Bill of Rights" did not generate much enthusiasm on Capitol Hill, it was received warmly in deliberation elsewhere. With minor changes, the text was unanimously adopted by the first International Conference for the Full Rights of Undocumented Workers, held in Mexico City from April 28 to April 30, 1980.[31]

The first Salvadoran immigrant political event occurred, according to writer Gary MacEoin, in July 1980, when a *coyote* (colloquialism for a professional smuggler), after collecting his bounty, promptly left his Salvadoran followers in the middle of the desert. MacEoin says that a "crash program of medical and emotional aid was immediately developed by the churches in Tucson, where the survivors were taken."[32]

Illegal Salvadoran entries and cruel smuggling deaths in the desert were, unfortunately, not unusual before 1980. Other sanctuary activists tell us that after the deaths of refugees left abandoned in the desert by the *coyotes*, MacEoin successfully persuaded the Tucson Ecumenical Council to fund legal work on behalf of Central American refugees. This effort was incorporated with, not surprisingly, the legal advocacy project of the Manzo Area Council to jointly provide "refugee resettlement services."[33] The highly visible front men for the sanctuary movement, "Quaker coyote" Jim Corbett and Reverend John Fife, began their campaign in 1981 while attempting to release on bond illegal Salvadorans on behalf of Manzo Area Council.[34]

According to one of its organizers, as the sanctuary movement developed, contacts were established with Bruce Bowman, a Los Angeles-area lawyer who was involved with El Rescate[35] and the Guild's National Immigration Project[36]; and with Gus Schultz, a Lutheran pastor (and now bishop) in the San Francisco Bay Area.[37] Schultz's congregation in San Francisco coordinated with Tucson Council for the first national declaration of sanctuary on March 24, 1982. Both groups hoped to attract the attention of San Francisco media and publicize the issue with area members of Congress. Unfortunately, a major problem cropped up: no Salvadoran could be found who was willing to take part! (A stark reminder of the sanctuary movement's own tendentious pecking order: political purposes first, illegal aliens second.) Three Salvadoran "refugees" did miraculously materialize in San Francisco just in time for the news conference: a teen-ager, a medical student and a survivor of the 1980 Arizona desert tragedy who was also a client of the Manzo Area Council.[38]

Who is Gary MacEoin, the man who was instrumental in patching together this first sanctuary event? His own book about the movement describes him as "a self-employed writer" and lawyer. Of his more than twenty books written on the issue of immigration and refugee policy, perhaps the most remarkable is *Revolution Next Door: Latin America in the 1970s*[39] which is dedicated to "the success of the revolution here and next door." As the editor of "Sanctuary: A Resource Guide," MacEoin writes that:

> [u]nattractive as military dictatorship is . . . it is the only transitional process which Latin American progressives see as capable of getting them out of their current satellite condition within the neocolonial system of Western capitalism. . . . It is accepted as a first principle that such a state would be organized along socialist principles, and with a harsh curtailment of individual liberties during the long process of development, or as they now prefer to say, of liberation. . . . Latin Americans, accordingly, interpret liberation to mean their escape from the values of American society no less than from political and economic manipulation. It is understandable, therefore, that they should give

major emphasis to the movements within the United States which challenge or seem to challenge those values—the revolt of students against the war in Vietnam . . . the radicalization of black movements . . . the emergence of a sense of identity and group power among Puerto Ricans and Chicanos. . . ."[40]

Thus we have seen that El Rescate and the Manzo Area Council initiated the sanctuary movement, with Gary MacEoin persuading the Tucson Ecumenical Council to become the "funding umbrella." MacEoin also wrote the first text published by sanctuary, *No Promised Land: American Refugee Policies and the Rule of Law*, Oxfam America, 1982.[41] Attorney MacEoin's sources for this material were *all* members of the National Immigration Project of the National Lawyers Guild: Marc Van Der Hout, director of the Central American refugee program of the Most Holy Redeemer church of the archdiocese of San Francisco; Antonio Rodriguez, director of the Los Angeles Center for Law and Justice (and a former leader of CASA); Michael Maggio of the Council on Hemispheric Affairs; and Linton Joaquin of the National Center for Immigrants' Rights. MacEoin also used as a source the 1980 *Haitian Refugee Center v. Civiletti* litigation, which was initiated by Peter Schey and Ira Kurzban of the National Lawyers Guild.

Salvadoran immigration work became the primary focus of the National Immigration Project, according to the official account of the National Lawyers Guild National Convention held February 17-21, 1982 in New Mexico, one month *before* the advent of "sanctuary." During an Immigration Committee workshop one woman later commented that "there are more people in this room representing Salvadoran refugees than there are immigration judges in the whole country." The Guild's National Immigration Project met throughout the convention, "providing an invaluable opportunity for immigration defense lawyers to strategize and improve their skills."[42]

THE GUILD AND THE FMLN

As noted previously, the Central Intelligence Agency described the National Lawyers Guild's parent organization, the International Association of Democratic Lawyers, as a Soviet front. The CIA is prohibited by its charter from monitoring or commenting on domestic issues, but it can report on international events. In a report to the House Intelligence Committee the CIA said that:

[n]umerous and well-attended rallies protesting U.S. policy toward El Salvador were held around the world on the eve of the Salvadoran national elections of March 28, 1982. The rallies were intended to discredit the elections themselves and U.S. efforts to organize them. Demonstrations were reported in Berlin, Frankfurt, Rotterdam, Mexico City, Bern, Stockholm, Luxembourg, Toronto, Calgary, London, Sao Paul, and Tel

Aviv . . . The decidedly anti-U.S. cast to these demonstrations, their timing, and their international scale suggest that the Soviet Union or one of its front groups was behind the protests. [43]

Coincidentally, sanctuary was first announced only a few days before the El Salvador elections. According to an Arizona Associated Press account, the incipient immigration movement was declared by "Margo Cowan, director of the Manzo Area Council in Tucson, an organization that has aided illegal aliens in Tucson for many years, [who] said a number of Tucson churches will give 'sanctuary' to Salvadorans to keep them from being captured by Border Patrol and Immigration agents." [44] This effort was in close cooperation with the Tucson Ecumenical Council, according to the Church World Service:

[I]n close cooperation with the community-based immigration counseling center Concilio Manzo [Manzo Area Council], [the Tucson Ecumenical Council] responds to the needs of Central American asylum seekers coming into South Arizona through four basic program areas: (1) Legal services to assure due process with adequate legal representation, (2) Bail bond strategy . . . (3) social and pastoral services and (4) advocacy and education work addressing the national issues. [45]

The task of organizing and funding support among national religious bodies for the sanctuary campaign fell to Patrick A. Taran of the Church World Service Immigration and Refugee Program, a project of the Ford-funded [46] National Council of Churches in New York. Duties were also given to Lauren Pressman McMahon of the Ford-funded Lutheran Immigration and Refugee Service. [47] Patrick Taran is a member of the Guild's National Immigration Project; [48] Lauren McMahon went on in 1987 to become the Executive Director of El Rescate in Los Angeles. [49]

At the end of 1987 El Rescate and CARECEN sponsored the visit to Los Angeles of Oscar Hernandez of the non-governmental (and Ford-funded [50]) Human Rights Commission of El Salvador. Far from being a non-partisan observer, Hernandez "support[s] the leftist guerrilla opposition, the FMLN," according to a straightforward account in *The Los Angeles Times.* "I am here to talk about human rights and make people aware of the situation in El Salvador so that [the United States] will stop military and economic aid. . . ." Hernandez was quoted as saying to "a dozen or so members of the National Lawyers Guild" who had gathered to hear him. Sandra Pettit, the activist lawyer who had her fingers in a number of legal battles, described the guild later as "an alternative to the American Bar Association for progressive lawyers." [51]

NO SANCTUARY FOR VIETNAMESE ORPHANS

Only once in its 15-year history has the Guild's National Immigration Project actually supported the exclusion of a group of aliens from the United States.

In 1975, upon the collapse of the American-supported South Vietnamese government, the Ford Administration moved to evacuate some 2,000 orphaned Vietnamese infants and children for adoption and resettlement in the U.S. This so-called "Operation Babylift" was popularly supported as a way to ensure that the children, all of whose parents had been lost because of the war—and who were bound to suffer under the often unkind dictates of the Vietnamese totalitarian state—would get a better upbringing in American families.

The National Lawyers Guild, whose bottomless wellspring of passion runneth over when migrants from American-supported countries were concerned, turned a cold shoulder to the Babylift operation. In the late summer of 1976 the *National Immigration Project's Immigration Newsletter* reported on the efforts of the Center for Constitutional Rights (a nonprofit law firm supervised by senior NLG members that concentrates on critical political litigation) to oppose Operation Babylift.[52] "CCR moved quickly, filing a class action suit on behalf of the children . . . to prevent the finalization of any adoptions," said the newsletter, assuming, of course, that blocking the childrens' migration was synonymous to "acting on their behalf." "The new government of South Vietnam, via telegram, has indicated its desire for the return of the children."[53]

The Center for Constitutional Rights demanded that the children be interviewed, identified, and their families traced in Vietnam. But the Catholic Committee for Refugees intervened, arguing that such a procedure would lead to communist government retaliation against those relatives still living in Vietnam. The Center responded by claiming that those relatives still in Vietnam were siding with the U.S. State Department anyway (and thus are deserving of harsh treatment from the communist government).

The CCR further argued that not repatriating the orphans would be unjust since "a large percentage of them are likely to undergo severe emotional problems when they reach adolescence, in part because they will be unprepared to deal with the racism of American society." Perhaps the Guild and its Center for Constitutional Rights felt at ease because, according to the *Immigration Newsletter*, "journalists and others returning from Vietnam report that the new government has been successfully reintegrating into families orphanage children and even the many children who survived in the streets."[54]

Even this effort was not too far beyond the pale for the Ford Foundation to support, as its Trustee, Harriet Schaffer Rabb, was a staff attorney for the Center for Constitutional Rights from 1966 to 1969 and served as a cooperating attorney for the organization in the period of the orphan litigation.[55]

CENTER FOR CONSTITUTIONAL RIGHTS

In 1975 CCR said, in its own self-stated purpose, that

It has always been necessary, in the United States, for the government to disguise its most repressive activities and intentions in a cloak of legality. . . . The illusion of lawfulness, so necessary for preserving the myth of democracy, has been at the center of the strategy and tactics of repression throughout this nation's history . . . .

It is in this context that the CCR has, since its founding in 1966, played a central role in advancing the goals of progressive organizations and individuals while protecting them as they engage in their struggles. Because it has been the 'law' that has been used as a tool of repression, it can be the law that is used as an instrument of resistance. . . . It can be the law that is used to strip away the facade of legitimacy where it exists and deprive it where it is sought. . . . The CCR's role in history is as a legal instrument of the people. . . . We are activists in a struggle for justice and against illusory democracy. . . . When the law is used as a weapon and the courtroom as a battlefield, the CCR is committed to insuring that the people never enter the fray unarmed. [56]

Several years after the Babylift litigation the NLG decided to expand upon the efforts of the National Immigration Project and its Center for Constitutional Rights. With much fanfare, the National Lawyers Guild announced the formation of the National Center for Immigrants' Rights, a legal advocacy center that would be partly funded through the federal government's Legal Services Corporation. As its first Executive Director, immigration lawyer Peter Schey was named. The Ford Foundation mentioned in its Annual Report that Guild members were "instrumental in lobbying for the creation of the support center." As the organization's primary functions, the Foundation said that NCIR will "engage in impact litigation in the area of immigrant's rights [and] lobby on issues important to the immigrant community." As for the Guild, the Ford Foundation's Annual Report said the "work of the NCIR can complement Guild work in the immigration field, [as] NCIR has the resources to engage in direct legal action around the country. While much of the Guild's work is political in nature, NCIR will concentrate more on lobbying and litigation. Joint projects can be undertaken in the future with NCIR contributing primarily legal resources." [57]

A 1984 listing of the Advisory Board for the National Center for Immigrants' Rights tells its own story about the iron triangle linking NCIR, the Guild, and the cash-rich Ford Foundation. Members of this group include many powerful lawyers in the radical alien rights forum, including: [58]

- Deborah Anker of the National Lawyers Guild [59] and Harvard Law School, whose immigration work has been funded by the Ford Foundation; [60]
- Ira J. Kurzban of the National Lawyers Guild, [61] and the Ford-funded Haitian Refugee Center; [62]
- Warren Leiden of the National Lawyers Guild [63] and Ford-funded American Immigration Lawyers Association; [64]
- Arthur C. Helton of the National Lawyers Guild [65] and Ford-funded Lawyers Committee for International Human Rights; [66]

- Wade J. Henderson of the National Conference of Black Lawyers[67] and Ford-funded American Civil Liberties Union;[68]

- Paula D. Pearlman of the National Lawyers Guild[69] and the Imperial Valley Immigration Project;

- Kristine A. Poplawski of the National Lawyers Guild[70] and now with the Ford-funded Farmworker Justice Fund;[71]

- Mark D. Rosenbaum of the National Lawyers Guild[72] and the Ford-funded American Civil Liberties Union;

- Michael H. Sussman of the NAACP, New York;

- Dale Frederick Swartz, formerly of the National Emergency Civil Liberties Committee[73] and head of the Ford-funded National Immigration, Refugee and Citizenship Forum.[74]

Since the Legal Services Corporation Act of 1974 prohibits its funds from being used to advocate particular public policies or encourage political activities,[75] and since LSC appropriations measures specifically forbid representation of illegal aliens,[76] NCIR's activity was naturally subjected to severe criticism. In response, Peter Schey simply established the National Center for Immigrants' Rights, *Inc.*, a supposedly private mirror corporation able to conduct litigation and advocacy outside federal-funding strictures.[77]

The U.S. government quickly pulled all federal funding out from under the blatantly partisan NCIR. Fortunately for the litigation group, the Ford Foundation came to the rescue with huge infusions of funds. In the now-familiar vapidness of Ford's Annual Report:

> When alien children come to this country from El Salvador, Afghanistan, Iran and other countries to avoid persecution or war or to join family members are apprehended by the Immigration and Naturalization Service (INS), it is not clear exactly what their rights are. The National Center for Immigrants Rights (NCIR), one of 18 national centers established by the Legal Services Corporation, has brought several important test cases against the INS to secure fundamental protections for indigent alien children. However, by law, corporation funding cannot be used for some activities relating to the defense of alien children. In 1986 the Foundation granted funds to the Legal Aid Foundation of Los Angeles for an expansion of NCIR's Immigrant Children's Rights Program to clarify this murky area and to secure for alien children access to education, health and other social services.[78]

The grant was for $150,000, with an additional follow-up check for $350,000 in 1987.

The Guild has even moved to supplant normal parent-child relationships among the illegal immigrants whose interests they purport to represent. A long-standing Immigration and Naturalization Service policy prohibits agency officials from releasing illegal alien-minors to anyone other than a parent or lawful guardian. A judge in Los Angeles found that minors released to other supposed claimants are often never seen nor heard from again. But in July 1985 Peter Schey and another radical lawyer, Carlos Holguin, both representing the "private" National Center for Immigrants' Rights, *Inc.*, filed a class action lawsuit on behalf of four Salvadoran children, challenging the INS policy. Their argument? "When parents do appear they are interrogated about their immigration status, risking deportation to civil war." [79]

Given the Guild's shamelessly partisan tilt, one wonders if the NCIR would have represented alien minors who have fled from totalitarian Vietnam, or from the repressive Sandinista regime in Nicaragua. But to the true ideologue, even children are nothing more than pawns to be moved this way or that as part of the larger game.

Chapter Eight
The American Civil Liberties Union

"The circumstances that endanger the safety of nations are infinite; and for this reason no constitutional shackles can be wisely imposed on the power to which the care of it is committed."

—Alexander Hamilton
The Federalist #23[1]

The American Civil Liberties Union has always prided itself on supporting the rights of legal aliens and the rights of illegal aliens for fair proceedings in deportation cases. Even during the height of the Cold War in the 1950s, the ACLU denounced the provision of the McCarran Internal Security Act (1950) which called for the deportation of all persons who were or had ever been members of the Communist Party. However, during this same period, the ACLU did not oppose the government policy of refusing permanent immigrant status to present members of Communist, Fascist, Falangist or other totalitarian parties.

As William A. Donohue notes in *The Politics of the American Civil Liberties Union*, "[t]he Union defended its policy by reminding us that government immigration must be selective due to the number of persons who may enter the United States each year. Therefore, it reasoned that 'it is not unjustifiable to exclude members of these organizations, since they are dedicated to the overthrow of democratic government.' "[2]

The ACLU extended this same reasoning to the denial of naturalization to members of all totalitarian groups. However, like so many other liberal advocacy organizations, the ACLU has lurched sharply to the left.

As an example of this trend, Donohue notes that in 1978 the ACLU came out against the Foreign Agents Registration Act (a widely-supported measure requiring lobbyists representing foreign powers and companies to register with the federal government) because "its system of regulation and disclosure has a chilling effect on the right to speak out on any issue." [3]

FARA, however, was a 40 year-old law by that time; in 1938, when originally passed, the ACLU did not utter a word of protest. Since the law was basically unchanged over the years, one must conclude that it is ACLU's attitude towards national security, and the sources of external threats to that security, that had changed.

Another sign of the changing times is ACLU's involvement in immigration policy, where it supports programs and proposals that are difficult to distinguish from the programs of MALDEF and the National Lawyers Guild. In 1977, for example, the ACLU came out against sanctions against employers hiring illegal aliens. [4] Although the rights of aliens were a concern, they were apparently not a priority. The ACLU's 1981 annual financial report listed twelve funds for specialized areas of legal advocacy; a special stance on aliens and sanctions, however, was not mentioned. [5]

Ford Foundation Trustee Harriet Schaffer Rabb, who was on the Board of the New York Civil Liberties Union from 1972 to 1983, played a pivotal role in activating the ACLU in the immigration struggle. [6] Ford's very first grant specifically devoted to the civil liberties of undocumented aliens went to the New York Civil Liberties Union in 1982. [7] Thereafter, the National Office of the ACLU was persuaded to undertake what was known as an Immigration and Alien Rights Project, with a 1983 Ford Foundation grant of $300,000 (as well as large-scale continuing general and some particular support from Ford to ACLU in following years). [8] Rabb continued to show her commitment to immigration law and policy by joining the board of MALDEF in 1986.

Since its adoption of a more radical agenda, the ACLU has built extensive ties to similarly-minded organizations. Lucas Guttentag, the Director of the ACLU's Immigration and Aliens' Rights Task Force, wears another hat as a member of the National Lawyers Guild's National Immigration Project. [9] In 1987 Guttentag also succeeded Harriet Rabb as head of the Columbia Law School Immigration Clinic.

The ACLU's primary immigration policy leader in its Washington, D.C. office is Wade Henderson, who is also a member of the National Conference of Black Lawyers (NCBL). [10] (The longtime leader of the NCBL, Haywood Burns, served from 1987 to 1988 as President of the NLG.) Since 1984, Wade Henderson has also had a seat on the Advisory Board of Peter Schey's National Center for Immigrants' Rights. [11]

Another ACLU leader involved with Schey's Center is Mark D. Rosenbaum, the head of the Union's Southern California Chapter and a strong advocate of an open immigration policy. Here the omnipresent National Lawyers Guild also plays an important role: Rosenbaum is a member, as is Board member Linda Wong, who is involved as well with the Mexican-American Legal Defense and Educational Fund. [12] In February 1982, Schey and Rosenbaum teamed up with Antonio Rodriguez, a Guild member with the Los Angeles Center for Law and Justice, to write a careful piece for the *Los Angeles Times* entitled "The Reagan Raids of 1982; Stepped-Up Sweeps by Immigration Agents are Flatly Illegal."

ATTACKING U.S. FOREIGN POLICY

In 1982 the ACLU and the newly-formed (and Ford-funded) Americas Watch Committee published a joint *Report critical of U.S. Central American policy called Human Rights In El Salvador.* This marked the first of many forays the organization would take into foreign policy.[13] Two years later the ACLU's National Immigration and Alien Rights Project issued its first report on *Salvadorans in the United States, The Case for Extended Voluntary Departure.*[14] This magnum opus on immigration policy was produced in part by Amit Pandya, a former research director and staff counsel for the Washington, D.C. office of Peter Schey's National Center for Immigrants Rights.[15] A second report from the National Immigration and Alien Rights Project was issued in April 1986, in conjunction with the Ford-funded American Friends Service Committee's Florida Project, called *The Hands that Feed Us: Undocumented Farmworkers in Florida.* Predictably, the report opposes employer sanctions, supports broad amnesty, and is critical of immigration enforcement. In 1985, when the "sanctuary" activists in Tucson were to stand trial for aiding illegal immigration, the ACLU announced that the accused were justified in their open defiance of the law. The rights organization openly participated in the legal defense.[16]

Perhaps the most complete statement of the ACLU's position on immigration can be found in an essay by Steven R. Shapiro of the New York Civil Liberties Union and Wade Henderson of the ACLU's D.C. office. Writing on "Justice for Aliens," Shapiro and Henderson said the desire to limit immigration is attributed to "hostility," motivated only by nativism, racism and red-scare.

> The tide of immigrants coming to this country in recent years from El Salvador and Nicaragua is inextricably tied to the Reagan administration's policy of promoting confrontation rather than conciliation in the region.
>
> It is widely believed, although there is little evidence to support this view, that illegal aliens are taking jobs at substandard wages that would otherwise be held by American citizens. . . Even without a national identity card or computerized data bank, a system of employer sanctions poses serious civil liberties risks . . . . proponents of the [Simpson-Mazzoli] bill consistently painted a mythical picture of a homogeneous society whose future is threatened by the arrival of outsiders. . .
>
> Once in this country and informed of their rights, many Salvadorans have applied for political asylum. Those applications pose an awkward problem for the Reagan administration. . . The treatment of Haitian boat people is a particularly vivid example of the Reagan administration's attitude towards political asylum. It is an attitude that views political asylum as a foreign policy tool . . . .[17]

After passage of the 1986 Immigration Reform and Control Act, the ACLU successfully got members of Congress to agree to review, at a later date, evidence of possible discrimination that resulted from employer sanctions. It was further agreed that, if sufficient evidence existed, that portion of the new law would be repealed.[18] Of course, the ACLU made sure that apparent cases of discrimination would be unearthed. In 1987 Lucas Guttentag explained just such a project: "The ACLU and

MALDEF have undertaken a joint effort to collect information about job discrimination caused by the new immigration act. The collection of data will permit nationwide documentation of discrimination resulting from employer sanctions." He also instructed members to "distribute the enclosed Discrimination Questionnaire as widely as possible." [19]

In 1990—only four years after the employer sanctions became law—pro-immigration Hispanic groups launched a serious effort to repeal them. This effort continues unabated. It did not matter that sanctions were part of the compromise the pro-immigration side accepted to gain amnesty.

ACLU IN THE 1990s

Today the ACLU is as active as ever in promoting uncontrolled flows of immigrants across our border. For example, the Texas Civil Liberties Union Foundation now tells its constituents that "[t]he ACLU has an Immigration Law Task Force which supports litigation to bring about systemic changes in our immigration law and enforcement." Ostensibly the Task Force plans action on forty litigation items and eleven education items. Among them:

- Weaken employer sanctions through 1) litigating establishment of search-warrant requirements; 2) representing job applicants who refuse to provide verification documents for "political reasons"; and 3) representing of employers who refuse to comply with sanctions for "religious reasons";
- Require free legal counsel, free translators, and release for illegal aliens contesting their deportations;
- Expand the amnesty by challenging the INS regulations in court;
- Contest the denial of welfare to newly-legalized aliens;
- Expand employment discrimination law to require employers to hire "newly arrived undocumented aliens."
- Work with MALDEF to distribute and collect discrimination questionnaires (as part of the 1990 effort to repeal the employer sanction provision of the Immigration Control Act).

In addition to these ambitious measures, the Texas Civil Liberties Union advocated the challenge and defeat of "citizen-only" job requirements imposed by governmental entities and government contractors. And, "[i]n light of the absence of" discrimination complaints, the advocates actually proposed establishing the use of so-called "testers", or phony job applicants, to act as magnets for any potential immigration-related discrimination complaints. [20]

Oddly, many of these goals contradict other celebrated causes of the alien rights crowd. The strong push for easier access to welfare programs, for example, belies the argument that immigrants do not increase the demand for welfare services paid for by the public. Similarly, the suggestion that "citizen-only" restrictions are barriers to immigrant job-seekers contradicts in practice the claim that immigrants create new jobs for themselves, or only take jobs no one else wants.

The Texas Civil Liberties Union Foundation tacitly admits that immigrants compete with citizens for available jobs, and therefore seeks legal/legislative methods to give the immigrants a better chance of winning this competition to the disadvantage of citizens. In the long run these measures could also be potential steps toward the incremental establishment of affirmative action programs for immigrants.

In 1988 the ACLU reached a new level of candor with the publication in its newsletter of "Helping Immigrants Stay in the USA," a celebration of the organization's recent history of hamstringing the country's immigration control laws. [21] Mentioned in the article was the ACLU's role in *Orantes-Hernandez v. Meese*, the landmark case that won asylum for illegal Salvadorans. "The ACLU of Southern California was instrumental in achieving this landmark victory," the article stated. "As chief counsel, staff attorney Mark Rosenbaum coordinated the work of a large coalition of legal services and immigration rights groups, including the national ACLU's Immigration and Aliens' Rights Task Force."

In addition, this grand statement of national ACLU policy formulated a number of other non-controvertible goals including: prohibition of workplace inspection for illegal aliens; prohibition of drugs and weapons searches of detained juvenile illegal aliens; release of rioting Marielito Cuban felons; a constitutional challenge to a major new law prohibiting immigration marriage fraud; and an increase in amnesty applications to take advantage of the enormous hole the ACLU and its brethren had blown into U.S. immigration laws.

The American Civil Liberties Union has now become, as it was during the 1988 presidential election, a political issue itself. Its agenda has undergone a profound shift away from the defense of individual rights and toward, as the *Wall Street Journal* said, "a new agenda of left-wing causes . . . fundamentally hostile to the processes of American constitutional government." [22]

This new agenda, beyond the obvious, substantive issues, accentuates liberalism's tendencies to push the notion of "individual rights" to the extreme. In this as-of-now uncharted zone of legal advocacy through which the ACLU is dragging its "constituents," the notion of individual rights has been polymorphed into the concept of "group" rights—where one "group" (i.e., illegal aliens, irrespective of their national origin) claims itself a "victim" of another (American citizens, at least those who are white). A victim, of course, has the right to proper redress by economic and political means. If magnified on a national scale, this concept can have ominous consequences.

Most disturbing to many of the ACLU's former supporters is the recognition that the organization's recent thrust has a pernicious underlying theme—hostility to the processes of constitutional democracy. This appears in three basic forms: first, an attempt to override democratic processes and replace them with judicial decrees; second, an attempt to expand individual "rights" without regard for countervailing public interests; and third, efforts to prevent certain viewpoints from being heard in the public arena.[23]

In "Justice for Aliens," the essay written by ACLU activists Steven Shapiro and Wade Henderson, the discussion of the word "alien" shows this pernicious technique:

> [The] use of the word 'alien' is both precise and powerful. In almost a primitive sense, it draws a line between members of the community and those on the outside. . . The Supreme Court has concluded that certain classes of aliens may not even claim the right to constitutional protection. . . Illegal aliens are not entitled to government benefits. . . The rationale for this limitation is not an economic one. . . The refusal to grant these often life-sustaining benefits can be explained only by a desire to punish illegal aliens for breaking the law. . .[24]

While it might be argued that this is merely equalitarian thinking carried to its extreme, which it most certainly is, it is more than pure nonsense. Citizenship is the issue; aliens are not citizens, by definition. Yet to propose that some constitutional injury exists when all residents, regardless of their legal status, do not have the same rights, is to revise the Constitution utterly. Instead of the rights of citizens, it is the global universalization of rights that the ACLU wishes to impose. As Abraham Lincoln said during the Civil War, the Constitution is not a suicide pact requiring its own destruction.

Chapter Nine
Other Open Border Groups

"We will continue to fight in the streets, the legislature, and the courtroom. Just because you lose on one path doesn't mean the struggle won't continue."
—Arthur Kinoy, *The Progressive* 1992.[1]

The list of organizations taking an aggressive approach to America's immigration policy, unfortunately, does not end with MALDEF, the National Lawyers Guild, and the ACLU. A number of other groups, some of them perched far on the "right" side of the political spectrum, have added their voices to the open borders choir.

NATIONAL IMMIGRATION, REFUGEE AND CITIZENSHIP FORUM

The Forum was first conceived as a tool to oppose the findings of Reverend Hesburgh's Select Commission on Immigration and Refugee Policy. In early February 1981, shortly after the findings of the Commission were made public, Rick Swartz of the Alien Rights Law Project (an adjunct of the Lawyers Committee for Civil Rights Under Law), with the generous assistance of the National Lawyers Guild, issued a call for a "Meeting of Public Coalition on Immigration and Refugee Policy."[2]

Along with Swartz's Project, seven other organizations answered his overture to form the nucleus of the National Immigration, Refugee and Citizenship Forum. The ledger of participants included: the American Friends Service Committee, the Mexican-American Legal Defense and Educational Fund, the National Lawyers Guild's National Immigration Project, and the Immigration Law Clinic of the Columbia School of Law, co-directed by Susan Susman and Ford Trustee Harriet Rabb.[3] At the time Susman was on the National Steering Committee of the Guild's National Immigration Project,[4] and Rabb was also on the Board of Swartz' parent organization, the Lawyers Committee for Civil Rights Under Law.[5]

This "Public Coalition" evolved into the purportedly neutral Forum. With the aid of a $5,000 start-up grant from the Samuel Rubin Foundation, it issued its first newsletter and call for membership on February 4, 1982.[6] The Forum's stated purpose was to "bring together a diverse group of local, national, and international organizations for the purpose of stimulating and coordinating systematic, policy-focused working relationships and communications networks that span the range of issues, interests and disciplines involved in immigration, refugee and related foreign policy matters."[7] However, given the makeup of its membership, the Forum could only be one more source of mischief in the immigration debate.

Predictably, the Ford Foundation was not far behind with huge infusions of cash. Its first benefit was a check for $50,000, which the Forum received in a merger with the American Immigration and Citizenship Conference, a fifty-year old advocacy organization based in New York. The Citizenship Conference swelled the ranks of the Forum and added greater legitimacy to its purpose.[8] Later donations were in the six-figure range: $300,000 in 1983, $450,000 in 1985 and $735,000 in 1987.[9] In its annual report, The Ford Foundation explained its purpose: "To help inform the often heated debate on immigrants' rights and status in the United States. . . . The Forum itself does not advocate specific positions. Instead on such controversial topics as the current immigration reform legislation in Congress, it seeks to provide unbiased information to all parties . . . "[10]

A casual reading of the Forum's bylaws and self-descriptive language gives one the impression of a neutral and unbiased agenda. Swartz, who became the Forum's first president, stressed this technicality in a letter to editor of *The Miami News*, when he scolded the paper for running a story on the incipient group with the headline "Area coalition comes out against immigration bill." As he explained: "The Forum does not take positions on policy issues and does not lobby. The Forum is not part of any coalition regarding Simpson-Mazzoli."[11]

If, however, an organization can be judged by the person who heads it, then the National Immigration, Refugee and Citizenship Forum was far from the image of an innocent bystander in the controversy over the Simpson-Mazzoli bill. Swartz himself has had a colorful history in the immigration debate. The Forum's first newsletter described him as an "advocate for diverse immigration and foreign policy interests."[12] He was a lead attorney in Haitian immigrant litigation, and in the 1981 Senate Immigration Hearings on Asylum Adjudication likened the United States to Nazi Germany and blamed illegal immigration on U.S. foreign policy. This provoked an annoyed response from the normally taciturn Senator Alan Simpson: "I do not think it has been very helpful, at least it is not to me. There have been references to Nazi Germany. Those things are not helpful in this debate."[13]

The model of a supposedly neutral and unbiased forum is now being reproduced at the local level. After the 1986 passage of the landmark Immigration Reform and Control Act, the Ford Foundation and the National Forum undertook an astonishing political initiative: the organization of "local" immigration coalitions in key locations across the country. [14] Existing smaller national coalitions are included in the effort as well: the Ford-funded National Coalition for Haitian Refugees received another $98,000 to handle Haitian immigration matters; and the Oakland-based National Network for Immigrant and Refugee Rights (an offshoot of the Guild's National Center for Immigrants' Rights) received $55,000 through the Center for Immigrants Rights of New York City.

These unfolding local efforts are exemplified by events in Texas, where the Forum's Texas office coordinated local organizations in an active, statewide effort. The National Forum, working as a funnel through which Ford monies were distributed, awarded funds to these local efforts, including the Dallas-based North Texas Immigration Coalition, the Lubbock-based Coalition for Immigration Policy and Education, and to the so-called Legalization Coalition, an advocacy group that concentrated its efforts in the valley of the Rio Grande. It was also reported that the North Texas Immigration Coalition was in active communication with then-Speaker of the U.S. House Jim Wright and John Bryant, a Representative from Dallas and member of the House Immigration Subcommittee. Both Wright and Bryant publicly urged the Immigration and Naturalization Service to address the issues raised by NTIC.

The National Immigration, Refugee and Citizenship Forum had previously worked with a "task force" headed by Texas Agriculture Commissioner Jim Hightower, with the purpose of lobbying Congress and putting pressure on the INS to delay implementing the new immigration reform law until amnesty was broadened and the employer sanctions reconsidered. "If that [the political effort] fails," warned Rick Swartz in the *Austin American Statesman*, "our last resort will be the courts" [15]—a boast that today appears more and more prophetic.

In Boston, half a continent away from the plains of Texas, the Forum's localization efforts were also taking shape. In cooperation with a "core group" from the sanctuary group Centro Presente—and with the help of a $35,000 grant the Ford Foundation funneled through the Action for Boston Community Development—Swartz's organization established the Massachusetts Immigrant and Refugee Advocacy Coalition (MIRA). A protest march organized by this new coalition was reported in the Communist newspaper *People's Daily World*: "The march, organized by a broad coalition . . . heard former State Rep. Mel King . . . and others demand the abolition of employer sanctions, extension and expansion of the current amnesty program, a fair application of the amnesty law and an end to local and state government cooperation with the Immigration and Naturalization Service (INS). The coalition also called for an end to INS abuses, such as workplace raids . . ." [16]

The seeds of agitation that the Forum scattered throughout the country produced a flowering of protest in other locations.

In Chicago, the Chicago Committee on Immigrant Protection was organized with the benefit of a $100,000 grant from Ford, directed through sanctuary leader Sid Mohn's Travelers and Immigrants Aid of Chicago organization.

In New York, the Governor's Task Force on Implementation, chaired by Arthur C. Helton of the Lawyers Committee for International Human Rights, had "taken a strong lead" on protesting immigration policy, according to the Forum; adding to the New York effort Ford provided $150,000 for lawyer-advocates through the Volunteers of Legal Services and for the creation of a Fund for New Citizens for immigration groups.

In Florida, according to the Forum, coalition work will be performed by existing (and Ford-funded) groups such as Haitian Refugee Center, the Greater Miami United and certain farmworker organizations.

In Los Angeles, the Coalition for Humane Immigration Rights of Los Angeles received $125,000 through Linda Wong of MALDEF, while MALDEF itself was provided an extra $200,000 from Ford for immigration work.

In northern California, Forum work would be performed by the San Francisco-based Coalition for Immigrant Rights and Services.

The newspaper *Unity*, a publication with sharply Marxist leanings, reported on a few of these coalition efforts in a favorable news piece:

> Already local coalitions are becoming increasingly broad and militant in their demands. On March 3, the Community Coalition for Immigrant Justice, a coalition of trade union, church and labor organizations, held a picket of over 200 people at the San Francisco INS to protest draft regulations, speak up against increasing workplace firings and harassment, and call for passage of the DeConcini-Moakley bill, which would grant temporary refugee status to thousands of Central American immigrants. In Washington, D.C., an ad hoc group of national organizations, including the National Immigration, Refugee and Citizenship Forum . . . will be holding a special lobbying day to mount a final protest of the draft regulations . . ."[17]

One of the major reasons for the success of Forum-aided community coalitions is a symbiotic coupling of local groups and national advocacy organizations and networks. For example, MALDEF and the ACLU lend a great deal of aid in coordinating the activities of these various localities; in turn, the larger organizations build connections with smaller coalitions found all over the country like the Washington-based "Ad Hoc Coalition for Immigration Reform Implementation" (CIRI), a Forum-founded national coalition for the establishment of which Ford granted $275,000.

The Forum also has no qualms about directing these small groups to the cash engines that make so much of this possible: "Foundations throughout the country have played a major role in helping fund coalitions, with the ultimate goal of enabling the largest number of eligible persons to apply for legalization. The Ford Foundation and the Rosenberg Foundation are by far the largest contributors. Ford has a deliberate strategy of funding coalitions in urban and regional areas."

Other Ford grants to organizations responding to the new immigration-reform law were: an additional $300,000 for the ACLU; $75,000 for the American Immigration Lawyers Association; $75,000 for the American Public Welfare Association, a group that loudly opposes immigration-control legislation; and $75,000 for the Farmworker Justice Fund to expand the agricultural-worker amnesty.

AMERICAN IMMIGRATION LAWYERS ASSOCIATION

The American Immigration Lawyers Association (AILA) is the national association representing the country's immigration lawyers. Although AILA has more than 2,000 members affiliated with the more moderate American Bar Association, the two hundred-odd National Lawyers Guild members have managed to co-opt the organization's message and have thrown it into the same net that snared MALDEF and the ACLU years ago. For example, in 1982, AILA members elected as their executive director Warren Leiden, whose immediate previous post was as the first permanent executive director of the Guild's National Immigration Project. [18]

In 1981 Leiden issued a report to Guild members critical of the Hesburgh Commission's findings, and trumpeted the formation of Rick Swartz's National Forum on Immigration and Refugee Policy as a way "to provide Congress with information and arguments upon which legislative alternatives may be built." [19] Since 1984 Leiden has also served on the Advisory Board of Peter Schey's National Center for Immigrants' Rights. [20]

Guild members have been inserted throughout the chain of command at AILA. Amy Novick, a member of the NLG's Immigration Project, was the assistant director. [21] Robert E. Juceam, an old supporter of the National Emergency Civil Liberties Committee, served as AILA's General Counsel. [22] Polly Webber, the organization's first vice president from 1987 to 1988, was the delegate of the National Immigration Project and the National Lawyers Guild to the "first International for the Full Rights of Undocumented Workers" in 1980. [23]

From 1987 to 1988 AILA's top position was held by Ira J. Kurzban, formerly of the National Emergency Civil Liberties Committee and the lead litigator on Haitian refugee issues for the National Lawyers Guild. One of his first acts in office was to present AILA's highest award to Ira Gollobin, longtime leader of the American Committee for the Protection of the Foreign Born, an organization often identified as pro-communist. [24] Gollobin is also Kurzban's colleague in the National Emergency Civil Liberties Committee, National Lawyers Guild and the Haitian operation. [25]

After these initial formalities, Kurzban moved quickly to reorganize AILA's committee structure, [26] sprinkling his allies (all NLG members) throughout the newly established committees. Appointed chair of the committee for liaison with the INS headquarters was Michael Maggio of the Immigration Project, while the committee for liaison on asylum appeals was packed by NLG members.

First vice president Webber was put in charge of the Section (supercommittee) on

Congressional and Public Affairs, where Carolyn Patty Blum, Co-Director of the Guild's Central American Refugee Defense Fund, chairs the Law School Committee.[27]

Under the Congressional and Public Affairs Section, Amy Novick headed the Section on Events and Publications.

The new Section on Litigation was headed by General Counsel Robert Juceam, and stacked with Guild members. Under the Section on Litigation, Guild member Lory Rosenberg headed the Amicus Curiae Committee, assisted by five vice-chairs (two of whom also have Guild affiliations).

Two of the three vice-chairs of the Pro Bono Service Committee were Guild members. On the Litigation Committee, by far the most important in planning AILA's agenda, the Guild has a stranglehold of six out of 13 total positions.[28]

In May 1987, as the Immigration Control Act came into effect and the largest mass-amnesty in history began, AILA sent out a memorandum to immigration lawyers and private organizations that were assisting in the alien legalization program advising that "experienced litigators" in public interest and private organizations "have joined with the principal organizations of legalization representatives to form an immigration litigation coordinating group."

The rights organization also announced that it was soliciting individuals as possible "plaintiffs for national class action litigation."[29] The coordinating organizations referred to (NCIR, Inc., NCIR, MALDEF, ACLU, NLG's National Immigration Project, and the Farmworker Justice Fund) are all, not coincidentally, major beneficiaries of Ford Foundation immigration grants with Guild members occupying many high-ranking positions in each.

During that same month the Ford Foundation approved a $50,000 grant to fund the AILA's new Legalization Assistance Project. According to the organization's "Monthly Mailing," this new venture "is working with the American Bar Association to establish a *pro bono* appeals project that will coordinate legal assistance for denied legalization applicants."[30] Chosen as the coordinator of this project was AILA member Carol Wolchok, who moved over from the Washington, D.C.-based (Salvadoran) Political Asylum Project of the American Civil Liberties Union.[31]

The strong-arm tactics of groups like AILA began to have an effect on immigration policy in 1987—barely a year after the landmark Immigration Control Act was passed—when the Immigration and Naturalization Service proposed revisions to the regulations on asylum. Huge backlogs of asylum claims, many resulting from the Cuban and Haitian invasions of 1980, had paralyzed the system, causing delay and inviting further abuse of this most generous of dispensations. Many of these asylum claims, no doubt, were the product of the litigation and lawsuit engines of extremist advocacy groups, and very often did not fit the original definition of "refugee."

This cynical exploitation of U.S. laws was all the more sinister, since many genuine claims of asylum were held up indefinitely by the litigious logjam. Personal liberty, however, is not at the top of AILA's agenda, which crowed about orchestrating "a tremendous campaign to rally support for AILA's opposition to INS's proposed asylum regulations.'' AILA's official comments on the asylum regulations filled up over eighty pages, and represented the opinions of fully twenty-two different lawyers.[32] Not surprisingly, nearly two-thirds, or 14 out of 22, of those lawyers are also members of the Guild's National Immigration Project.

LAWYERS COMMITTEE FOR INTERNATIONAL HUMAN RIGHTS

The LCIHR is part of the campaign to apply the ''equal protection'' clause of the U.S. Constitution to aliens on the same basis as to American citizens. Its director, Arthur C. Helton, is a prominent expert in immigration law and active in the precedent-setting litigation surrounding the Haitian refugee controversy. Helton is also an advisory board member to the National Lawyers Guild's National Immigrant Project, and has contributed widely to creating a link between the left's definition of foreign policy, ''imperialism,'' and the immigration problem.

Helton has long litigated in federal courts against alien exclusion, especially the federal government's denial of entry visas to Communists, suspected terrorists, and other subversives. The 1952 McCarran Act, for example, allows the State Department discretion in granting visas to suspected subversives. [Liberal Massachusetts Representative Barney Frank introduced legislation to remove the discretionary provision from the McCarran Act.] The argument, drawing substantial support now from liberals who earlier would have considered it insidious, is that those rights enjoyed by American citizens under the First Amendment should be extended to all foreigners as well.[33]

This push to block the Executive branch from interposing the federal courts between aliens and other non-citizens has resulted in the emergence of a pattern of litigation—which has since made some startling progress—in destroying the legal meaning of ''alien.'' As an example of this, one need search no further than the protracted, excruciating litigation over the Haitians ''boat people'' who entered the country illegally in the early 1980s.

When the thousands of Haitians who fled their homeland in the closing months of the Duvalier regime washed up on the shores of south Florida, the INS classified them as economic migrants, not political refugees. This drew an immediate hailstorm of litigation sponsored by the Haitian Rights Center, an organization now under the auspices of the National Coalition for Haitian Refugees. Among the lawyers were Ira Kurzban[34], Rick Swartz, Peter Schey, Vera Weisz (later to join Schey's National Center for Immigrants' Rights), and Timothy Barker[35] of the National Center for Immigrants' Rights in Los Angeles.[36]

The avalanche of cases filed in behalf of the Haitians drew criticism from many corners of the American political spectrum, including the normally liberal *Washington Post*, which noted that ''. . .because of [activist] lawyers, the Haitians who are coming illegally are perhaps being accorded more legal rights than those who obey the law. To force the government to provide due process for the Haitians, the lawyers have raised not only the merits of individual cases, but also virtually every possible legal issue to trap the government in its own bureaucratic tangle . . .'' Kurzban was quoted in the same article as saying "[f]ighting [the INS] is like shooting fish in a barrel."[37]

Years later the issue is still not settled. New suits were filed alleging discrimination, lack of due process, and failure to comply with provisions of the Immigration Reform and Control Act granting special treatment to the Haitian and Cuban refugees. Unfortunately, this endless succession of legal challenges can only sharpen the skills of the LCIHR's lawyer-advocates. In the "Immigration Newsletter," Helton boasted of how the Committee had assembled "practice materials on . . . how to prepare an asylum application, and on how to conduct a hearing and/or appeal in connection with an asylum claim . . ."

The effort also brought into their orbit a surprising number of allies, making it what Helton called "one of the most ambitious pro bono enterprises ever attempted by the legal community in the United States . . . [involving] the ABA, and AILA [American Immigration Lawyers Association], the Association of the Bar of the City of New York, the Legal Aid Society of the City of New York, the New York Civil Liberties Union, the National Lawyers Guild, the Washington Lawyers Committee for Civil Rights Under Law . . . and the American Civil Liberties Union."[38]

THE CENTER FOR CONSTITUTIONAL RIGHTS

The Center for Constitutional Rights is the work of William Kunstler and Arthur Kinoy, two veteran leftists with impeccable pedigrees in extremism. In his student days at Harvard, Kinoy was on the executive committee of the American Student Union, a widely-known radical group, and later went on to become a representative of the International Workers Order. Kinoy was also an attorney for the United Electrical Workers, one of the few unions expelled by George Meany from the CIO for retaining Communist leadership.

During the 1950s Kinoy offered his services in helping with a last-ditch defense of the Rosenbergs, the couple convicted of atomic espionage; at one time he also represented Steve Nelson before the Supreme Court. Nelson was identified by the House Committee on UnAmerican Activities as a pro-Soviet activist. Kinoy has twice been Vice President of the National Lawyers Guild, and was a member of the National Council of the National Emergency Civil Liberties Committee, as well as having worked with the American Committee for the Protection of the Foreign Born. These pieces of Kinoy's career obviously add up to a commitment to far-left organizations. The skeptical reader can resolve doubts about this assessment by reading *Rights on Trial*, Kinoy's own autobiography.[39]

Kunstler and Kinoy together led the march of the National Lawyers Guild into the civil rights movement of the early 1960s. The Guild's presence was denounced by mainstream progressives and liberals, including then-U.S. Attorney General Robert

F. Kennedy, among others. In *Rights on Trial*, Kinoy discloses that liberal Democrats, such as Joe Rauh of the Americans for Democratic Action, wanted "to drive out the Lawyers Guild" because it was "immoral to take help from Communists." At a meeting called by the NAACP in 1963, writes Kinoy, "foundation funding and substantial material resources were openly tied to eliminating the influence of the 'Guild lawyers.' "[40] Despite their loud belly-flop into the civil rights debate, Kunstler and Kinoy's contribution to the effort was negligble; their largest triumph, a successful constitutional attack on southern states' anti-subversion laws, was of dubious benefit to African-Americans.[41]

While few Americans may remember the startling 1966 news photo of Professor Kinoy being dragged kicking and screaming from an attempt to disrupt the House Committee on Un-American Activities, the vain and histrionic figure of William M. Kunstler is immediately recognizable from his role as the chief lawyer for the defendants in the case of the infamous "Chicago Seven," the organizers of the violent "peace" demonstrations at the 1968 Democratic Convention. During the proceedings Kunstler was cited for contempt of court for his disruptive defense tactics. [Arthur Kinoy was also chief author of the Chicago Seven appellate brief.[42]]

Earlier, Kunstler had defended the "Catonsville Nine", a group of antiwar protesters led by the Berrigan brothers (Daniel and Philip, both Catholic priests) who had pioneered the practice of breaking into government offices and destroying local draft records.[43] Through their association with the National Emergency Civil Liberties Committee, Kunstler and Kinoy involved themselves in the defense of Daniel Ellsberg, the National Security Council staffer who made public large amounts of classified information concerning military plans during the Vietnam War.[44]

At the 1971 National Lawyers Guild convention, the flamboyant Kunstler described himself "as 'a double agent' in the system" according to *The New York Times*. "I want to bring down the system through the system" he said.[45] Although "the system" still remains intact (at least for the most part), Kinoy and Kunstler certainly threw several well-aimed bombs into it. During the high water mark of 60s radicalism, the two lawyers could be found at the very center of the New Left's agenda, advising and defending its numerous campaigns.

Arthur Kinoy's writings offer several relevant lessons on advocacy and agitprop. First, drawing on events leading to the expulsion of the United Electrical Workers from the CIO, Kinoy notes that the creation of a legal network is essential in order to confront similar crises in the future. "Whenever a new problem developed in one part of the country," he wrote in *Rights on Trial*, "all of the lawyers in the network were fully briefed and received copies of all necessary papers in order to be ready when the same crisis hit them." Kinoy notes that this network opened up other needs for organization, a process that eventually led to "the National Lawyers Guild's massive mobilization of legal resources to support the civil rights struggles of the 1960s, and the organization of the Center for Constitutional Rights."[46]

Next, Kinoy's political strategy emphasizes exploitation of bourgeois "forms," such as human rights, constitutionalism and political democracy, against the "ruling class.'' In his book *Law Against The People* (in a chapter entitled ''The Role of the Radical Lawyer and Teacher of Law'') Kinoy makes this startling claim:

> [R]adicals and radical lawyers must fight skillfully and tenaciously for every scrap of democratic liberties. It is within this context that the role of radical . . . teacher of law begins to emerge more clearly. On the one hand, the radical lawyer must assist in the increasing and exploding radicalization of masses of people learning from their own political experience. On the other hand, all of the lawyer's skills and energies must be utilized to resist in every way the efforts of the dominant sections of the ruling class to solve their crisis, even if temporarily, by substituting the open terrorist dictatorship for the present forms of bourgeois democracy, both within the parliamentary and judicial systems.[47]

With Cuban dictator Fidel Castro as his example, Kinoy advocates disruption of ''capitalist'' democracy to the point that ''revolutionary military measures are correct and will receive the support of the people . . . when people are convinced . . . that all other channels of struggle are closed and futile.''[48]

Kinoy also found that the method of teaching law in America's schools was not adequate. His suggestion: that every ''American law school today must have the clinic at its heart''—that is, that school curriculum should revolve around the so-called clinical approach of teaching, as opposed to the conventional (and widely-used) case-study approach.[49] This piece of advice grew directly out of Kinoy's own experience in the mid 1960s at Rutgers Law School, where he was professor of constitutional law. Finding a tenured position no adequate vehicle for conveying his political causes, he set out with William Kunstler to organize the Law Center for Constitutional Rights.

But Kinoy and Kunstler had reasons other than education for forming the Law Center. They desired an organization that could operate in tandem with their law firm, Kunstler, Kunstler and Kinoy, to carry out their political work.[50] Although law clinics can give law students hands-on experience in real cases, the Rutgers Center shows the major academic flaw of such endeavours: being co-opted by radical political agendas. Witness also the Columbia Law Center under Hariett Rabb and Susan Susman to appreciate this point.

Harriett Rabb cut her own teeth at Rutgers in Kinoy's Constitutional Litigation Clinic in 1966, and then worked with the clinical operation of the Center for Constitutional Rights in its earlier years. It was this experience in legal agitation that she took to Columbia in 1971 when she was hired to head the school's National Employment Law Project.[51] Later, as professor of clinical education at Columbia Law School, Rabb actively involved students in policy-oriented immigration litigation from 1980 to 1986.

Finally, through his leading role in the formation of a National Interim Committee for a Mass Party of the People (NIC) in 1973 and 1974, Kinoy demonstrated the cornerstone Marxian trait of strategic fidelity with tactical flexibility. NIC was an early attempt to unite the varied radical left sects remaining from the collapse of the

New Left into a popular-front type of organization. In April 1975, Kinoy toured the United States as NIC's "national traveler" in order to make contacts with Mexican-American political organizations, including the Centro Accion Social Autonoma (CASA), the illegal-alien organizers in Los Angeles. [52] Kinoy and other NIC leaders, including CASA's Antonio Rodriguez, also served on the Puerto Rican Solidarity Committee, a significant support group at the time for the pro-Castro and far-left Puerto Rican Socialist Party. [53]

While Kinoy insisted that the strategy of the Marxist-Leninists who took over the Soviet Union, China, Vietnam and Cuba "must remain central in the thinking of all who would attempt to chart out a strategy to take power in this last powerful stronghold of world capitalism," [54] the NIC was advocating a mass party, mainly because that was the traditional American forum for seeking to take and hold political power. Political campaigning, according to the NIC's advocates, provided a useful propaganda platform as well as "traditional legitimacy," giving it the ability to "maintain its legality and ability to function openly as long as possible." [55] Kinoy's NIC foreshadowed the Rainbow Coalition of today.

THE AMERICAN FARM WORKERS UNION AND THE INTERNATIONAL COORDINATING COMMITTEE

A resolution of the XXII Convention (1979) of the Communist Party, USA (CPUSA) called for a "Charter of Rights of Immigrant Workers" and for the "trade unions of the United States to energetically work for bi-lateral and world-wide conferences of the trade unions to establish mutually-agreed upon programs, policies and strategies to strengthen world labor unity against the divisive, exploitative policies of the transnational corporations and the imperialist governments which do their bidding." [56]

In December later that year the CPUSA's newspaper, *Daily World,* publicized the Arizona Farm Workers Union (AFWU), an organization promoting illegal migrant workers. [57] An outgrowth of the Maricopa County Organizing Project, the AFWU was the brainchild of the leftist leader Lupe Sanchez. In 1977 Sanchez had split with United Farm Workers of America (UFWA) in 1977 over the UFWA's violent opposition to the employment of illegal aliens.

Because of this enthusiastic support for undocumented workers, financial assistance from the AFL-CIO or the Agency for International Development was not forthcoming. However, the Ford Foundation was more than glad to fill the void. According to a "special report" in the Ford *Letter,* the Arizona Farm Workers Union "works simultaneously to upgrade the working and living conditions of the migrants in the United States and to help create conditions in Mexico that will reduce the flow of migrants." By its own report, most of the AFWU's alleged membership of 10,000 are illegal aliens, while the organization enjoys only a handful of U.S. labor contracts covering a few hundred workers.

A subsidiary of the AFWU, the Farmworkers Economic Development Corporation (FEDC), funds a cooperative called "Advice and Development for Migration Zones," which is supposed to finance irrigation projects and the like for illegal Mexican migrants in their home villages. Ford stepped in with $115,000 of funds for this project since, according to the *Letter*, the project "is based on the theory . . . that most undocumented Mexican workers are in the U.S. out of economic necessity." [58]

However, AFWU organizers disclose that the real reason for diversion of wages to the Mexican "development" fund is that the union's "wage gains and benefits would attract citizen workers, curtailing job opportunities for undocumented Mexicans." [59] That is, an organization that is supposed to exist to improve the conditions of migrants actually works to keep their wage levels depressed!

In 1981, Lupe Sanchez and Jesus Romo, the leader of the Florida Farm Workers Union, presented their organizing experiences at Wayne Cornelius's Center for U.S.-Mexican Studies. They recited a list of "accomplishments" that included: apprehending Mexican-American "coyotes" (alien smugglers) and subjecting them to "workers' trials"; forming strike committees and "security committees" in Mexico; and indoctrinating organizers. In addition, beginning in 1977 AFWU "infiltrated" 23 committees into Arizona citrus. Sanchez concluded with the typical Marxian diatribe against Western capitalism: "We are all subject to the same underlying disease: the inhumane and ethereal transnational corporation that has regard only for profit. . . One of our main objectives was to internationalize the struggle of the undocumented." [60]

The Arizona Farm Workers Union, in fact, was integrated into an effort to "internationalize the struggle": the International Coordinating Committee. The ICC was formed at the 1980 "undocumented" conference in Mexico City, and later changed its name to the American Federation of Workers (AFW). In addition to Sanchez' AFWU, the Committee has as its principal affiliates the Texas Farm Workers under the leadership of Antonio Orendain, Romo's Florida Farm Workers Union, and the Los Angeles-based International Brotherhood of General Workers under the leadership of Jose "Pepe" Medina. [61] Radical intellectual James D. Cockcroft informs us that the leaders of these so-called "independents", including Ramon Danzos Palomino, a top leader in the Mexican Communist Party, were promoting nothing less than a working-class revolution on both sides of the border.

In April 1980 these groups came together in Mexico City for the International Conference for the Full Rights of Undocumented Workers, where they helped to draft a "Bill of Rights for the Undocumented Worker." [62] As mentioned in a previous chapter, other groups attending this revolutionary confab represented the cream of the radical left, including an official delegate of the National Lawyers Guild and other members of its National Immigration Project, and a representative from the Soviet-front World Federation of Trade Unions. Participants were also treated to "solidarity messages" from the Cuban Confederation of Workers, the Palestinian Liberation Organization and the Revolutionary Coordinating Committee of El Salvador. [63]

THE SAMUEL RUBIN FOUNDATION

Although Samuel Rubin was a staunch leftist, he made his fortune in the capitalist cosmetics business by founding Faberge, Inc. in 1936. The name was suggested to him by Armand Hammer in order to play on the reputation of Carl G. Faberge, the creator of the famous "Faberge Eggs" who had served as jeweler to the court of Imperial Russia. Not only was there no blood connection between Rubin and Faberge, but an ideological division separated the two men as well. While Rubin was attacking a system that made him rich, Faberge risked his life to escape from a Soviet gulag in 1920, and remained an anti-communist the rest of his life.

The Rubin Foundation is a major contributor to a host of left-wing groups. But for the purposes of this study, it is the foundation's support for organizations like the Institute for Policy Studies, the ACLU, the National Emergency Civil Liberties Committee Foundation, National Immigration, Refugee and Citizenship Forum and the Center for Constitutional Rights, which associates it with the cause of open borders and full civil and political rights for undocumented aliens. [64]

The Rubin Foundation is now run by Rubin's daughter, Cora Rubin Weiss, who came to national prominence as a leader of the New Left during the Vietnam War. She is the head of the Disarmament Program at Riverside Church (Ford funds the refugee and migrant program of Riverside, [65] a "sanctuary" church). Her husband, Peter Weiss of the National Emergency Civil Liberties Committee and National Lawyers Guild, oversees the Institute for Policy Studies and the Center for Constitutional Rights.

Chapter Ten
Aliens, the Alienated and the "Ultimate Domino"

"American democracy may well be the ultimate domino."

—James D. Cockcroft [1]

F or the alienated radical, there is only one truth over all time: America is a bad country and its "conservative" native-born are a defective people; only distant lands are on the road of progress; only other peoples are intimate with social justice. This is less of a caricature than the defamations that radicals are typically wont to hurl at their opponents on immigration policy or on any other matter.

The yearning of American leftists today for a more receptive proletariat is more than just a sentiment; it is a plea for spiritual employment. The radical left's fortunes have risen and fallen in concert with the proportion of the foreign-born in the United States, not entirely a coincidence. The ever-cautious Nathan Glazer, in a major sociological study of the movement, tells us that "the most striking characteristic of Communist Party membership throughout the 1920s was that it was overwhelmingly composed of relatively recent immigrants. Probably only one in 10 of the members was a native American." [2]

The early Communist Party was so un-American, says Glazer, that even by 1930 its organizers could complain that, "Whenever an American joins the Party there is open opposition that he is a spy." [3] Still, native intellectuals materially benefitted, in an odd way, from their role as political foremen for the unassimilated. Paul Buhle, one of today's Marxist intellectuals favoring more new immigration, explains the bargain: "The Party encouraged the uncertain relationship between revolutionary politics and ethnic culture, providing the immigrants with essential services: labor defense, propaganda, English-language spokesmen and organizational contacts. The

groups in return gave the bulk of funds for the Party's operation, produced enthusiastic crowds, and formed an authentic radical proletariat. And by the thousands these
immigrants proved doggedly loyal, unlike the American recruits . . . "[4]

The collapse of Communism in most of the world has not dampened the desire of
radicals in the United States to remake the country into their own image. As Jeane J.
Kirkpatrick, the former U.N. Ambassador under President Reagan and now Professor of Government at Georgetown University, has argued:

> It is possible that the collapse of Communism as a world revolutionary movement, its
> elimination as a framework for the critical analysis of capitalism and as an alternative
> focus of loyalty, may eventually have an effect on the relationship of the American left
> with the United States, but I doubt it. I believe the left's attitudes toward America have
> influenced its attitudes towards Communism rather than the reverse . . . . I believe one
> of the distinctive attributes of the American Left is a broad, though not universal, alien-
> ation from the dominant American society and culture.[5]

The views of Samuel Bowles, a Marxist economics professor at the University of
Massachusetts-Amherst, provide a good example of this feeling of estrangement.

> In discipline after discipline, what Marx said about capitalism has been shown during
> the Reagan and Bush years to be transparently true, because we have experienced the
> mounting social inequalities and tensions [foreseen by Marx] . . . And the collapse of
> central planning and public ownership in Eastern Europe really is far less important in
> influencing students and intellectual opinions about Marxism than the fact that we live
> in a highly unjust society which is becoming increasingly an armed camp of haves
> against have-nots.[6]

Other leftists lament the demise of the USSR. As Daniel Singer wrote in *The Nation*, "the Soviet Union was the only check on the Pax Americana, the only external
obstacle to U.S. imperialism . . . it is this chapter of Soviet resistance that is now
coming rapidly to an end."[7] But in domestic affairs, they have counted not on the
Red Army, but on an underclass revolution to bring themselves to power. And they
see control of immigration as part of the struggle to build and direct a revolutionary
underclass.

Frank Donner, who in his earlier years was a law partner of Arthur Kinoy and
later served as the director of the American Civil Liberties Union Project on Political
Surveillance, equates anti-communism with nativism. "As a vital ideological resource of American capitalism, nativism has kept the countersubversive tradition
burning . . . "[8]. Donner's testament, the 500-page *Age of Surveillance*, continually
blames America's rejection of the leadership of a radical cadre on a supposed tradition of ignorance and bigotry. "The nativist counter-subversive tradition has always,
as I have tried to show, seized on a foreign-inspired conspiracy as the fountainhead
of subversion. But such external plots have merely served as a rhetorical setting, a

metaphor for the evil threatened by domestic movements which, it is claimed, pose the real danger." [9]

SAVING WORKERS BY DESTROYING THEM

A review of Marxist-Leninist doctrine is impossible in the space of this text, but a salient point requires mention. Marx predicted that socialism and proletarian power would come first to the developed countries; Lenin and his successors, having created a thriving and successful revolutionary movement in a backward country, revised Marxism with a theory of imperialism that posited the oppressed nations and the colonies of the world as the strategic ally of the industrial proletariat.

Imperialism's super-exploitation of cheaper labor of oppressed nationalities in the home state and the colonies allows the bourgeoisie to bribe a "worker aristocracy" that misleads the metropolitan proletariat onto the reformist road. While this "Soviet" orthodoxy describes the worker-aristocracy as a narrow circle of reformist trade unionists and socialists, an increasingly common Third-World "deviation" has emerged that describes the entire "white" working class of the United States (or the world, for that matter) as a compromised aristocracy requiring "leadership" from oppressed nationalities (such as blacks or "Mexicano/Chicanos" in the United States) or from "internationalists" reigning in some politically correct Third World country, or both. For almost a century now, leftists have searched for a theoretical and emotional explanation that accounts for the American proletariat's heroic indifference to "liberation."

The solution? Increase immigration, especially that of undocumented, illegal workers. The Communist Party USA, in its publication, *Political Affairs: Theoretical Journal of the Communist Party USA*, understands well the cause-effect relationship of this: "undocumented workers in any work . . . have the effect of depressing wages and lowering the quality of working conditions." [10] In other words, CPUSA and its fellow travelers suggest that, in order to "save" workers, the working class must first be destroyed through declining wages and living standards!

CPUSA has been displaying a willingness throughout the late 1970s and 1980s to "rebuild" its immigrant heritage in order to achieve this remarkable end. At the 22nd Convention (1979) the Party first gave modern recognition to questions of "Asian-Pacific Islander" immigration. At the 23rd Convention in 1983, the Party resolved not only to promote bilingualism, but to agitate among the "undocumented" from the Caribbean and Central American countries, to organize and lead those "new peoples who have been coming to the United States in large numbers . . . from countries like Iran, Greece, Egypt, as well as Lebanon and other Arabic-speaking countries," and to "more effectively help to mobilize the movement and struggle against passage of the Simpson-Mazzoli bill and to more effectively lead and participate in the struggles against all forms of discrimination against the workers without documents." [11]

A detailed theoretical declaration appeared after the passage of the Immigration Reform and Control Act of 1986. The Party, which for both practical and personal reasons denounces the anti-communist leadership of the AFL-CIO, correctly identifies organized labor as the key political force holding back massive illegal immigration, and instructs its cadre to undermine labor's consensus on the issue. The party also recommends that "[s]olutions [to] the problems of undocumented immigration must be put forth as a necessary part of the political and ideological struggle against the bill." Those solutions, most of which have nothing at all to do with the problem of undocumented migration, include: an end to the arms race, an end to transnational corporations, a non-interventionist foreign policy, an end to anti-communism, a charter of rights for labor (including immigrant labor) and the advancement of American "socialism." [12]

Marxist theoretician Mike Davis is one of many who find it necessary to resort to the comforting deviation that the (white) American working class is worthless as the agent of revolutionary change. In his book, *Prisoners of the American Dream*, Davis offers "a prospective alliance of non-white Americans and Third World revolutionaries, all taking their marching orders from white Leninists." To be sure, the dream of a black 'vanguard' is not a new one; it was popular in both Old and New Left circles during the 1960s. But the rise in America's Hispanic population has given it a fresh twist: the "real weak link in the domestic base of American imperialism is," Davis proclaims:

> a black and Hispanic working class, fifty million strong. This is the nation within a nation, society within a society, that alone possesses the numerical and positional strength to undermine the American empire from within. In tandem with the Communist resurgence in Central America, this 'nation within a nation' can act to bring 'socialism' to North America by virtue of a combined hemispheric process of revolt that overlaps boundaries and interlaces movements. [13]

Paul Buhle, a more flexible theorist, envisions greater diversity within the revolutionary left, and through Latin American liberation theology a return of communism to its chiliastic roots. The collapse of secular socialism and its replacement by religious radicalism, the "rise of religious-based support groups for international revolution and the Sanctuary movement" are significant for Buhle. Again, the failure of the American revolutionary project leads to a frightening solution, the racial and religious liquidation of the undeserving native proletariat. Writing in a 1987 issue of *Against the Current*, Buhle said that "immigration patterns to the United States have altered drastically from the very geographical direction of the new revolutionary faith, just as they did from the European hotbeds of socialism in the early years of the twentieth century. At the present rate, in less than a century, more than half of the U.S. population will be of Caribbean Basin origin. Unlike the European immigrants, their radicalism is based not in the secular left but in the Church." [14]

THE MOOD OF ALIENATION

American sociologist Paul Hollander, in his acclaimed book *Political Pilgrims*, found a pattern of estrangement *and* affirmation that an intense alienation from one's own place requires. To avoid cynicism or moral collapse, one finds the location of virtue elsewhere. If the distant society (or, as argued here, alien peoples) also represent some kind of overt opposition to the home society for whatever reason, then so much the better.

Although Hollander does not name it, this pattern may be called "xenophilia," the love of the foreign and distant over the known and close. Xenophilia is as irrational and pathologic as the more familiarly denounced xenophobia—the fear of strangers. And, just as with Hollander, such alienation may be relieved by affirmation of the distant society. Hope and mission can be found in identification with those visibly "alien" in the home society. Says Hollander, "The repository of all this 'natural goodness,' harmony, and authenticity was the Noble Savage, whose image continued to exert a powerful influence on the fantasies and wishes of Westerners and who keeps re-emerging in forever new incarnations . . . incorporating the same core elements—whether he is projected as the preliterate 'native,' the robust proletarian, earthy peasant or tenacious Third World guerrilla." [15] Or he may be the honest immigrant or endangered refugee, one might add, for members of the National Lawyers Guild and their followers in the "sanctuary" cult.

Peter Collier and David Horowitz, former editors of the revolutionary *Ramparts* magazine and among the leading founders of the New Left, have since had profound second thoughts. They have aptly described Hollander's alienated attitude with additional comment on a common consequence:

The post-Vietnam Left . . . not only colludes with totalitarianism but tries to delude people about its aims. It . . . has an inexhaustible cynicism about American motives and a perpetual inability to locate America's virtues. It is an 'us-them' mentality in which 'us' are the dictators in Cuba, Nicaragua and elsewhere in the Third World, while 'them' is the United States . . . . The post-Vietnam left is effective because of its deceitful layering of the apparatus through which it works and also because it has found a way to support totalitarian movements while appearing to be interested only in improving America's international morality. [16]

A POLITICALLY UNBIASED IMMIGRATION POLICY?

Peter Schey of the National Center for Immigrants' Rights was interviewed for a 1982 "60 Minutes" segment on the Tucson sanctuary movement. Speaking as if an independent authority, he said, "The United States government, as you say, has set out the welcoming mat to literally hundreds of thousands of refugees, primarily fleeing Communist-dominated countries or other countries with which the United States was not maintaining friendly relations. On the other hand, with regard to Salvadoran refugees, Haitian refugees and other refugees coming from countries which are primarily supported by the United States, we find an almost across the board denial of political asylum—again, I believe, for foreign policy reasons . . ." [17] To those who stand with Schey on the left, any suggestion that the United States might base its immigration and refugee policies on its own national interests (be it foreign policy or domestic economics) is to condemn the policies adopted.

Speaking at a February 1975, NLG-Immigration Committee seminar on U.S. refugee policy, Guild attorney William Waterman, Jr. was far more blunt than Schey could afford to be: "[T]o adopt a liberal policy would provide the basis for thousands of non-white, often left-leaning and politically conscious individuals to remain lawfully in the United States." [18]

Those who still doubt that there is a rigid ideological motivation behind immigration-policy agitation, or who doubt the close relationships among the National Lawyers Guild, the Center for Constitutional Rights and the National Center for Immigrants' Rights and other interests, should examine *The Illegality of U.S. Intervention: Central America and Caribbean Litigation*, published in 1984 by the National Lawyers Guild Central America Task Force in conjunction with the Kinoy and Kunstler's Center for Constitutional Rights. Sounding out the now-familiar paranoid mantra, the publication states that the Reagan Administration "is fostering a new wave of anti-Soviet hysteria," and that both groups are actively involved in bringing "numerous lawsuits to expose the lawlessness of the Reagan Administration . . . . Exposing the illegality of these actions is important to counteract the constant immersion of the American people in miseducation and disinformation . . ." [19]

At the time that *The Illegality of U.S. Intervention* was published, the Guild had also set up a "War Crimes Tribunal on Central America and the Caribbean" to convict the entire Reagan Administration *in absentia* for their apostasy. Serving on the Tribunal's "Legal Secretariat" was radical lawyer Ellen Yaroshefsky, who also was Chair of the Guild's Central America Task Force, who remains a staff attorney with the Center for Constitutional Rights, and who was lead counsel in the mid-1980s for the convicted Tucson "sanctuary" defendants.

FORD BUILDS A NEW LEFTIST CADRE

Among the Ford Foundation working paper responses to the situation of the Hispanics, three themes are prominent. First, leadership development:

> The continuing development of a leadership cadre is needed to focus attention on and to support the diverse needs of the Hispanic community . . . . A strong cadre of leaders . . . through their involvement can create opportunities for greater Hispanic participation in the national mainstream . . . . The Foundation has thus initiated a Hispanic Leadership Development Program (HLDP) that is designed to meet the following objectives:

to identify potential Hispanic leaders; to reinforce their commitment to serving the Hispanic community; and to provide them with . . . training and practical experience . . .[20]

"Cadre development," of course, is an unusual choice of words, one that would ring sweetly in the ears of many radicals and Marxists who often use the term "vanguard" to describe just such a group.

Second, Ford wants to increase Hispanic participation in the political process by registering them to vote and by naturalizing permanent resident aliens so they can vote. Although registration of *legal* Hispanic-Americans is a commendable and laudable goal, Ford's aims seem to go far beyond that. Drawing from the expanded Constitutional application argument—that illegals should have all the constitutional rights accorded to natural American citizens and the right to become citizens—the Foundation actively supports steps to enfranchise illegals. *Because many illegals can't gain citizenship*, Ford explained in its April 1 *Letter*:

a growing number of Hispanic-Americans are unable to hold public office, serve on juries, or obtain federal employment or entitlements such as student aid . . . Among [some of the reasons for Hispanics' reluctance to seek citizenship] . . . may be allegiance to their native countries, a belief that seeking U.S. citizenship could result in deportation, a sense that citizenship confers no special benefits, apprehension about the English-language requirement for naturalization, and administrative obstacles such as backlogs at the Immigration and Naturalization Service.[21]

One of the proposals for mass-enfranchisement was to give those obtaining driver's licenses the option of registering to vote. This was accomplished by the so-called "motor voter" legislation. It proposed to increase the number of voting citizens, no doubt a fact that won "motor-voter" the support of many mainstream liberal groups. However, since little documentation is required to get a driver's license—meaning that non-citizens can just as easily get approval—many in government decried the measure as a way to sign up mass numbers of illegals to vote without any background check. (Republican Senator Mitch McConnell of Kentucky has mocked "motor-voter" as "auto-fraudo.")

Despite these complaints, Ford has poured money into the Hispanic "voter registration" movement: fully $1 million to the National Association of Latino Elected Officials alone, and almost $2 million combined from 1983 to 1988 to several groups, including the National Puerto Rican/Hispanic Voter Participation Project, the Midwest Voter Registration Project, and the Southwest Voter Registration Education Project, headed by Willie Velasquez.[22]

During the 1984 Presidential election the Southwestern Voter Project came under controversy when it received a large donation from the Democratic Party's "Hispanic Force '84." Then New Mexico Governor Toney Anaya, a far-left liberal and Chair of the "Hispanic Force '84" effort, predicted that the election would hinge on Texas, which would be carried for the Democrats by the Southwest Voter Registration Education Project. Anaya made sure that the Project received fully $500,000—one-fourth of its total budget—to perform this task. (The money, however, was wasted, as Republican Ronald Reagan swamped Democrat Walter Mondale in the state by a Texas-sized margin of 64 to 36 percent.)[23] More importantly, the Southwest Voter Registration Project was a tax-exempt venture, meaning that the "nonpartisan" facade of such enterprises had all but crumbled away.

The Southwestern Project also might have stepped over the partisan line in the Denver mayoral election, where, according to author Thomas Weyr, "Velasquez had his people . . . help Federico Pena become mayor."[24]

The third leg of Ford's approach to the Hispanic immigrant problem is forging a coalition between blacks and Hispanics, the two largest minorities in the country. An early attempt at this alliance between the two minorities took form in the Ford-funded National Committee on Hispanics and Blacks, which made promising gains for its short duration.[25] Several years later the Foundation funded the Joint Center for Political Studies, a far-left think tank stressing black electoral goals.

In an article entitled "A Changing Black Electorate" in the April 1987 *Letter*, the Foundation noted that demographic trends will eventually turn America's minority populations into an absolute majority, outnumbering whites for the first time in history. (In this context "minority" means all blacks, Hispanics, Asians, and other "people of color" lumped together into one mass; the left often suffers from severe racial myopia by assuming that these people behave and vote in conformity, simply because of their shared non-white skin color.) "The time has come for black and white leaders to change some of the references and terms of the public policy debate in America," the article said. "Blacks are already approaching 20 percent of the American labor force. The number of Hispanics, meanwhile, increased by 56 percent from 1970 to 1982."[26]

Naturally, refugees and illegal immigrants (with the vote franchise, no doubt) would play a pivotal role in Ford's greater *Weltanschauung*. In 1986 a special issue of "Refugee Reports" (funded by the Foundation through the American Council for Nationalities Service[27]) was devoted to the theme "Refugees Learn to Flex Political Muscle."

"Most assessments still rate refugee political clout as minor right now, but with great potential for the future," according to the Report. "One key to their success will be the degree to which refugees can play coalition politics within their wider immigrant and refugee communities. The combined Hispanic and Asian demographic strength in five of the heaviest electoral-vote states—California, Texas, New York, Illinois, and Florida—is growing dramatically . . . . Demographers project that the Asian and Hispanic proportions of the population will continue to grow nationwide, with particular impact on the vote-rich, sun-belt states."

In the 1986 World Refugee Survey (published by the Ford-funded U.S. Committee for Refugees[28]), Robert Rubin, a Guild member with the Ford-funded Refugee Rights Project of the San Francisco Lawyers Committee for Urban Affairs[29], wrote about "The Empowerment of the Refugee Community."[30] In the article Rubin explains that "[t]he advocacy efforts of mutual assistance associations and other community-based organizations will be crucial in developing the community's awareness of legal rights and the political process." Naturalization, enfranchisement, petitioning for immigration of relatives, and political empowerment are the immediate tasks, according to Rubin. The Southeast Asians, Mexicans, and recently hundreds of thousands of Central American refugees must unite now for opposing immigration reform and English-language laws, and later for more important political objectives.

THE RAINBOW COALITION

Arthur Kinoy, National Lawyers Guild member, Vice President of the Center for Constitutional Rights, "mentor" to Ford Trustee Harriet Rabb and founder of the National Interim Committee for a Mass Party of the People (NIC), also wears another hat as a member of the National Board of the Reverend Jesse Jackson's Rainbow Coalition. According to Sheila D. Collins, Jesse Jackson's "national rainbow coordinator" in 1984, the Kinoy forces were crucial in laying the groundwork for the Rainbow Coalition.[31] Collins also says in her long revolutionary tract *The Rainbow Challenge: The Jackson Campaign and the Future of Politics*, that "the organizational apparatus provided by [the Ford-funded] Operation PUSH became indispensable to the Jackson campaign."

Further, she says that the Rainbow forces calculate that "if current immigration and birthrates continue, by the year 2000, Latinos will be the largest ethnic group in the United States. Since 85 percent of all Spanish-speaking people are concentrated in nine states and 20 cities that control 193 (or 71 percent) of the electoral votes needed to win the presidency, they constitute a critical swing vote in future elections."

Elsewhere in the book Sheila Collins pays special tribute to her close friend Renny Golden, the Chicago sanctuary leader. She also explains the plans of Jackson's international affairs advisor, former CPUSA Central Committee member, Jack O'Dell, "who sees the Jackson campaign of 1984 as a pivotal point in a longer term transference of power from the military-industrial complex to the majority of the people, whose needs and desires are not now represented in the national government." O'Dell also advocates the eventual replacement of the Democratic party with the so-called "progressive trend" that the Rainbow Coalition represents—a bold move that would horrify most of today's Democratic party leaders.

During the 1984 Presidential primary, Jackson was the only one of three final candidates who not only opposed the Simpson-Mazzoli bill, but also espoused the entire open-borders platform. Jackson still vigorously supported programs for bilingual education (even though American opinion was turning widely against this measure), defended the "sanctuary" movement, and even refused to utter the word "illegal alien," utilizing instead the politically correct verbiage of "undocumented worker." Jackson also journeyed to Central America to criticize American policy in the region. He paid homage to the Mexican state, where he criticized the U.S. policy toward the country and led a rally at the border to protest "reactionary immigration policies."

In return, Jesse Jackson and his Rainbow Coalition received some early endorsements, including one from 36 Southern California Chicano leaders led by Antonio Rodriguez. According to the Communist Party's newspaper, the New York *Daily World*, Jackson was commended for his opposition to the Simpson-Mazzoli immigration bill "and his support for a fair and just immigration policy." [32]

Running again for the nomination in 1988, Jesse Jackson addressed the national convention of the National Lawyers Guild and sought its endorsement for his presidential campaign. The convention adopted a resolution expressing Guild support for the Rainbow Coalition's program. [33]

Jackson's California campaign launched Coalition 88, the so-called "March and Rally: The March to Build a Progressive Precinct Network"—but billed it as an honor to Martin Luther King. The event was headquartered at the Ford-funded Southern California Ecumenical Council, and Antonio Rodriguez and Bert Corona served on the Steering Committee. [34] A number of religious groups and other organizations that had endorsed the march only because of the Martin Luther King advertisement, publicly withdrew after the coalition officially endorsed the actions of the Palestine Liberation Organization and its inclusion of the Communist Party U.S.A. [35]

Despite the aura of legitimacy surrounding Jesse Jackson's national campaign as he battled Massachusetts governor Michael Dukakis for the nomination, by the "U.S. League for Revolutionary Struggle, Marxist-Leninist" and its allies claimed to have strong influence in his California campaign. [36] The League was quite pleased with the Jackson effort, saying in its paper *Unity* that "[a] Democratic victory will . . . also mean that Jesse Jackson, the leading representative of . . . progressive social forces, will have more access to the highest levels of government, be able to place more of his people in positions of power, influence policy, and be heard." [37]

Picking up on this theme, the Marxist-Leninist newspaper *Frontline* reflected at the close of the primary campaign that "[w]hat the progressive forces led by Jesse Jackson have accomplished in 1988 is the deepest penetration of the bourgeois political arena at least since the 1930s . . . . The process has also presented those of us on the organized left with our best opportunity in decades for ending our marginalization from U.S. politics." [38]

Sure enough, this influence was felt, at least at the Democratic Convention, when the first major demand of the Jackson forces was party endorsement of the Cranston-Conyers bill, the Universal Voter Registration Act of 1988, which would mandate mail-in and same-day voter registration on the states and localities. [39] As with "motor-voter," there was concern that such a scheme would promote considerable election fraud, as well as effectively granting the franchise to numerous ineligible, and politically tractable legal and illegal aliens.

THE ULTIMATE DOMINO

When radical professor James D. Cockcroft used the term "Ultimate Domino" for U.S. democracy in connection with immigration policy, he used the reverse logic for which leftists are so well known. Arguing in *Outlaws in the Promised Land* that American society in the post-Vietnam era "has displayed a deepening 'anti-communist,' racist, nativist, and class-biased character in its treatment of immigrants and in its immigration policy," Cockcroft claimed that the country "has also experienced a wave of legislative, administrative, and court decisions that may curtail the basic civil rights of not only immigrants but of all U.S. citizens."[40]

His particular examples of these presumed threats to civil liberties were in the areas of law enforcement: allowing the police more discretion in questioning suspects and submitting evidence. Most Americans, when polled, think that recent laws have in fact "tied the hands" of law enforcement officers, and would gladly support a greater latitude for police. Cockcroft, however, derides such considerations, condemning in generic terms "the dangerously open-ended grounds of 'over-riding considerations of public safety.' " He also dismissed measures prompted by " 'national security' and the specter of 'terrorism.' "

In particular he attacked the Prohibition Against the Training or Support of Terrorist Organizations Act (1984) that "makes it a crime to 'act in concert with,' train, or serve in any organization designated by the Secretary of State as an intelligence agency or armed force or any foreign government, faction or international terrorist group." Cockcroft was afraid that these proposed laws "could make it illegal to protest U.S. government policy anywhere."[41] Clearly the concept of what people should be at liberty to do is quite broad according to Cockcroft. There is also apparently no acceptable limit of the form or magnitude their protests might take if conspiring with terrorist groups and foreign governments is to be allowed. This is especially true if they happen to be "anti-interventionist and anti-nuclear groups," for which Cockcroft naturally has a special concern.[42]

Political scientists Aaron Wildavsky and Carolyn Webber have written that "Protecting a way of life, modifying it or rejecting it in favor of another, are the global objectives of political regimes." Therefore, policy "matters most when it is centrally implicated in a web of explanation strengthening one culture and weakening another."[43] This is especially true of immigration policy, where questions of cultural conflict or assimilation are explicit.

Taken together, these statements identify the fault line in democracy that the radicals hope to use to destabilize and bring down the established order of state and society. It is the aim of the radicals to increase the level of conflict as much as possible, to kick over the "melting pot" that has served in the past to transform a "nation of immigrants" into the United States. Neo-conservative advocates of increased immigration want to give preference to professionals, anti-communists and Europeans because these groups will strengthen the United States.

In contrast, leftists advocate an open border to the south in hopes of building a larger underclass of alienated anti-Western proletarians who can be recruited to causes that will weaken the United States. Cockcroft maintains that "[t]he emergence of a Latino minority outnumbering American blacks and the likelihood of its rapid growth during the spread of turmoil in Latin America adds to an ever more assertive bloc of voters anxious to affect national and foreign policies in ways not necessarily compatible with the goals of recent presidents and the transnational corporations."

Nothing better illustrates the ultimate goal of this movement than the increased demands that non-citizens be allowed to vote. "Increasingly, advocates for immigrants in New York—as in Washington, Los Angeles and several smaller cities across the nation—have begun exploring the sensitive issue of securing voting privileges for immigrants who are not citizens." writes American University law professor Jamin Raskin in a July 1992 letter to the *New York Times*. Raskin is a leader in this movement and claims "immigrants' rights are the civil rights of the 1990s." By the same logic, he claims that "noncitizen voting is the suffrage movement of the decade." [44]

Non-citizen voting for local government has already been implemented in the liberal suburban enclave of Tacoma Park, Maryland, home of the University of Maryland. Nearby in Washington, D.C., City Councilman Frank Smith has endorsed legislation to allow non-citizens to vote in local elections in the nation's capital. [45] The direction of the movement, Raskin argues, is going in the radicals' direction. "[I]f picked up by large cities—like Los Angeles, Washington, New York and Houston—it could strengthen American democracy by including in the crucial processes of local government many hundreds of thousands of people born elsewhere."

Of course, there is no absolute bar to becoming a U.S. citizen and thus earning the privilege of voting. All a person has to do is enter the country legally and go through the naturalization process. This properly requires a long-term commitment to the United States, its laws, and its Constitution.

That is what citizenship really means; not mere residence. One needs to become part of the national community to share in its direction. But this is exactly the opposite of what the Left wants. It wants political power for those who are alienated from American society, for people who have not yet become part of the nation or who refuse to become part of the nation. "There are 10 million legal immigrants who are not United States citizens," Raskin concluded. "In number, at least, they represent a potential political force of some diversity and dimension, particularly in such cities as New York."

INTERNATIONALIZING THE STRUGGLE

In his writings, Chicano insider Estevan Flores recalled the alarming quote from former Mexican President Luis Echeverria that "Chicanos through the electoral processes were moving the border northward daily because of political victories."

Flores also reveals that Mexican sources (or conduits) have helped to finance immigration agitation in the United States. Included in the funding were major litigious assaults on U.S. immigration laws, especially the crucial Supreme Court case *Plyler v. Doe*, which bestowed a "right" to education for illegal-alien schoolchildren. Said Flores, "[c]oncrete support for the struggles of the undocumented in the United States have been demonstrated through monetary contributions to various struggles such as the education case in Texas." [46]

Former Mexican President Echeverria became involved himself in the Mexican Peace Movement (part of the World Peace Council) and other organizations described by diplomatic sources as Soviet fronts. [47] According to a Central Intelligence Agency report presented to the House Intelligence Committee in February of 1980, "A leader of the Mexican Peace Movement affiliated to the World Peace Council met recently with leaders of the North American Peace Movement (NAPM) in Los Angeles." According to the CIA the parties involved in this session agreed on many goals, including: protesting U.S. "repression" of Mexican illegals and Chicanos; and preparing an "open meeting of the Mexican Peace Movement. . .in Mexico City which would include Mexican government support and participation." [48]

Further support from within Mexico was uncovered in a 1981 bulletin from the American Friends Service Committee. It confirmed that four large Mexican trade unions (the Telephone Workers of Mexico, the Mexican Electrical Workers, the Federation of Government Workers, and the Revolutionary Confederation of Transport Workers) contributed huge sums of money as a means of "moving from 'verbal support' to political action."

In addition, it was reported that various unions in Arizona, Texas and Los Angeles also helped the organizational effort. Donated funds would be put to use in aiding "workers in the U.S. who are threatened with deportation because of attempting to struggle for their rights." [49] Not surprisingly, two of the Mexican unions, the Telephone Workers of Mexico and the Mexican Electrical Workers, are associated with the "Democratic Tendency," a far-leftist political movement in Mexico, while the government-workers union is a surrogate for elements of PRI, the ruling party of Mexico.

Traditionally the Mexican government has been reluctant to involve itself in U.S. politics. Today, however, the government has developed a plan to deploy the 12 million Mexican-Americans in the United States as a lobbying force beneficial to Mexico's interests in expanded immigration and in trade and debt issues, according to the *Wall Street Journal*.

The plan, termed an *acercamiento* (reconciliation or bonding), mentions the fast growth of the Mexican-American population in the United States, and also notes their potential in "changing the 'equilibrium of power' in the border states of California, Arizona, New Mexico and Texas." Americans of Mexican descent have traditionally distanced themselves from the Mexican government, says the *WSJ*, but now, "it is first generation immigrants . . . that make *acercamiento* possible today."

Mexico-born Antonia Hernandez of MALDEF urges the Mexicans to act with even larger boldness, saying "[i]t is reaching a point where the paciencia [patience] is wearing thin." [50]

Lester D. Langley, a professor of Latin American history at the University of Georgia, has found wide-spread irredentist sentiments throughout Mexico, and not just among left-wing intellectuals and politicians. Mexico's loss of its northern lands after the war with the United States, according to Langley, forms "part of the nation-alist mythology where factual accuracy is incidental to the unforgettable shame of the gringo victory over the cosmic race." [51] Speaking in terms of "MexAmerica" to emphasize his belief that Mexico and the United States are "two countries with one future," Langley even refers on occasion to the United States as "MexAmerica Norte." He argues that Americans "have to accept a painful reality about Mexico, Mexicans and even the Mexican in America. Mexico is defiant. Mexicans are defiant . . . . They have brought this defiance into MexAmerica." [52]

THE CONTINUING APPEAL OF ASSIMILATION

Of course, these plans, whether of American leftists or Mexican nationalists, have no guarantee of success. American citizens of Mexican and Latin American descent are as good, as hard-working, as patriotic and as individually diverse as Americans of any other ethnic heritage. Nor are "Hispanic" Americans necessarily susceptible to demagogic appeals: witness the dismal showing among Latino voters of Jesse Jackson's "Rainbow Coalition" during the 1988 Presidential election, a defeat that cast radical-left political ranks into turmoil. In California, Jesse Jackson polled only 40 percent of Hispanic voters in the 1988 Democratic primary and only 21 percent in Texas. [53]

However, the hostile forces involved in the immigration debate tend to ignore such inconvenient statistics. James D. Cockcroft maintains that "[t]he emergence of a Latino minority outnumbering American blacks and the likelihood of its rapid growth during the spread of turmoil in Latin America adds to an ever more assertive bloc of voters anxious to affect national and foreign policies in ways not necessarily compatible with the goals of recent presidents and the transnational corporations." [54] A recent development in Los Angeles is the emergence of an organization called the Mexican Assembly for Effective Suffrage, which agitates for the right of "Mexicans" in the United States to vote in Mexico's elections!

In December 1992, the results of one of the most thorough studies of Hispanic opinion, the Latino National Political Survey, found very little difference between Hispanic-Americans and non-Hispanic white Americans regarding immigration and assimilation. Conducted by a team of academic experts under the direction of Rodolfo O. de la Garza of the University of Texas, the 2,817 Americans questioned revealed some interesting numbers, including:

- Among U.S. citizens, 74 percent of non-Hispanic whites and 75 percent of Mexican-Americans agreed with the statement "There are too many immigrants."

- Among Mexicans living in the U.S. who are not citizens, 84 percent agreed there were too many immigrants. This higher percentage indicates that newly arrived immigrants feel an intense competition with other new arrivals for jobs.

- Among other Hispanic citizen groups, 66 percent of Cuban-Americans and 79 percent of Puerto Ricans agreed that America has too many immigrants.

- Although 60 percent of those interviewed preferred to speak in Spanish, 93 percent of Mexican-Americans, 92 percent of Cuban-Americans and 91 percent of Puerto Ricans said that citizens and residents of the U.S. should learn English.

- Among non-citizen Hispanics, 92 percent of Cubans and 93 percent of Mexican immigrants agreed. While there was still "strong" support for bilingual education, respondents thought the objective should be to teach English, not preserve Spanish.

- Only 30 percent of Cuban-Americans, 38 percent of Mexican-Americans and 37 percent of Puerto Ricans said that immigration preference should be given to Hispanics. However, 74 percent of Mexican immigrants (non-citizens) did favor a preference for Hispanics.

The authors of the study concluded that "Their positive views on their experiences with government and their optimism about their future suggest that the relationship between these groups and mainstream society is not so harsh as to isolate the Hispanic community and make it easily mobilized around narrow ethnic appeals." In fact, an "overwhelmingly large" majority of respondents rejected the collective terms "Hispanic" and "Latino" to describe themselves.

Angelo Falcon, a co-researcher on the project who is president of the Institute for Puerto Rican Policy, noted that a majority of all Hispanic groups call themselves moderates or conservatives in contrast to the self-appointed "Hispanic community leaders," who are overwhelmingly liberal in orientation. "The implication is that there is a growing gulf between Latino leadership and the community," said Falcon.

Thus it appears that assimilation still has a strong appeal. However, if nothing is done to offset the concerted radical effort to undermine this appeal, over time it may weaken thus giving the Left the opening they dream of.

REVOLUTIONARY HOPES SPRING ETERNAL

Many on the left saw the May 1992, Los Angeles riots as a harbinger of an underclass revolution. The three days of non-stop violence was sparked by the acquittal of four white L.A. police officers of all but one charge relating to the video-taped beating of black motorist Rodney King. Following such episodes, left-wing activists often exploit the political fallout to further their own agenda, and Los Angeles was no exception. Many liberal civil rights spokesmen were quick to condemn a racist, exploitive capitalist system that created an intolerable environment for minorities. Although much of the criticism was cast in a black v. white mold, it was estimated by Attorney General William Barr that approximately 30 percent of the 15,000 people arrested during the rioting were illegal aliens, primarily Hispanics.[55] In order to connect the Hispanic looting with issues similar to the King beating, Juan Jose Gultierrez, director of the open border group One Stop Immigration, told the *San Francisco Chronicle* that the riot was in response to "decades of abuse by the immigration authorities and U.S. Border Patrol officers."[56]

A year earlier, the Mount Pleasant area of Washington, D.C., was torn by rioting after a black police officer shot and wounded a fleeing Hispanic suspect. This time, much of the violence was committed by refugees from El Salvador, many of whom probably owe the sanctuary movement for getting them into the country.

Once again, many of today's left-wing activists try to paint urban violence in the stark colors of white v. non-white or underclass v. upper-class. But this analysis does not hold under closer scrutiny. Much of the violence in America's cities stems from animosity between competing minority groups. For example, Los Angeles is plagued by an internecine war between black gangs and Hispanic gangs, who vie for turf and the control of the drug trade in demographically mixed neighborhoods. A similar situation has been afflicting other cities as their neighborhoods become increasingly diverse. Violence is quickly becoming common among powerful Puerto Rican, Haitian, Vietnamese and Cambodian gangs.[57]

Recent irredentist claims by Chicano leaders should set off alarms in every corner of the United States. Activist Rudolfo Acuna stated in an article for *The Nation* that "the black community is going to have to come to grips with the fact that this land [California] was once ours and it was taken away from us—the whole history of colonialism, conquest, repression of Latinos."[58] A fast-growing radical Hispanic group in the Los Angeles area goes by the name "NEWS for America"—NEWS standing for North, East, West and South, conveying the increased Hispanic presence in all parts of the United States.

Unlike other organizations on the far end of the political spectrum, NEWS for America refuses to work with other ethnic groups, in particular blacks. According to Fernando Guerra, director of Chicano Studies at Loyola University "NEWS combines '60s rhetoric with '90s numbers. They're waking Latinos up to the fact they're not a minority anymore." John Mack, president of the Los Angeles Urban League feels that the "notion that 'it's our turn and it's time for blacks to move over' is very destructive."[59]

Many blacks harbor an irredentist feeling of their own for neighborhoods taken over by immigrants, especially when the immigrants have done better economically. A case in point is the Koreans in Los Angeles. Mike Davis travelled through L.A. after the riots to report on attitudes for the *The Nation*. He wrote:

the arson was ruthlessly systematic. By Friday morning 90 percent of the myriad Korean-owned liquor stores, markets and swapmeets in South Central L.A. had been wiped out . . . The Koreans suffered damage or destruction to almost 2,000 stores from Compton to the heart of Koreatown itself . . . I saw graffiti in South Central that advocated "Day one: burn them out. Day two: we rebuild." The only national leader whom most Crips and Bloods seem to take seriously is Louis Farrakhan and his goal of black economic self-determination is broadly embraced . . . At the Inglewood gang summit, which took place on May 5, there were repeated references to a renaissance of black capitalism out of the ashes of Korean businesses. "After all" an ex-Crip told me later, "we didn't burn our community, just *their* stores.[60]

Perhaps the leftists can make something out of the growing instability that is flowing from the rapid fragmentation of America's "multicultural" urban centers. Anarchy has often paved the way for totalitarianism. But the clash of interests between separatist ethnic groups is hardly susceptible to neatly ordered ideological solutions. *Washington Times* columnist Samuel Francis quotes former Colorado Governor Richard Lamm's argument that "One lesson of history is that all successful nations have a social glue that holds them together. Nations must have a common language and common core of assumptions and beliefs. We need only look at Lebanon, Sri Lanka, Quebec, the Balkans to observe what happens when people don't develop a common core and believe in a common destiny. Societies that don't melt, fragment."

Francis adds "if they don't fragment, it's because they're held together only by force, like the multicultural and multi-ethnic empires of ancient times and the late unlamented Soviet Union. In Los Angeles it was force that put the city back together again; it will be force alone that holds it and other American megapolises in one piece."[61] This also explains why most riots are sparked by clashes between minority groups and the police—the armed guardians of the large society.

There are, of course, many Mexicans who are willing to make a strong commitment to the United States. East Los Angeles, where large numbers of Mexican-Americans live, was untouched by the riots. The essential difference between East L.A. and South-Central L.A. is that those who live in East L.A. have been long-term residents, while South Central has been heavily infiltrated by recent immigrants. A different level of attachment and degree of assimilation is obviously indicated here.

During the Persian Gulf War, U.S. Army recruiters were swamped with calls from young men south of the border who wanted to volunteer to fight. This occurred despite the stand of most Mexican intellectuals and liberal-left political leaders who were strongly opposed to the war as another example of Yankee imperialism. Apparently a rumor spread in Mexico that volunteers would be rewarded with American citizenship. Although the rumor was false, if the United States had needed volunteers, such a reward would have been fitting.[62]

The purpose of this study, however, has not been to analyze or predict the future of American politics. It has been to expose the motivations of certain radical groups engaged in the immigration debate; to explain why they advocate or oppose different immigration policies; and to reveal their vision of what America should be. This vision—or, more appropriately, apparition—should startle everyone, because when radical forces promise to flood the country with illegal and large-scale legal immigration in the open hope of seizing power by fraud or force, then Americans of all origins have a legitimate concern.

Appendix One
Harriet Schaffer Rabb: Profile of a Ford Foundation Activist

W hen Henry Ford, Jr. resigned in 1976 from the board of the largest foundation in the world, established by the wealth of his family, he occasioned
considerable controversy. ''I'm not playing the role of the hardhearted ty-
coon who thinks all philanthropists are socialists and that university professors are
communists. I'm just saying the system that makes the Foundation possible is very
probably worth preserving,'' Ford declared in his resignation statement.[1] The vacan-
cies created by the departure of Ford and several other trustees were filled by, among
others, Harriet Schaffer Rabb, a professor at Columbia University School of Law.
New York magazine offered a friendly profile of ''Harriet Rabb, Scourge of Male
Chauvinism,'' in its issue of June 26, 1978 (p. 38):

> It was, in fact, at William Kunstler's denim knee that Rabb got her early training as
> a 'Movement' attorney . . . 'She's doing all this radical work, but she's really straight.'
> Despite a certain post-Watergate pride in the size of her FBI file ('I had a friend whose
> file was longer, but *he* didn't have a CIA file'), Rabb herself would probably agree
> . . . if it weren't for her politics, Rabb would probably be the token lady fat cat at the
> firm of her choice . . .
>
> It was after her second year at Columbia that she happened to be placed in a summer
> job with a civil-rights law firm headed by William Kunstler and Arthur Kinoy . . .
> Kinoy, according to Rabb, was her 'mentor' in the 'Gail Sheehy-*Passages* sense.' She
> continued to work for him—briefly as his assistant at Rutgers but mainly for his Center
> for Constitutional Rights, which had just been formed—until a personal-professional
> crisis in 1969. After her divorce, she had started dating an old friend from law school,
> Bruce Rabb, who came from a prominent Republican family (his father, Maxwell Rabb,
> was formerly Secretary to the Eisenhower Cabinet) and was then with the Nixon White

118

House ('He was on the Domestic Council, and had some title—something-to-the-president'). One of her firm's clients was SDS, then the administration's official Red Menace. Harriet began finding herself at the center of a menage of strange bedfellows: The White House, say, would engineer the banning of an SDS demonstration, and Harriet would call Bruce and tell him it wasn't fair and Bruce would fix it.''

This unusual situation led to Harriet Schaffer Rabb's departure from the staff of the Center for Constitutional Rights, and she was then unable to find satisfactory employment in Washington, D.C. because of her political record, according to her account related in *New York* magazine. "The Rabbs moved to New York in 1971 and she's been with Columbia University ever since." Rabb continued as a "cooperating attorney" of the Center for Constitutional Rights until her appointment as a Trustee of the Ford Foundation in 1977.

Harriet Schaffer Rabb's profile compiled from *Who's Who*:[2]

- Columbia Law School, 1966.

- Staff attorney, Center for Constitutional Rights, 1966-1969.

- Staff attorney, Stern Community Law Firm, Washington, D.C., 1970-1971.

- Assistant Dean Urban Affairs, Columbia University Law School, 1971-1984; co-director Immigration Law Clinic, 1980-1986, clinical professor of law, director of clinical education, 1984-.

- Board of Directors, Ford Foundation, 1977-.

- Board of Directors, New York Civil Liberties Union, 1972-1983.

- Board of Directors, Lawyers Committee for Civil Rights Under Law, 1978-1986.

- Board of Directors, Mexican-American Legal Defense and Educational Fund, 1986-.

Summing her career in brief: Mrs. Rabb was a cooperating attorney for the Center for Constitutional Rights up to 1976; served on the Lawyers Committee for Civil Rights Under Law which established an Alien Rights Project in 1978; served on the New York Civil Liberties Union Board when it began immigration agitation in 1981; participated as the Columbia Immigration Law Clinic with Rick Swartz of the Alien Rights Project and the National Lawyers Guild in establishing the National Immigration Forum in 1981; worked arm in arm with successive co-directors of the clinic who were leaders of the National Immigration Project of the National Lawyers Guild; and served as Ford Trustee as that Foundation granted tens of millions of dollars to immigration-policy projects for the most part run by members of the National Lawyers Guild; and lately has joined the Board of the Mexican-American Legal Defense and Educational Fund (MALDEF).

The profile of Mr. Bruce Rabb, as extracted from *Who's Who*:[3]

- Columbia Law School, 1966.
- Clerk to Judge John Minor Wisdom, 1966-1967.
- Staff Assistant to the President of the U.S., 1969-1970.
- Board of Directors, Lawyers Committee for International Human Rights, 1977-.
- Board of Directors, Helsinki Watch, 1985-.
- Board of Directors, Americas Watch, 1982-.
- Member, International Advisory Committee, International Parliamentary Group for Human Rights in the Soviet Union, 1984-.

Mr. Rabb is Vice Chair of the Lawyers Committee, and on the Board of Americas Watch and Helsinki Watch; while Aryeh Neier is Vice Chair of Americas Watch and Helsinki Watch, and on the Board of the Lawyers Committee. All three groups are at the same address, and together receive millions of dollars a year from the Ford Foundation to act in the areas of U.S. immigration policy and foreign policy. Bruce and Harriet Rabb graduated from Columbia Law School in 1966. Vilma Martinez, for ten years the leader of MALDEF and of its efforts to defeat the first Carter immigration-reform plan, graduated Columbia Law in 1967.

Franklin A. Thomas, President of the Ford Foundation beginning in late 1979, graduated from Columbia Law School in 1963, became University Trustee from 1969-1975, and joined the Ford Board of Trustees in 1977, the same time as Rabb.

Appendix Two
Ford Foundation Immigration and Related Grants 1983-1989

"**F**FY85" would mean a one-year or multiple-year grant *approved* in Ford fiscal year 1985, which runs from October 1, 1984, to September 30, 1985. Ford documents report both on grants approved and funds disbursed. For the sake of simplicity and accuracy, these summaries report only on approvals. All descriptions are quotations or accurate paraphrasing from Ford Foundation publications. The survey covers Ford Foundation Annual Reports from 1983 through 1991, supplemented by Ford newsletters from those years. Though the list is long and the dollar values substantial, the list is not a complete picture of Ford Foundation activity. For example, in the 1989 Annual Report, the statement is made "In response to the legal needs of asylum seekers, the Foundation granted funds for the development of a program for *pro bono publico* recruitment, training and representation" involving the American Bar Association, the Texas Bar and the American Immigration Lawyers Association. Yet no dollar figure was provided so this program does not show up on the list.

FORD FOUNDATION IMMIGRATION AND REFUGEE GRANTS

Action for Boston Community Development, Boston.

*FFY88, $35,000 for refugee and immigrants' rights.

"Advice and Development for Migration Zones", Mexico.

*FFY84, $115,000, to enable migrant agricultural workers to develop small-scale irrigation projects in their home communities (Arizona Farmworkers Union).

African-American Institute, New York.

*FFY85, $35,000, listed under refugees and migrants, for a newsletter for South African students and refugees in the U.S.

American Bar Association Fund for Justice and Education, Chicago.

*FFY89, $50,000 for refugees and migrant's rights; $150,000 for access to social justice legal services.

*FFY88, $7,500 for refugees and migrant's rights.

*FFY86, $49,500, for a conference to encourage the development of pro bono publico legal programs for refugees seeking asylum and to help strengthen existing programs.

*FFY85, $38,000, for refugee and migrant rights.

American Civil Liberties Union Foundation, New York City. (see additional ACLU entries under ''Supporting Organization Grants'' below)

*FFY91, $440,000 for migrant rights.

*FFY90, $650,000 for access to social justice.

*FFY89, $275,000 for ACLU's Immigration Project for ''litigation, training and educational activities on behalf of aliens''; $500,000 for civil and political liberties.

*FFY88, $550,000 access to social justice/legal services.

*FFY87, $300,000 for refugee and migrant's rights; $430,000 for access to social justice legal services.

*FFY83, $300,000, to establish a National Fund for Alien and Immigration Rights. ''The fund will provide support to ACLU affiliates for public education, litigation, and advocacy to define and protect the civil liberties of aliens in the United States. ACLU and its affiliates have been challenging the legality of various government practices with regard to aliens, including prolonged detention, raids and arrests at places of employment, and restrictions on health and social service benefits.''

American Council for Nationalities Service, New York City.

*FFY86, $550,000 for U.S. Committee for Refugees.

*FFY84, $450,000, for international refugees and migration.

*FFY83, $227,000, ''for the public information activities of the U.S. Committee for Refugees.''

   The U.S. Committee for Refugees, which recently merged with ACNS, publishes the *World Refugee Survey*, a comprehensive yearbook of statistics on refugees around the world; *Refugee Reports*, a biweekly newsletter for re-

settlement workers, refugee groups, and public service organizations; and issues papers that deal with specific refugee populations and protection questions.

American Friends Service Committee, Philadelphia, PA.

*FFY88, $225,000 for refugees and migrant's rights.

*FFY87, $135,000 for refugees and migrant's rights.

*FFY86, $200,000, ''These groups hold that conditions in Central America are so
life-threatening for most of the refugees that it would be inhumane to force
them to return . . . . The religious groups base their actions not only on compas-
sion, but also on the principle that refuge is a basic human right . . . . AFSC has
played an important role in alerting American citizens and policy makers not
only to the plight of Central American refugees in the United States but also to
the events in Central America that are generating the refugee flows. In addition
to issuing several publications about the refugees, AFSC staff have testified
before Congressional hearings, briefed local media and human rights groups,
and helped lawyers representing refugees in remote areas.''

*FFY86, $160,000, for Florida Project.

*FFY85, $20,000, for a project to monitor and report on the drafting of the U.N.
Convention on Migrant Workers and Their Families.

*FFY84, $130,000, refugee and migrant rights, for ''Florida Project for Undocu-
mented Workers . . . . The Florida Project is bringing foreign farmworkers
together to define their common problems. It also provides paralegal training
on immigration problems, monitors the practices of the INS to ensure fair treatment of workers, and disseminates information on the working and living conditions of farmworkers.''

*FFY84, $150,000 for U.S. rural employment generation (Arizona Farmworkers
Union?).

*FFY83, $160,000, for U.S. rural employment generation.

American Immigration Law Foundation, New York and Washington.

*FFY89, $275,000 ''To encourage the fair and effective implementation of IRCA
. . .[to] help low-income and poor immigrants apply for legalization.''

*FFY88, $ 75,000 for refugee and migrants' rights.

*FFY87, $ 75,000 for refugee and migrants' rights.

American Public Welfare Association, Washington, DC.

*FFY88, $75,000 ''to assist state agencies in implementing the law [the Immigra-
tion Reform and Control Act of 1986].

Asian Pacific American Legal Center of Southern California, Los Angeles.
*FFY88, $15,000 for refugee and migrants' rights.

Bay Area Institute, San Francisco.
*FFY 85, $75,000, to enable Pacific News Service to circulate newspaper articles on contributions and problems of Hispanic citizens, refugees and migrants in the U.S.

Bilateral Commission on U.S.-Mexican Relations, Cambridge, MA and Mexico.
*FFY86, $600,000 for "an independent bilateral commission recently formed at the Foundation's initiative . . . . Of major concern to both countries are the two million Mexicans who annually cross the border, many of them illegally, in search of jobs . . . . The Commission held its first meeting in October in Tijuana and San Diego where it heard current and former government officials, Chicano leaders, and prominent citizens speak on immigration and other issues."

Brandeis University, MA.
*FFY82, $65,000, for Lawrence Fuchs, former Staff Director of the Select Commission on Immigration and Refugee Policy, for a study of American pluralism.

British Refugee Council, England.
*FFY87, $35,000 for refugee and immigrants' rights.
*FFY86, $35,000, for seminar on developing an international system for indexing and exchanging information among worldwide refugee documentation centers.
*FFY85, $70,000, for a series of meetings of European and North American attorneys specializing in asylum law, where participants will discuss judicial interpretations in various western countries of protections provided by the United Nations Convention and Protocol relating to Status of Refugees, including a "seminar for developing an international system for indexing and exchanging information among worldwide refugee documentation centers."

California Rural Legal Assistance Foundation Sacramento.
*FFY89, $40,000 for refugee and migrants' rights.

California State University, on behalf of the Consortium for Employment Communication.
*FFY88, $75,000 for refugee and migrants' rights.

*FFY86, $50,000, for vocationally related English-language program and bilingual teaching and counseling materials.

Casa de Proyecto Libertad, Harlingen, Texas.
*FFY89, $50,000 for refugee and migrants' rights.

Center for Constitutional Rights, New York.
*FFY88, $200,000 for access to social justice/legal services.

Center for Economic and Social Studies of the Third World, Mexico.
*FFY84, $44,900, for research on U.S., Mexican and Central American relations.

Center for Migration Studies of New York, Brooklyn, NY.
*FFY85, $10,000, for refugee and migration policy.

*FFY84, $5,000, for a conference on immigration laws, on the rights of undocumented aliens, and policies affecting refugees.

*FFY83, $7,500, for a conference on immigration and refugee policy.

*FFY83, $140,242, for six special issues of the scholarly journal, *International Migration Review*. Topics to be addressed include illegal migration, measurement of international population flows, women refugees and migrants, and the civil rights and participation of aliens.

Center for Northern Border Studies, Tijuana, Mexico.
*FFY85, $225,000, for a center "established in 1981 to study the politics, economy, and culture of the border region and to generate data on cross-border migrant flows. . .to enable U.S. scholars to participate in its research and training programs."

*FFY83, $130,000, "for research on U.S.-Mexican border issues. . .including migration of Mexican laborers to the U.S."

Center for Southeast Asian Refugee Resettlement, San Francisco, CA.
*FFY85, $200,000, "to provide loans, technical assistance and training to refugee entrepreneurs in the Bay Area."

Center for Teaching and Research in Economics (CIDE), Mexico.
*FFY84, $300,000, to study and publish on migration, U.S.- Mexican border relations, and U.S. foreign policy in Central America.

Central America Resource Center, Austin, TX.

*FFY88, $75,000 for refugee and migrants' rights.

*FFY87, $59,989 for refugee and migrants' rights.

*FFY86, $100,000, "for the center's Refugee Legal Support Service, which provides up-to-date information on conditions in Central American countries for use by policymakers, by lawyers representing refugees seeking asylum or safe haven, and by others interested in protecting the rights of Mexican aliens."

*FFY84, $40,000, "for the Refugee Legal Support Service, which provides background information to lawyers representing Central American refugees seeking asylum in the U.S."

Centro Presente, Cambridge, MA.

*FFY85, $45,500 for health, social service and community education projects for Central American refugees.

Chinatown Resources Development Center, San Francisco,

*FFY83, $150,000, for project to increase employment opportunities for refugees and migrants in the U.S.

Christian Community Service Agency, Miami, FL.

*FFY84, $112,000, for project to increase employment opportunities for refugees and migrants in the U.S.

*FFY83, $102,000, for same.

Church Council of Greater Seattle, Seattle, WA.

*FFY84, $26,000, for organizing refugees.

City University of New York, New York City.

*FFY86, $25,000, listed under refugee and migrants rights, to enable 20 Nicaraguan officials to meet with U.S. legal scholars on ways to safeguard civil liberties in Nicaragua's draft constitution.

*FFY84, $206,795, "The links between U.S. foreign policy and various waves of immigration into this country from Cuba, Haiti, Mexico, the Dominican Republic, and Central America is the subject of a study by a group of researchers led by Christopher Mitchell of New York University. They are analyzing the role U.S. foreign policy considerations play in governmental decisions to admit or exclude aliens. The researchers are also assessing how various interest groups in the United States, such as labor, business, farmers, and human rights organizations, influence U.S. immigration policy."; $50,000, for a study of the interactions between immigrants and other residents in the Elmhurst-Corona section of Queens.

*FFY83, $4,840, for refugee and migration policy.

*FFY82, $49,500, for refugee and migration policy.

*FFY82, $50,000, for international human rights law.

Clinica Monsignor Oscar A. Romero, Los Angeles, CA.

*FFY85, $46,600, for health, social service, and community education projects for Central American refugees.

*FFY84, $49,000, for refugee and migrant resettlement.

Coalition for Immigrant and Refugee Rights & Services, San Francisco
*FFY91, $50,000

College of Jalisco, Mexico.

*FFY86, $61,000, "for studies of the costs and benefits of migration from the State of Jalisco to the United States, in particular its effects on Jalisco's economy."

*FFY86, $27,000, for study of women in transnational industries.

College of Mexico, Mexico City.

*FFY83, $37,600, for participation of Mexican scholars in international conferences.

*FFY83, $5,000, for publication of papers on U.S.-Mexican economic relations.

*FFY82, $20,000, for research on U.S.-Mexican border relations.

Columbia University, New York City.

*FFY89, $100,000 for access to social justice/legal services.

*FFY88, $150,000 for access to social justice/legal services.

*FFY87, $5,000 for access to social justice/legal services.

*FFY86, $1,310,000, "Last year, it granted funds to Harvard Law School [q.v.] for an expanded program of human rights teaching, research and internships. Now, Columbia University is establishing the first university-wide human rights program, for which the Foundation has made a $310,000 grant for the first eighteen months of the program, and a challenge grant of $1 million, to be matched by the university two-to-one, to establish a permanent fund to support the program. Columbia's program will consist of interdisciplinary teaching, research, and work with human and civil rights organizations. The program is being coordinated by the university's Center for the Study of Human Rights. Since its founding in 1978 by three senior faculty members, the center has encouraged interest in international human rights throughout the university community. Visiting researchers from the United States and abroad have joined Columbia's faculty and students in studying themes ranging from the rights of aliens to human rights and development. The Center. . .has worked with such organizations as the Lawyers Committee for International Human Rights [q.v.], Helsinki Watch, and Americas Watch. Building on these activities as well as existing teaching and research on U.S. civil rights and refugee issues, Columbia's new program will integrate the study of human rights. . .''

*FFY85, $40,000, to study the role of self-help associations formed by Dominican immigrants in New York City's Washington Heights section.

*FFY84, $20,000, for a study of the role of churches in providing services to immigrants and in helping them organize self-help projects.

*FFY82, $150,000, for international human rights law, including meetings to promote international human rights research and to discuss issues related to national security, migrants and refugees.

*FFY84, $20,000, for refugee and migrant resettlement.

*FFY84, $40,000, for refugee and migrant rights.

Community Board Program, San Francisco, CA.

*FFY85, $200,000 for refugee and migrants rights.

Community Consolidated School District 15, Chicago, IL.

*FFY84, $115,000 for refugee and migrant resettlement.

*FFY83 $102,000, to improve employment opportunities for refugees and migrants to the U.S.

Community Training and Assistance Center, Boston, MA.

*FFY85, $100,000, ''which is providing training in organizational and leadership skills to members of the refugee self-help organizations. It is also exploring the formation of a multi-ethnic refugee coalition in the Boston area.''

Community Funds, New York.

*FFY91, $50,000 for refugee and migrants' rights

*FFY89, $50,000 for refugee and migrants' rights.

*FFY88, $150,000 for refugee and migrants' rights.

Farmworker Justice Fund, Washington, D.C.

*FFY89, $400,000 for refugee and migrants' rights.

*FFY87, $75,000 for refugee and migrants' rights; $319,500 for access to social justice/legal services..

*FFY85, $250,000 "to expand its public education activities on behalf of alien farmworkers . . . . In coordination with the Arizona Farmworkers Union, the fund will recruit attorneys to represent alien farmworkers."

Frederick Burk Foundation, San Francisco, CA.

*FFY84, $206,000, for refugee and migrant resettlement.

Haitian Centers Council, New York City.

*FFY84, $300,000, for technical assistance, leadership training, public education, and social services for Haitians living in New York.

*FFY83, $150,000, "in New York, where the great majority of Haitian immigrants have settled, the Haitian Centers Council coordinates the activities of five local Haitian self-help programs."

Haitian Refugee Center/Sant Refijie Ayisyin, Miami FL.

*FFY91, $300,000.

*FFY89, $275,000 "To encourage the fair and effective implementation of IRCA . . .[to] help low-income and poor immigrants apply for legalization."

*FFY88, $75,000 for refugee and migrants' rights.

*FFY88, $100,000 for refugee and migrants' rights.

*FFY87, $225,000 for refugee and migrants' rights.

*FFY85, $265,000, ". . .the Foundation continued to support the efforts of the Haitian Refugee Center to clarify and protect the rights of aliens in detention or in exclusion, deportation, and asylum hearings. Serving as the legal representative of Haitians in southern Florida, the center has sought to establish before the U.S. Supreme Court, and other federal courts aliens' rights to due process and equal protection under the law, and to educate the public about the rights of aliens."

*FFY83, $255,000, "the center has used test-case litigation and public education to bring to national attention mass deportations, interdiction on the high seas, and prolonged detention of undocumented Haitians. . ."

Haitian Task Force, Miami, FL.

*FFY84, $290,100, for refugee and migrant resettlement, small business development loans, survey of jobs and working conditions.

*FFY84, $450,000, program-related investment for same, *not* grant.

*FFY83, $30,000.

Harvard University, Cambridge, MA.

*FFY91, $50,000 for Refugees and migrants' rights.

*FFY89, $200,000 for refugee and migrants' rights; $100,000 for access to social justice/legal services.

*FFY88, $400,000 for exchange of ideas and information; $150,000 for access to social justice/legal services.

*FFY87, $190,000 for refugee and migrants' rights; $50,000 for access to social justice/legal services.

*FFY85, $300,000, "to establish a teaching and research program in international human rights law. Harvard will initiate several new courses covering such topics as economic and social rights and immigration and asylum, and it will also expand an internship program that enables students to work with public interest and human rights groups."

Health and Community Services Council of Hawaii, Honolulu.

*FFY86, $25,000, for operation of bilingual hotline for non-English-speaking immigrants.

Immigrant Legal Resource Center, East Palo Alto, CA

*FFY91, $350,000 for refugees' and migrants' rights.

*FFY89, $90,000 "To encourage the fair and effective implementation of IRCA . . .[to] help low-income and poor immigrants apply for legalization."..

*FFY88, $58,000 for refugee and migrants' rights.

Indochina Resource [Refugee] Action Center, Washington, D.C.

*FFY91, $170,000 for refugees' and migrants' rights.

*FFY89, $170,000 "the primary national organization representing Southeast Asian mutual assistance associations. . .for public education, information dissemination and networking activities."

*FFY85, $200,000, serves as an advocate for refugees.

*FFY84, $15,600.

*FFY83, $350,000, "The center will represent the interests of Southeast Asians on refugee admission issues and will also work with their community organizations in training leaders, obtaining funding, and in preserving the Indochinese ethnic heritage."

Institute for Regional Education, Santa Fe, NM.

*FFY85, $15,000, for U.S. rural employment generation.

*FFY84, $10,000, for feasibility study of new programs for migrant workers in Arizona (possibly for Resource Center).

International Refugee Center of Oregon, Portland.

*FFY85, $16,000.

*FFY84, $200,000, for six mutual assistance associations and for a loan fund that refugees can draw on to start small businesses.

*FFY84, $500,000, program-related investment, *not* grant, for same.

Inter-University Program on Latino Research.

*FFY85, $1,500,000, for "a consortium of four Hispanic research centers at Stanford University [q.v.], University of California at Los Angeles [q.v.], University of Texas [q.v.], and Hunter College [see City University of New York], and the Social Sciences Research Council." They ". . .will invite applications for grants to support research on the effects of Hispanic migration into the United States, on Hispanic's participation in U.S. politics, on their opportunities for education and employment, and on their participation in income support programs." (Note: Fernando de Necochea, Assistant Provost at Stanford University, was MALDEF Board Chair for 1984-1985.)

Intertect Institute, Dallas, TX

*FFY91, $151,000 for refugees' and migrants' rights.

*FFY88, $100,000 for refugees' and migrants' rights.

Jewish Federation for Metropolitan Chicago, IL.

*FFY83, $100,000, for referral services on immigration and to train leaders of local refugee and migrant groups.

Lawyers Committee for Civil Rights Under Law, Washington, D.C.

*FFY91, $370,000 for refugees' and migrants' rights.

*FFY88, $50,000 for refugee and migrants' rights; $766,000 for access to social justice/legal services.

*FFY83, $30,000, "The Alien Rights Law Project. . .received a grant to coordinate legal representation for aliens appealing administrative decisions to deny them asylum. Most requests for asylum based on claims of persecution at home are denied at the initial hearings, but important precedents have been established on appeal by the Board of Immigration Appeals in Washington, D.C. and by the federal courts. The project recruits and trains volunteer attor-

neys from the Washington area, assigns cases, and draws on specialists to provide advice on conditions in various countries in support of asylum appeals.''

Lawyers Committee for International Human Rights, New York City.

*FFY87, $700,000 for refugee and migrants' rights.

*FFY86, $6,880, for a workshop on emerging priorities in international human
rights.

*FFY85, $330,000 for two-year supplement for promoting human rights, includ-
ing rights of those seeking asylum.

*FFY84, $125,000, ''Foreigners who enter the United States without proper pa-
pers are subject to detention until their status is determined . . . . The. . .Law-
yers Committee. . .received support for a program to recruit and train volunteer
lawyers near each detention center to provide representation for asylum applicants.''

*FFY83, $300,000, ''. . .over the last three years the Political Asylum Project of
the Lawyers Committee. . .has arranged for *pro bono publico* legal representation for some 250 aliens from more than thirty countries, and has trained many
young lawyers in the intricacies of immigration law and asylum claims. The
project has also worked with other groups in arranging legal assistance that
secured the release of 1,800 detained Haitians seeking asylum in the United
States.''

*FFY82, $85,000, ''. . .put forward a plan that permitted parole of Haitians who
had been detained by the government pending determination of their asylum
petitions. With other groups, the committee is providing legal representation
for between 1,700 and 1,900 Haitians under this parole program.''

(The Lawyers Committee is a project of the Fund for Free Expression,
which also includes in the same offices Americas Watch, Asia Watch and Helsinki Watch. Each of these other projects receives substantial Ford funding;
also, see Columbia University Human Rights.)

Legal Aid Foundation of Los Angeles, California.

*FFY91, $275,000 for refugees' and migrants' rights.

*FFY89, $250,000 for National Center for Immigrants' Rights.

*FFY87, $350,000 for refugee and migrants' rights.

*FFY84, $150,000, ''When alien children come to this country from El Salvador,
Afghanistan, Iran and other countries to avoid persecution or war or to join
family members are apprehended by the Immigration and Naturalization Service (INS), it is not clear exactly what their rights are . . . . The National Center
for Immigrants Rights (NCIR), one of eighteen national centers established by
the Legal Services Corporation, has brought several important test cases

against the INS to secure fundamental protections for indigent alien children. However, by law, corporation funding cannot be used for some activities relating to the defense of alien children. This year the Foundation granted funds to the Legal Aid Foundation of Los Angeles for an expansion of NCIR's Immigrant Children's Rights Program to clarify this murky area and to secure for alien children access to education, health and other social services.''

Lehrman Institute, New York City.

*FFY86, $48,500, for seminars on the impact of immigration on U.S. foreign policy.

Lutheran Council in the U.S.A., New York City.

*FFY86, $400,000, ''. . .Central Americans are seeking refuge in the United States in increasing numbers . . . . the vast majority of whom are believed to be undocumented. Thus far the Central American refugees' main sources of assistance have been churches and religious organizations . . . . The Immigration and Naturalization Service, contending that the Central Americans are primarily fleeing economic, not political difficulties, continues to arrest, detain and deport them . . . . One of the first national efforts by a church group to aid Central Americans came from the Lutheran Immigration and Refugee Service of the Lutheran Council in the U.S.A. In 1981, it established Central American Concerns (CAC), which makes small grants to projects throughout the country that provide Central American refugees with direct assistance or referrals in obtaining food, clothing, shelter, jobs, health care, and language instruction. Most of the projects also have legal units that help with asylum applications and provide legal representation in deportation proceedings. In addition to grants, CAC gives the projects technical assistance and works to inform the public about the problems faced by the refugees here and the conditions that drove them from their countries. CAC also serves as an advocate for the refugees on pending legislation and on such issues as their detention while they await asylum hearings and the low rate at which asylum is granted to Central Americans.''

*FFY85, $50,000, for access to social justice and legal services.

Lutheran Immigration and Refugee Service, New York City.

*FFY91, $175,000 for refugees' and migrants' rights

*FFY89, $500,000 for refugees' and migrants' rights.

Mexican-American Legal Defense and Educational Fund, San Francisco, CA.

*FFY91, $350,000 for human rights; $442,000 for public policy and civic participation.

*FFY90, $1,575,000 for civil and political liberties.

*FFY89, $295,000 for civic participation.

*FFY88, $1,350,000 for access to social justice/legal services; $135,000 for "training, advocacy, and litigation activities on behalf of aliens." "MALDEF focuses on education, immigrants' rights, language-based discrimination and voting rights."

*FFY87, $200,000 for refugee and migrants' rights.

*FFY86, $1,300,000, two year supplement for general support.

*FFY85, $240,000, to "provide training and placement services for young Hispanic professionals who wish to serve on local boards and commissions" (Hispanic Leadership Opportunity Program).

*FFY84, $1,365,000, "to defend the rights of U.S. Hispanics."

*FFY83, $320,000, to improve Hispanic access to higher education.

*FFY83, $270,000, for policy analysis and dissemination.

*FFY83, $33,600, for policy research on Hispanic political participation (see National Chicano Council for Higher Education).

*FFY82, $900,000, for civil and political liberties.

Miami Urban Ministries, FL.

*FFY84, $41,000, for United Methodist Church health education project for Haitian women and children.

Michigan State University,

*FFY82, $40,833, for refugee and migration policy.

Minnesota Department of Public Welfare, Saint Paul MN.

*FFY82, $93,000 for encouraging businesses to train and hire qualified refugees and migrants.

Migrant Legal Action Program, Washington, DC

*FFY89, $50,000 for refugee and migrants' rights.

Multicultural Education Training and Advocacy Center, Somerville, MA.

*FFY89, $162,000 "for legal advocacy on behalf of children who are denied their right to education because of language or other cultural barriers."

*FFY87, $50,000 for refugee and migrants' rights.

National Association for the Southern Poor, Washington, D.C.

*FFY85, $50,000, listed under migrants and refugees: "for support and expansion of community self-help organizations serving the poor in the 'black belt' region of the South."

National Bureau of Economic Research, Cambridge, MA.

*FFY85, $500,250, "to examine the impact of immigration on jobs, wages, and working conditions in the United States and other developed countries—an issue at the heart of discussions on immigration law reform . . . . Questions addressed by the study include: Does the immigration of low-wage workers reduce imports of labor-intensive products? If the United States restricts the flow of low-wage workers, will it export more capital to low-wage countries and import more foreign goods? Is the recent recovery of the U.S. economy at least partially attributable to readily available labor from other countries?" Martin Feldstein, Project Director.

National Chicano Council on Higher Education, Berkeley, CA.

*FFY83, $34,014, to synthesize the results of five Hispanic public policy task forces: U.C.L.A. [q.v.], employment and economic opportunities; University of Houston [q.v.], education; MALDEF [q.v.], political participation; National Council of La Raza [q.v.], social services and community development; University of Wisconsin [q.v.], statistical and other data needs.

*FFY81, $202,500, for education and research.

National Coalition of Advocates for Students, Boston, MA.

*FFY89, $ 50,000 for its report on "the educational experiences of immigrant school-children. Although every immigrant child has the legal right to a free public education, the report state that many schools, often inadvertently, discourage immigrant children from enrolling. Once inside the classroom, these children continue to confront barriers to an effective education."

*FFY86, $250,000, "for a nationwide study of alien children in public schools. The coalition will recommend changes in educational policy and practice that will benefit newcomer children."

*FFY85, $25,000, to plan a study of the status of alien children in public schools.

*FFY84, $150,000, for general support of organization advocating for English-limited students.

National Coalition of Haitian Refugees, New York City.

*FFY88, $24,500 for refugee and migrants' rights.

National Council of Churches of Christ, New York.

*FFY85, $50,000, under migrants and refugees, for a demonstration project to improve the capacity of local churches to provide social services in inner-city neighborhoods.

National Council of La Raza, Washington, D.C.

*FFY91, $1,000,000 for public policy analysis; $150,000 for urban poverty, social revitalization; $55,000 for urban poverty, youth employment.

*FFY90, $162,000 for public policy analysis; $100,000 for social revitalization.

*FFY89, $402,000 for public policy analysis; $50,000 for teen pregnancy.

*FFY88, $830,000 for public policy analysis.

*FFY87, $110,000 for public policy analysis.

*FFY86, $300,000, one-year supplement for technical assistance to community-based Hispanic groups and for research, advocacy, and public information on policy issues important to Hispanics; $25,000, for improvements in its financial and management system.

*FFY84, $500,000, for development of Hispanic-oriented television programming, "to educate the public about the history and contributions of Hispanic Americans," program-related investment, *not* a grant.

*FFY83, $500,000, ". . .La Raza, which received renewed support, has shifted its emphasis to policy analysis as federal support of its technical assistance to local groups has been cut back. Recent studies disseminated to policy makers and other Hispanic organizations include an analysis of Black and Hispanic perspectives on immigration. . ."*FFY83, $37,732, for policy research on Hispanic social services and community development, see National Chicano Council on Higher Education.

National Economic Development and Law Center, Berkeley, CA.

*FFY86, $575,000, two-year supplement, "for legal services to community and refugee self-help organizations."

NALEO Education Fund, Washington, DC.

*FFY87, $300,000 for refugee and migrants' rights.

National Immigration Project of the National Lawyers Guild, Boston, MA.

*FFY91, $50,000 for refugees' and migrants' rights

*FFY89, $48,000 for refugees' and migrants' rights.

*FFY85, $15,000, for conference of local legal organizations working on behalf of Central Americans seeking asylum or temporary safe haven in the U.S.

National Immigration, Refugee and Citizenship Forum, Washington, D.C.

*FFY91, $460,000 for migrant rights.

*FFY89, $435,000 "for information and other services for U.S.-based organizations working on behalf of immigrants and refugees."

*FFY88, $235,000 for refugee and migrants' rights.

*FFY87, $600,000 for refugee and migrants' rights.

*FFY85, $450,000, "To help inform the often heated debate on immigrants' rights and status in the United States, the Foundation granted $450,000 to the . . .Forum. A membership organization of more than 100 groups, the forum includes ethnic, refugee, Black, Hispanic, and voluntary organizations; academic institutions; and representatives of business and labor. The forum itself does not advocate specific positions. Instead, on such controversial topics as the current immigration reform legislation in Congress, it seeks to provide unbiased information to all parties, to help diverse groups work together on common concerns, and to communicate regularly with policy makers. The forum will use the grant for publications, conferences, technical assistance to member groups, and various other activities designed to keep channels of communication open."

*FFY83, $300,000, "The United States. . .is considering major changes in its immigration laws . . . . The forum sponsors national and regional workshops on such topics as the international factors influencing the migration of peoples, publishes a newsletter on the proposed immigration legislation, and reports on the effects of immigration on different U.S. regions. It also collaborates with such organizations as the Foundation-supported Refugee Policy Group, which conducts research on refugee matters."

*FFY83, $50,000, to the American Immigration and Citizenship Conference, for research, information exchange, and public education activities of the National Forum; "The Foundation also provided start-up funding for the National . . .Forum, a group formed in 1981 to promote public understanding of immigration, refugee, and related foreign policy issues."

National Opinion Research Center, Chicago, IL.

*FFY82, $25,000 for study of American immigration policy.

National Womens Law Center, Washington, D.C.

*FFY88, $775,000 for access to social justice and legal services.

*FFY85, $50,000, for access to social justice and legal services.

*FFY84, $485,000, for access to social justice and legal services.

*FFY83, $440,000, for continued support for litigation and public education efforts on employment, education and needs of low-income, refugee and immigrant women.

New Hampshire College.
*FFY85, $95,000, to enable a team of experts to evaluate the effectiveness of. . .[a San Francisco project for Southeast Asian resettlement]. . .and two others involving Haitians in Miami and the refugee community in Portland, OR.

New School for Social Research, New York City.
*FFY83, $113,111, ''for a study of the causes, characteristics, and outcomes of refugee flows in the Third World since 1960. The Study, to be conducted by Professors Aristide Zolberg of the New School, Astri Suhrke of American University, and Sergio Aquayo of El Colegio de Mexico, will analyze the different outcomes of refugee flows and their relation to the types of tension that gave rise to them.''

New York Association on New Americans.
*FFY86, $100,000, for the Refugee Urban Skills Community Development Project, which addresses housing, tenants' rights, and personal safety of refugees in New York City.

New York Circus, New York City.
*FFY86, $49,000, for refugee and migrant resettlement.
*FFY84, $35,000, for Central American emigres.

New York Civil Liberties Union, New York City.
*FFY82, $45,000, ''seeks to safeguard the constitutional rights of aliens—for example, by challenging the government's practice of conducting sweep arrests—-without a warrant—-of suspected illegal aliens.''

Orange County Refugee Community Resources Opportunity Project, Garden Grove, CA.
*FFY85, $100,000, for ''a pan-Asian coalition of mutual assistance organizations . . . . It received funds to train refugees in English language skills so that they may qualify for work in the county's garment industry.''

Overseas Education Fund of the League of Women Voters, Washington, D.C.
*FFY85, $25,000, for refugee and migrant rights.

*FFY84, $250,000, "for its Refugee Women in Development Project, which helps local groups address the special problems of female refugees and ensures that women's interests are included in discussions of refugee policy."

*FFY83, $155,850, to expand an array of programs for refugee women.

Policy Sciences Center, New York City.

*FFY84, $16,000, to complete a volume by Professor Atle Grahl-Madsen on refugee protection and international law.

Population Council, New York City.

*FFY84, $45,368, for refugee and migration policy.

Population Reference Bureau, Washington, D.C.

*FFY83, $10,000, for dissemination of information.

Potomac Institute, Washington, D.C.

*FFY84, $25,000, migrants and refugees, "for activities aimed at expanding housing opportunities for the urban poor and at preventing their displacement from neighborhoods undergoing revitalization."

Radio Bilingue, San Joaquin, CA.

*FFY88, $100,000 "to produce news and information programs for newcomer and established resident communities throughout the Southwest."

*FFY86, $100,000, for information on immigration laws and social services for Mexicans and Central Americans.

Refugee Policy Group, Washington, D.C.

*FFY86, $300,000, two-year supplement for same.

*FFY84, $425,000, for refugees and migrants.

*FFY82, $339,900, Group "was created in 1982 to provide a continuing source of information and analysis on three principal themes: refugee resettlement in the industrialized world, refugee assistance programs in Third World countries, and the legal rights of aliens. Among the topics it has investigated are welfare dependency and residency patterns of refugees in the U.S. and standards of proof in asylum claims."

Refugee Women in Development

*FFY88, $160,000 "to help address the social and economic needs of newly resettled refugee women in the United States."

Riverside Church, New York City.

*FFY84, $49,500, for program of instruction in English as a second language for refugees and migrants in New York City.

Saint Johns Presbyterian Church, Berkeley, CA.

*FFY85, $46,000, for health, social service, and community education projects for Central American refugees.

*FFY84, $40,000, "Groups in Chicago and the San Francisco Bay area are experimenting with methods to coordinate and improve housing, language training, and other services provided by local churches." (See also Travelers Aid Society of Metropolitan Chicago.)

Salvadoran Humanitarian Aid, Research and Education Foundation,, Washington, D.C.

*FFY86, $25,000, for social services to women and children refugees from Central America.

*FFY84, $47,000 for a project of the Committee of Central American Refugees on Long Island, NY.

San Francisco Lawyers Committee for Urban Affairs, San Francisco, CA.

*FFY88, $175,000 for National Refugee Rights Project to provide "legal assistance in the areas of health, education, employment and public benefits".

*FFY87, $87,500 for refugee and migrants' rights.

*FFY86, $175,000, "to expand the committee's National Refugee Rights Project, which addresses policies and practices that restrict refugees' access to public benefits or that impede their efforts to become self-sufficient."

*FFY84, $50,000, for National Refugee Rights Project.

Social Science Research Council, New York City.

*FFY86, $1,835,000, for research on U.S. Hispanic employment, political participation, income security, education and migration.

*FFY85, $64,600, for competition-based program of research on issues concerning U.S. Hispanics.

*FFY86, $350,000, "for the Indochina Studies Program, which administers a nationwide competition for research on Indochina history and culture."

*FFY83, $300,000, "For an oral history project, that will gather information on the recent history and social and economic fabric of Vietnam, Laos, and Cambodia through interviews with Indochinese refugees in the United States."

Southeast Asian Mutual Assistance Associations Coalition, Philadelphia, PA.

*FFY85, $50,000, "advises and serves as a voice for self-help organizations representing the city's 15,000 Southeast Asian refugees."

Southern Arizona Legal Aid, Tucson.

*FFY89, $50,000 for refugee and migrants' rights.

Southern California Ecumenical Council, Los Angeles.

*FFY86, $156,000, "for a project called El Rescate (Rescue) which provides indigent Central American refugees in Los Angeles with such social services as emergency food and shelter, classes in English, job and psychological counseling, and legal assistance."

Stanford University, Stanford, CA.

*FFY86, $380,000, "for policy-focused academic and training internships for Hispanic college students."

*FFY85, $240,000 for planning of Inter-University Program on Latino Research [q.v.].

*FFY85, $87,000, for U.S.-Mexican working group that is studying interactions between agricultural policies and rural development in the two countries, under Professor Clark Reynolds.

State University of New York, Albany.

*FFY88, $275,000 for access to social justice/legal services.

*FFY87, $24,000 for refugee and migrants' rights.

*FFY86, $50,000, to compile curricular resources in Chicano studies.

*FFY84, $158,000, for refugee and migration policy.

*FFY84, $250,000, for access to social justice and legal services.

State University of New York, Binghamton.

*FFY89, $965,000 "for a study of the relations between new immigrants and longtime residents in six communities."

*FFY87, $1,075,000 for refugee and migrants' rights.

*FFY84, $158,000, "for an analysis of the characteristics of the 125,000 Cubans who came to this country in the Mariel boatlift in 1980. Working with Cuban researchers, Professor Robert Bach is using heretofore unavailable data from both countries to compile demographic, social, and economic profiles of the Mariel entrants. The information will be used to identify the causes of migration and factors that may affect the assimilation of the Cubans into American society.''

Statue of Liberty—Ellis Island Foundation, New York City,

*FFY86, $30,500, to videotape symposium on U.S. Constitution and Bill of Rights.

*FFY84, $50,000, for research and a survey of materials to be used in the Ellis Island Centennial celebration.

Temple University, Philadelphia, PA.

*FFY86, $50,000, for an intergenerational program for elderly Southeast Asian and Hispanic migrants in Philadelphia.

Texas Legal Services, Austin.

*FFY89, $49,000 for refugee and migrants' rights.

*FFY88, $49,000 for refugee and migrants' rights.

Travelers and Immigrants' Aid Society of Metropolitan Chicago, IL.

*FFY89, $ 50,000 ''To encourage the fair and effective implementation of IRCA . . .[to] help low-income and poor immigrants apply for legalization.''

*FFY88, $100,000 for refugee and migrants' rights.

*FFY86, $ 45,000, for refugee and migrant resettlement.

*FFY84, $ 46,600, ''Groups in Chicago and the San Francisco Bay area are experimenting with methods to coordinate and improve housing, language training, and other services provided by local churches.''

United Nations High Commissioner for Refugees, Geneva, Switzerland.

*FFY91, $142,000 for refugees' and migrants' rights.

*FFY89, $130,000 ''To coordinate a worldwide network of nongovernmental organizations that collect data and document the conditions of refugees in various countries. The network sponsors an information clearinghouse, training seminars, technical assistance and conferences.''

United Way of Orange County, Los Angeles, CA.

*FFY91, $50,000 for refugees' and migrants' rights.

*FFY89, $50,000 for refugees' and migrants' rights.

*FFY83, $123,000, for ''encouraging businesses to train and hire qualified refugees and migrants.

University of Arizona, Tucson.

*FFY83, $30,500, for conference of Mexican and American scholars to discuss regional development problems, labor migration, and Mexican economic crisis.

*FFY82, $15,000, for conference on economic relations between U.S. and Mexico.

University of California, Los Angeles.

*FFY85, see Inter-University Program on Latino Research.

*FFY83, $35,967, for policy research on Hispanic employment and economic opportunities, see National Council Chicano Higher Education.

University of California, San Diego, Center for U.S.-Mexican studies.

*FFY86, $54,800, for supplement for a study of Hispanic women in the U.S. garment and electronics industries.

*FFY85, $75,000, for research on "Hispanic women's employment conditions in the garment and electronics industries in Los Angeles and New York."

*FFY84, $448,000, "A child is born to undocumented Mexican migrants in California. As an American citizen, the child is entitled to a range of social services, including free or low-cost health care, but how do the parents lay claim to those services without revealing their undocumented status and risking deportation? What happens to the child if the parents are deported? These are some of the questions being studied by researchers at the Center for U.S.-Mexican Studies . . . .

". . .the center will. . .conduct research under two broad categories: the causes and consequences of the flow of workers and capital between the United States and Mexico; and Mexico's efforts to solve its development problems . . . .

"The center will continue its analysis of the use of documented and undocumented workers in various industries in California and of how those industries might be affected by proposed changes in immigration laws. A key issue is whether reliance on migrants by some companies deprives American workers of jobs, as is often alleged by those calling for stricter immigration controls.

"The center is also examining the role of expanded households in maintaining the pool of migrant labor. It is common for two or three families to live together . . . . This provides economies in living costs not available to American workers . . . . In another project, the center will publish a case study of efforts by the Arizona Farmworkers Union to obtain union contracts for undocumented Mexican agricultural laborers. Research will continue on an unusual development program organized by the union . . . . Among other topics to be explored are the access of migrants to social services, the protection of their legal rights, and the special needs of the children of undocumented migrants.''

University of Florida, Gainesville.

*FFY85, $13,000, for access to social justice and legal services.

*FFY82, $50,000, for research and training related to Caribbean migration to the southeastern United States.

University of Houston, Texas.

*FFY83, $35,300, for policy research on Hispanic education, see National Chicano Council on Higher Education.

University of Maryland, College Park.

*FFY84, $26,000, for a study of the use of social services and informal networks by newly arrived Hispanic immigrants.

*FFY83, $62,993, for research and a conference of experts on the links between migration to the United States and economic development in the Caribbean; researchers will examine such issues as the effect on Caribbean emigration of different development strategies and U.S. government efforts to inhibit the flow of migrants.

University of Michigan, Ann Arbor.

*FFY82, $40,000, for a conference on the effects of immigration on the U.S. black community.

University of Notre Dame.

*FFY84, $15,000, under migrants and refugees, for a conference to explore ways of combining economic development and social justice within a democratic framework in Latin America.

*FFY82, $135,000, ''for a study of the evolution of United States refugee admissions policy since World War II.''

University of San Diego, California.

*FFY88, $15,000 for refugee and migrants' rights.

*FFY85, $16,250, for research on Mexican policies toward Central Americans seeking asylum.

University of Texas, Austin.

*FFY85, $1,240,600, for five-year supplement for research in ''such areas as employment, political participation, income security, education, and migration.'' See, Inter-University Program on Latino Research.

*FFY85, $45,770, for conference on ways to include more Hispanics in national opinion polls.

University of Wisconsin, Madison.

*FFY86, $69,580, for comparative research on the effects of migration and resettlement on Puerto Ricans, Cubans, and Mexicans in the U.S.

*FFY85, $63,210, for conference comparing causes and consequences of poverty for Blacks and Hispanics.

*FFY84, $25,000 for access to social justice and legal services.

*FFY83, $26,900 for policy research on Hispanic statistical and data needs.

Urban Institute.

*FFY86, $56,900, to assess the economic impact of foreign agricultural workers on resident farm workers in California.

Wellesley College.

*FFY85, $49,000, for refugee and migrant rights in Mexico and Central America.

World Council of Churches, Switzerland.

*FFY88, $20,000 to advance refugee and migrants' rights in the United States and worldwide.

Yale University.

*FFY84, $5,500, for conference on U.S. exclusion of aliens on ideological grounds.

Youth Project, Washington, D.C.

*FFY82, $339,900, for the Refugee Policy Group [q.v.].
   (Also administered the Center for Third World Organizing)

FORD FOUNDATION HISPANIC AND RELATED GRANTS

Accion International, Cambridge, MA.

*FFY85, $15,000, for technical assistance to organizations promoting Hispanic small business development in the Southwest.

Arts Council of San Antonio, TX.

*FFY85, $111,415, for national conference to improve communications among Hispanic performers and to develop touring circuits for Hispanic theater groups.

ASPIRA of America, New York City.

*FFY86, $100,000, supplement for Hispanic Leadership Opportunity Program.

*FFY85, $474,640, "ASPIRA will use the funds to support the high school component of the Hispanic Leadership Opportunity Program (HLOP). Leadership training and public policy workshops will be provided for 150 students at ten sites. Fifty of these students will then be placed in local internships, and ten of them will be awarded summer policy internships in Washington, D.C." Also involves LULAC and Youth Policy Institute.

Asian-American Legal Defense and Education Fund, New York City.

*FFY84, $25,355, for governance and public policy.

Asian, Inc., San Francisco, CA.

*FFY84, $1,500,000, program-related investment, *not* a grant, to ensure sufficient bank financing of business condominiums that will be sold to enterprises employing low-skilled Asian-Americans.

Association of Puerto Rican Executive Directors, New York City.

*FFY86, $5,500, to disseminate materials for a conference on problems of Puerto Ricans living in New York.

Ballet Hispanico, New York City.

*FFY84, $150,000, for Hispanic ballet.

Barrio Education Project, San Antonio, TX.

*FFY83, $150,000, to help Hispanic women in San Antonio obtain small business loans.

Bilingual Foundation of the Arts, Los Angeles, CA.

*FFY85, $225,000, to strengthen administration and fund raising; " 'To deny anyone the opportunity to sing from the heart is to deny us all,' says Luis Valdez, founder of El Teatro Campesino, a leader in a Hispanic cultural renaissance, especially in theater, that is emerging all across the United States."

Border College Consortium, Laredo TX.

*FFY84, $82,150, for mathematics education of community college Hispanics.

Caribbean Cultural Center, New York City.

*FFY84, $138,000, to make the cultural traditions of the Caribbean known to a wider public.

Center for Applied Linguistics, Washington, D.C.

*FFY85, $750,000, ''It is regularly consulted on questions ranging from English-language instruction for refugees and migrants to ways of improving the teaching of foreign languages in American colleges and universities.''

*FFY84, $100,000.

*FFY83, $300,000.

Center for Border Workers, Mexico.

*FFY86, $50,000, ''for an innovative social service program for Mexican women along the Texas-Mexico border.''

Center for Cuban Studies, New York City.

*FFY85, $46,000, for cultural preservation and interpretation.

*FFY83, $23,000, for a cultural exchange program that brings together writers from the U.S. and Cuba for scholarly discussions and lectures.

Center for the Development of Nonformal Education, Austin, TX.

*FFY84, $400,000, for bilingual outreach.

*FFY82, $178,191.

Chicanos por La Causa, Phoenix, AZ.

*FFY86, $300,000, for supplement for organization engaged in revitalizing depressed urban community.

*FFY84, $32,000, for teenage pregnancy program.

*FFY83, $150,000.

*FFY82, $150,000.

Citizens Housing and Planning Council of New York, New York City.

*FFY86, $36,776, to translate into Spanish and distribute tenant's rights books.

City University of New York, New York City.

*FFY84, $1,267,337, for "preparing material for a new introductory course in American history . . . . It integrates new scholarship—on such topics as women's economic roles, the changing composition of the working class, and the struggle of minority groups for equality—with the political emphasis of traditional American history courses."

City University of New York, Center for Puerto Rican Studies, Hunter College of the City University of New York, New York City.

*FFY86, see Inter-University Program on Latino Research.

*FFY84, $277,800, for "documentation of the Puerto Rican experience in the U.S.," Ford has been "a principal supporter of the Center since its founding in 1973."

Claremont McKenna College, CA.

*FFY86, $35,000, for publication of *The California Latino Atlas*.

Columbia University, New York City.

*FFY85, $82,500, "for an evaluation of a program directed to Hispanic residents in the neighborhoods surrounding Columbia Presbyterian Medical Center . . .resulting in substantial changes. . .including placement of a patient advocate . . .and the hiring of a staff person to assist patients with Medicaid applications."

*FFY82-FFY84, $355,000, for same.

Congressional Hispanic Caucus, Washington, D.C.

*FFY86, $347,600, over 28 months to create a clearinghouse for governance and public policy leadership training and internship opportunities for Hispanic graduate students.

*FFY85, $15,800, for same.

Cuban National Planning Council, Miami, FL.

*FFY85, $61,000, for analyses of public policies affecting Hispanics in Miami.

DePaul University, Chicago, IL.

*FFY84, $250,000, for the Hispanic Alliance, to improve college preparation of Hispanic students.

*FFY84, $150,000, for the Hispanic Alliance, to assist Hispanics who aspire to careers.

Educational Foundation Ana G. Mendez, Puerto Rico.

*FFY86, $40,000, to disseminate to mainland and island colleges new interdisciplinary humanities curriculum developed for Hispanic students.

El Teatro de Campesino, San Juan Bautista, CA.

*FFY86, $50,000, for Hispanic theater.

El Teatro de la Esperanza, Santa Barbara, CA.

*FFY86, $115,000, for Hispanic theater.

Greater Kansas City Community Foundation, MO.

*FFY86, $75,000, for a development fund to help stabilize Hispanic community-based organizations, and for an assessment of the needs of the area's Hispanics.

Greater Miami United, FL.

*FFY84, $25,000, for housing for Cuban refugees.

Harvard University, Cambridge, MA.

*FFY85, $6,687, for completion of first edition of *Journal of Hispanic Politics*. *Hispanic Office of Planning and Evaluation*, Boston, MA.

*FFY84, $7,550, for public policy analysis.

Hispanic Policy Development Project, New York City.

*FFY86, $250,000, over two years for research and analysis of public policies affecting U.S. Hispanics; the project concentrates on education and employment problems of Hispanic youth.

*FFY85, $125,700, for analysis of Hispanic school drop-outs.

Institute for Puerto Rican Policy, New York City.

*FFY86, $150,000, for analyses of public policies facing Hispanics in New York City.

*FFY84, $20,000, to increase research capacity.

International Arts Relations, New York City.

*FFY86, $250,000, for experimental Hispanic theater.

La Casa de Don Pedro, Newark, NJ.

*FFY86, $150,500, "for policy-focused training and placement of Hispanic mid-career professionals on local public boards and commissions."

Latin Center/Centro Latino, Chicago, IL.

*FFY86, $169,000, over three years for a native-language literacy program, the center provides legal assistance and other services to Chicago's large Hispanic population.

Latino Institute, Chicago IL.

*FFY82, $250,000, for "a program to increase participation by Hispanic parents in public school activities."

League of United Latin American Citizens (LULAC)

*FFY91, $330,000 for public policy, civic participation.

*FFY90, $145,000 for civic participation.

*FFY89, $134,000 for civic participation.

Massachusetts Institute of Technology, Cambridge, MA.

*FFY85, $50,000, for study of migration policies in South Asia and Middle East.

Mexican-American Unity Council, San Antonio, TX.

*FFY84, $402,000, for supplement for organization engaged in revitalizing depressed urban community.

*FFY83, $102,000, for community development.

*FFY82, $300,000, for community development.

Mid-America Arts Alliance, Kansas City, MO.

*FFY86, $120,900, for a tour of the Midwest and Texas by the Bilingual Foundation of the Arts, a Hispanic theater company based in Los Angeles.

Midwest Voter Registration Project, Columbus, OH.

*FFY86, $200,000, for supplement for research and nonpartisan voter education and registration activities, primarily among Hispanics, in ten Midwestern states.

*FFY85, $50,000, same.

*FFY84, $50,000, same.

National Association of Latino Elected Officials Fund, Washington, D.C.

*FFY86, $160,000, two-year supplement to expand a citizenship hotline that provides toll-free information to resident aliens on the naturalization process.

*FFY86, $705,000, over two years for the second phase of a project to increase naturalization rates among Hispanics and other resident aliens.

*FFY85, $236,000, ". . .a growing number of Hispanic-Americans are unable to hold public office, serve on juries, or obtain federal employment or entitlements such as student aid. Lack of citizenship also hampers reunification with family members who would otherwise be eligible to petition for legal entry into the U.S . . . . Among [some of the reasons for Hispanics' reluctance to seek citizenship]. . .may be allegiance to their native countries, a belief that seeking U.S. citizenship could result in deportation, a sense that citizenship confers no special benefits, apprehension about the English-language requirement for naturalization, and administrative obstacles such as backlogs at the Immigration and Naturalization Service (INS).

"The funds will help NALEO with the initial stages of a project to encourage naturalization among Hispanics and other permanent resident aliens. NALEO will study data on the characteristics of Hispanic legal residents. . .and analyze their attitudes towards citizenship . . . . will . . .recommend ways to improve INS naturalization procedures and practices. . .and to build a network of people and resources to encourage naturalization. The Foundation expects to make additional grants to assist the process."

National Catholic Educational Association, Washington,D.C.

*FFY85, $37,940.

*FFY83, $363,950, to identify special needs of Hispanic students.

National Puerto Rican Coalition, Alexandria, VA.

*FFY91, $165,000 for public policy analysis.

*FFY89, $50,000 for teen pregnancy.

*FFY88, $460,000 for public policy analysis.

*FFY87, $130,000 for public policy analysis; $50,000 for civic participation.

*FFY86, $260,000 supplement for organization dealing with Puerto Rican issues, such as tax policy, budget cuts and migration.

*FFY84, $20,805, to study establishment of a philanthropic entity in Puerto Rico.

*FFY83, $200,000 for general support of Puerto Rican advocacy organizations.

National Puerto Rican Forum, New York City.

*FFY85, $50,000, for youth employment research and training.

National Puerto Rican/Hispanic Voter Participation Project, Union, NJ.

*FFY85, $50,000, to encourage greater political participation on a nonpartisan basis by Hispanics in Northeastern states.

National Urban Fellows, New York City.

*FFY86, $276,000, ''for national policy-focused training and internships for Hispanic mid-career professionals.''

New York Shakespeare Festival, New York City.

*FFY85, $50,000, for Hispanic theater.

Old Globe Theatre, San Francisco, CA.

*FFY86, $75,013, for Hispanic theater.

Partners for Livable Places, Washington, D.C.

*FFY86, $20,000, for national touring exhibit illustrating the impact of Hispanic culture on buildings and towns in the Untied States.

*FFY85, $15,000, for a conference on the impact, needs and contributions of Hispanics in U.S. cities.

Puerto Rican Family Institute, New York City.

*FFY84, $26,647, for conference on migrating families.

Puerto Rican Legal Defense and Education Fund, New York City.

*FFY91, $500,000 for human rights and civil liberties.

*FFY89, $425,000 for civil/political liberties.

*FFY87, $208,750 for legal services.

*FFY86, $167,500 for legal services.

*FFY85, $375,000, supplement for litigation, advocacy and education in such areas as voting rights, employment, education and housing (includes $123,750 for legal services).

*FFY84, $200,000 unspecified.

*FFY83, $168,750 for legal services.

Remediation and Training Institute, Washington, D.C.

*FFY85, $143,000, to help Hispanic employment training organizations.

*FFY83, $299,000.

Rocky Mountain SER/Jobs for Progress, Denver CO.
*FFY85, $50,000 for youth employment research and training.

SER/Jobs for Progress, Milwaukee, WI.
*FFY85, $50,000, for youth employment research and training.

Southwest Voter Registration Education Project, San Antonio, TX.
*FFY91, $200,000 for human rights and civil liberties.
*FFY90, $300,000 for human rights and civil liberties.
*FFY88, $150,000 for legal services.
*FFY86, $236,000 for human rights and civil liberties.
*FFY85, $300,000, for supplement for nonpartisan voter registration programs on behalf of Hispanics.
*FFY84, $300,000, same as above.
*FFY83, $300,000, same as above.

Spanish-Speaking Unity Council, Oakland, CA.
*FFY86, $450,000, for supplement for organization engaged in revitalizing depressed urban community.
*FFY83, $170,000, same.
*FFY82, $300,000, same.

Spanish Theatre Repertory Ltd., New York City.
*FFY86, $300,000, for Hispanic theater.

University of South Carolina.
*FFY86, $80,000, for a study of the transfer rates of Hispanic students at six public community colleges in the Southwest.

University of Texas.
*FFY86, $49,600, for planning a national survey on the political beliefs, values, opinions, and behavior of Hispanics.

SUPPORTING ORGANIZATION GRANTS

This is a list of grants which are not necessarily devoted wholly to immigration and refugee policy. Listings here include groups which sometimes appear as political allies on immigration policy issues, which provide occasional legal support on immigration policy issues, or which provide student or law student interns to immigration advocacy groups among others. Every effort is made to narrow the number of grants listed here, but some of the grants are not well understood, and this particular list is imprecise.

American Civil Liberties Foundation New York City.

*FFY91, $1,100,000 for civil liberties; $1,125,000 for access to social justice; $65,000 public policy analysis.

*FFY90, $625,000 for dissemination of information; $137,000 for public policy analysis.

*FFY86, $600,000, supplement for litigation and advocacy on race-based discrimination, voting rights, employment, capital punishment.

*FFY86, $50,000, to study feasibility of mounting an endowment campaign.

*FFY84, $600,000, for access to social justice and legal services.

*FFY83, $50,000, for litigation, advocacy and public education on minority voting rights.

American Society of International Law, Washington, D.C.

*FFY85, $50,000, for international human rights law.

*FFY85, $49,075, for study of jurisdiction of International Court of Justice and U.S. policy toward court.

Asia Watch.
    See Fund for Free Expression

Aspen Institute for Humanistic Studies, New York City.

*FFY84, $16,000, for seminars for federal judges on possible domestic applications of international human rights law.

Center for Community Change, Washington, D.C.

*FFY85, $230,000, for U.S. rural employment generation.

*FFY85, $20,000, for access to social justice and legal services.

*FFY84, $295,000, for economic development, technical assistance and evaluation.

*FFY84, $340,596, for Coalition on Block Grants and Human Needs.

*FFY83, $175,000, for U.S. rural employment generation.

*FFY82, $370,000, for economic development, technical assistance and evaluation.

Center for Law and Social Policy, Washington, D.C.

*FFY86, $200,000, for explorations of new ways to provide legal services to the poor.

*FFY84, $150,000, for study of possible new directions in legal services.

*FFY83, $100,000, same.

Center on Social Welfare Policy, New York City.

*FFY85, $275,000, for research on the effects of changes in welfare eligibility regulations, by a Legal Services support center.

*FFY83, $100,000.

Council on Foundations, Washington, D.C.

*FFY84, $250,000, to enable Council's new leadership to implement administrative reorganization and outreach.

Food Research and Action Center, Washington, D.C.

*FFY85, $120,000, for a Legal Services support center "which seeks to protect the rights of the poor to federal food assistance programs."

*FFY84, $150,000.

*FFY82, $110,000.

Fund for Free Expression, (subsidiary organizations: Americas Watch, Helsinki Watch [q.v.], Asia Watch, Lawyers Committee for International Human Rights [q.v.]) New York City.

*FFY91, $700,000 for civil and political liberties, U.S. and world-wide; $34,000 for human rights education and scholarship, Southeast Asia.

*FFY89, $710,000 for civil and political liberties, U.S. and world-wide; $20,000 to exchange ideas and information, U.S. and world-wide.

*FFY87, $665,000 for civil and political liberties, U.S. and world-wide; $95,000 for civil and political liberties in Asia.

*FFY84, $20,000, for exchange of ideas and information.

*FFY84, $395,000, for civil and political liberties in Latin America (Americas Watch).

*FFY84, $245,000, for Asia Watch.

*FFY82, $180,000, for Americas Watch Committee, "The committee. . .was organized in 1981 to bring human rights violations in the Americas to the attention of the news media and international organizations. . ."

Funding Exchange, New York City.

*FFY85, $95,000, for coordination of small "progressive" foundations (not Ford description).

Helsinki Watch, (see Fund for Free Expression) New York City.

*FFY85, $250,000, the organization "maintains an even-handed attitude . . . . will . . .look into accusations that broadcasting by the Voice of America and Radio Free Europe/Radio Liberty is less objective than the BBC overseas broadcasts."

*FFY83, $150,000, for a program to promote compliance with the human rights provisions of the 1975 Helsinki Accords.

*FFY82, $78,000, for "an American group that monitors domestic and international compliance with the human rights provisions of the 1975 Helsinki accords. . ."

Human Rights Internet, Cambridge, MA.

*FFY86, $255,000, two-year supplement for same.

*FFY85, $225,000, for an international communication network and clearinghouse for human rights activists, scholars and policy makers (also assists lawyers in U.S. asylum cases, works with Harvard Law School Human Rights Program).

*FFY83, $200,000, for same.

Institute of International Education, New York City.

*FFY84, $475,000, for civil and political liberties.

*FFY83, $300,000, for program which "places highly qualified young people from the U.S. and abroad in international human rights programs."

International Human Rights Law Group, Washington, D.C.

*FFY85, $200,000, "Working through a network of pro bono publico lawyers, the Law Group pursues a variety of activities to advance human rights and to increase awareness of them among public officials, lawyers, and the public. The grant will also support a new effort to assist human rights legal centers in developing countries and a study of the independence of the judiciary in Central America."

*FFY83, $135,000, ". . .the Foundation renewed support for two organizations . . .the New York-based Lawyers Committee on International Human Rights and the Washington-based International Human Rights Law Group. Both organizations advise human rights groups and bar associations in the two cities and have developed a network of pro bono attorneys who work on particular cases. The two groups also urge U.S. courts to consider international human rights standards in their findings in domestic cases, thus helping to make the body of human rights laws more effective.''

Joint Center for Political Studies, Washington, D.C.

*FFY82, $1,544,500, for a four-part study, one component of which is the effect of refugee resettlement on cities with large black populations.

Law Students Civil Rights Research Council, New York City.

*FFY86, $100,000, two-year supplement for same.

*FFY85, $50,000, for summer internships of law students in civil rights and human rights organizations.

*FFY84, $50,000, same.

*FFY83, $40,000, same.

Lawyers Committee for Civil Rights Under Law, Washington, D.C.

*FFY86, $550,000, two-year supplement, for litigation, advocacy and public education in such areas as voting rights, employment, education and housing.

*FFY85, $350,000, for access to social justice and legal services.

*FFY83, $375,000, ''$100,000 over two years for voting rights activities, and $175,000 over two years to combat race and sex discrimination in employment.''

Mozambique Ministry of Justice.

*FFY85, $117,000.

National Conference of Black Lawyers, New York City.

*FFY83, $31,400, for human rights and social justice.

National Council of the Churches of Christ, New York City.

*FFY84, $50,000, listed under migrants and refugees, ''for a demonstration project to improve the capacity of local churches to provide social services in inner-city neighborhoods.''

National Housing Law Project, Berkeley, CA.

*FFY85, $165,000, for a Legal Services support center that advises on housing issues.

*FFY82, $200,000.

National Legal Aid and Defender Association, Washington, D.C.

*FFY85, $100,000, "The association has kept a close watch on the controversy over the nominations of Legal Services Corporation directors, and on the operation of state and national support for legal services."

*FFY83, $100,000, "a tradition of legal services to the poor. . .may be threatened by cutbacks in funds. . .and by new restrictions on the kind of legal assistance that may be offered."

PUSH for Excellence, Chicago, IL.

*FFY83, $150,000, terminal support for program to decentralize the management of PUSH/Excel.

Southwest Research and Information Center, Albuquerque, NM.

*FFY86, $174,500, for a project to help Hispanic and Indian communities in northern New Mexico protect their water rights.

*FFY84, $50,000, for poor Hispanic communities in New Mexico.

TransAfrica Forum, Washington, D.C.

*FFY83, $150,000, for U.S. foreign policy, including aspects relating to U.S. immigration policy.

Urban Institute, Washington, D.C.

*FFY85, $1,284,854, general support.

*FFY84, $2,500,000, general support.

*FFY83, $3,000,000, general support.

*FFY82, $3,000,000, general support.

FORD FOUNDATION CENTRAL AMERICA FOREIGN POLICY GRANTS

Center for Research and Studies of Agrarian Reform, Ministry of Foreign Cooperation, Nicaragua.

*FFY86, $92,000 for research on Nicaragua's rural sector.

Central American Historical Institute, Nicaragua.

*FFY86, $24,500, for supplement for research on contemporary social, economic, and political developments in Nicaragua.

*FFY84, $25,500, for scholarship and scholarly resources.

Central American Institute of Business Administration, Nicaragua.

*FFY85, $250,000, for research on the management of state-run Nicaraguan agricultural enterprises.

*FFY85, $90,000, for scholarships to enable Nicaraguans to participate in a training program for senior managers and regional directors of state enterprises.

*FFY84, $94,000, for agrarian reform policy development.

*FFY84, $200,000 for strengthening public service, "to provide scholarships for senior managers from the government and from state-run and private enterprises."

Central American University, "Jose Simeon Canas," El Salvador.

*FFY85, $260,000, for Central American human rights. *Central American University*, Nicaragua.

*FFY85, $200,000, for scholarship and scholarly resources.

Columbia University, New York City.

*FFY86, $322,000, for a joint research program with the Cuban Ministry of Health on infant mortality in Cuba.

*FFY84, $5,000, for conference on political and economic problems in Central America.

Commission for the Defense of Human Rights In Central America, Costa Rica.
*FFY85, $14,500

Committee for the Defense of Human Rights in Honduras, Honduras.
*FFY84, $77,000.

Evangelical Committee for Aid to Development, Nicaragua.
*FFY85, $8,500, for land and water development.

Guatemalan Human Rights Commission, Guatemala.
*FFY85, $31,500.

Human Rights Commission of El Salvador, El Salvador.
*FFY85, $9,600.

Institute for Policy Studies, Washington, D.C.
*FFY85, $24,471, for U.S. foreign policy.
*FFY83, $22,131, for U.S. foreign policy.

Institute of Economic and Social Research, Nicaragua.

*FFY84, $95,000, for study of alternative approaches to cattle production, processing and marketing.

*FFY83, $32,976, for employment generation.

Inter-American Institute of Human Rights, Costa Rica.

*FFY82, $300,000, ''Among new groups receiving grants this year were the Americas Watch Committee and the Inter-American Institute of Human Rights, both concerned with promoting civil and political liberties throughout the Americas.''

International Reconstruction Fund of Nicaragua, Nicaragua.

*FFY84, $68,000, for land and water management.

*FFY84, $74,000, for agrarian reform policy development.

*FFY84, $25,000, for international economics and development.

*FFY83, $100,000, for research on small-scale cotton-production in Nicaragua.

*FFY83, $34,820, for bilingual, bicultural education for Miskito Indians.

*FFY83, $20,000, for international economics and development.

*FFY82, $33,000, for agricultural productivity.

Johns Hopkins University School of Advanced International Studies, Washington, D.C.

*FFY85, $10,000, for exchange program with University of Havana, begun in 1980 and the first such exchange since 1959.

*FFY84, $9,500, same.

*FFY83, $256,000, same.

Latin American Studies Association, Austin, TX.

*FFY86, $25,000, for annual meeting.

*FFY85, $40,000, for international relations.

*FFY83, $17,000, to enable Latin American and Caribbean scholars to participate in annual meeting.

*FFY83, $5,000, same for Mexican scholars.

Legal Aid Office of the Archbishopric of San Salvador, El Salvador.

*FFY85, $21,000, for civil and political liberties.

Mexican Academy of Human Rights, Mexico.
*FFY85, $150,000.

National Autonomous University of Nicaragua.
*FFY86, $87,000, for faculty training at University of Nicaragua and for research on employment in the coffee sector.

National Public Radio, Washington, D.C.
*FFY86, $140,000, over one year to expand news coverage in Thailand, the Philippines, and Central America.
*FFY84, $137,500, to expand on-the-scene reporting from Central America.

University of Texas, Austin.
*FFY86, $50,000, for a study by U.S. and Nicaraguan researchers of public sector administration in Nicaragua.

Washington Office on Latin America, Washington, D.C.
*FFY86, $213,000, for two-year supplement.
*FFY83, $220,000, "to continue a program of information gathering and advocacy on human rights in Latin America. Through extensive contacts in the region, publications, and conferences, WOLA provides information to policy makers, members of Congress and the media."

Appendix Three
The Anti-American Worldview

Those who doubt that there may be a rigid ideological motivation behind the immigration-policy agitation that has so far been described, or who doubt the close relationships among the National Lawyers Guild, the Center for Constitutional Rights and the National Center for Immigrants' Rights and other interests, should examine *The Illegality of U.S. Intervention: Central America and Caribbean Litigation*, published by the National Lawyers Guild Central America Task Force, in conjunction with the Center for Constitutional Rights, in 1984. This text is not special because of its uniqueness, but because it is typical of the flood of such documents that have poured forth from Left-wing groups since the 1960s.

The Illegality of U.S. Intervention begins by claiming that "the [Reagan] administration is fostering a new wave of anti-Soviet hysteria . . . The National Lawyers Guild and the Center for Constitutional Rights have been involved in numerous lawsuits to expose the lawlessness of the Reagan Administration . . . exposing the illegality of these actions is important to counteract the constant immersion of the American people in miseducation and disinformation . . ."[1]

The Chair of the NLG's Central America Task Force in 1984 was Ellen Yaroshefsky, who also served on the "Legal Secretariat" of the War Crimes Tribunal on Central America and the Caribbean. Today she remains a staff attorney with the Center for Constitutional Rights, and was lead counsel for the Tucson "sanctuary" defendants. The defense of the sanctuary advocates was the subject of a paper she presented at the Ford-funded National Lawyers Guild conference on Central American refugee work.[2]

Yaroshevsky indicates the connection between sanctuary and the Guild when she describes a conference in an article reprinted in the September, 1986 *Basta!*, a publication of the Chicago Religious Task Force on Central America. The conference was held following the January, 1985, federal indictments against sixteen members of the

162

"sanctuary" movement, and prior to their trial. "The Central American Refugee Defense Fund [an effort of the National Immigration Project of the National Lawyers Guild] organized a conference in San Francisco, June 15-17, 1985, for those engaged in refugee defense work to come together for an intensive two days of training and strategizing . . . The program was as follows . . . Running a Refugee Center . . . Sanctuary, Political Action and Alternative Remedies for Refugees . . . Developing a Political and Legal Strategy for your case . . ." [3]

The following litigation was listed in *The Illegality of U.S. Intervention*, (case descriptions are paraphrased and summarized, supporting organizations are taken verbatim):

Dellums v. Smith, 573 F. Supp. 1489 (N.D. Cal., 1983). Rep. Ron Dellums and others alleged criminal violations of Neutrality Act by President Reagan with respect to Nicaragua, and sought to direct the Attorney General to investigate the allegations. Judge ordered Attorney General to investigate, government appealed.
National Lawyers Guild with the Center for Constitutional Rights.

Sanchez-Espinoza v. Reagan, 568 F. Supp. 596 (D.D.C., 1983). Nicaraguan citizens alleged damage resulting from U.S. support for contra forces under the Alien Tort Claims Act, and Congressional plaintiff Rep. Ron Dellums alleged Presidential violations of warmaking statutes. Dismissed as political question.
National Lawyers Guild with the Center for Constitutional Rights.

Crockett v. Reagan, 558 F. Supp. 893 (D.D.C., 1982). Rep. George Crockett and other Congressmen alleged that 55 U.S. military advisors in El Salvador violated the War Powers Resolution, and that presidential certification of human rights progress in El Salvador was unfounded. Dismissed as political question.
Center for Constitutional Rights, National Lawyers Guild *amicus*.

Sixty-eight Unnamed Salvadoran Refugees v. Reagan, 83-0426-AWT (KX) (C.D. Cal., Nov. 1983). Religious and political organizations and unnamed Salvadorans in the U.S. alleged that presidential certification of human rights progress in El Salvador was in bad faith. Dismissed as moot.
National Lawyers Guild with the National Center for Immigrants' Rights, Inc.

Orantes-Hernandez v. Smith, 541 F. Supp. 351 (C.D. Cal., 1982). A nationwide action alleging that the Immigration and Naturalization Service systematically mistreats Salvadoran "refugees." (For result, see section on Recent Asylum Litigation).
National Lawyers Guild with the National Center for Immigrants' Rights, Inc. and the Center for Constitutional Rights.

In the Matter of Luis Armando Escobar Trujillo and Luis Alonso Sanchez Trujillo, No. A24 235 796, No. A 24 224 793, before the Board of Immigration Appeals. Young male Salvadorans sought political asylum on the basis that they belong to a persecuted social group—young urban males who have never served in the military. Denied.
National Lawyers Guild Central American Refugee Defense Fund.

Peres-Funes v. District Director, No. CV 81-1457-ER (C.D. Cal., Feb. 1984).

Challenges Immigration and Naturalization Service practices relating to detention of illegal-alien minors. Court injunction.

National Lawyers Guild, with the National Center for Immigrants' Rights, Inc., the ACLU of Southern California, and Los Angeles Center for Law and Justice.

N.C.I.R., Inc. v. I.N.S., 83-7927-KN (C.D. Cal., Dec. 16, 1983). National Lawyers Guild, National Center for Immigrants' Rights, Inc. and 21 other individuals and organizations challenged a new Immigration and Naturalization Service regulation denying work authorization to alleged illegal aliens in deportation proceedings. Court enjoined INS regulation.

National Lawyers Guild, National Center for Immigrants' Rights, Inc. and other organizations.

Dellums v. Smith, 82-0040-G (S.D. Cal., June 19, 1982). Rep. Ron Dellums and other plaintiffs challenged closed deportation hearings. Court issued preliminary injunction prohibiting closed hearings.

National Lawyers Guild with National Center for Immigrants' Rights, Inc.

Conyers v. Reagan, No. 83-3430 (D.D.C., Feb. 1984). Rep. John Conyers and other Congressmen challenged U.S. action in Grenada, alleging violation of War Powers Clause. Dismissed as political question.

National Conference of Black Lawyers, National Lawyers Guild, ACLU of Southern California, and the Center for Constitutional Rights.

Nation v. Haig, No. 81-2988-MA (D. Mass., 1982). Action by *Nation*, *Guardian*, and *Progressive* publications and other parties challenged U.S. embargo on Cuban publications. Settled with government.

National Lawyers Guild with the Center for Constitutional Rights and the American Civil Liberties Union.

Wald v. Reagan, Civ. No. 82-1690-T (D. Mass., 1982). Center for Cuban Studies and other parties challenged Treasury regulation limiting travel to Cuba.

Center for Constitutional Rights, National Emergency Civil Liberties Committee, and the American Civil Liberties Union.

THE CUBAN CONTRIBUTION

The Center for Cuban Studies in New York City promotes favorable understanding of the Cuban government. Cuban leader Fidel Castro praised the organization on its tenth anniversary.[4] The Center helps arrange student and academic visits to Cuba.[5]

In 1985, the Ford Foundation granted $46,000 to the Center for Cuban Studies, for cultural preservation and interpretation.[6] In 1983, Ford gave the Center $23,000 for a cultural exchange program that brings together writers from the U.S. and Cuba for scholarly discussion and lectures.[7] In Washington, D.C., a Cuban intelligence defector alleged that a vast spy-recruitment network relies on friendly gestures and emotional pressure to win the favor of U.S. journalists, scholars and other prominent citizens . . . He also said Cuban intelligence officers recruited spies through Johns Hopkins University . . . Johns Hopkins spokesman Ron Sauder said . . . "We know that on our end there is absolutely no Cuban government funding involved in this program. It's completely independently funded through the Ford Foundation." [8]

The Second Seminar on the Situation of the Black, Chicano, Cuban, American Indian, Puerto Rican, Caribbean and Asian Communities in the U.S. was held in Havana, Cuba, December 4-6, 1984. [9] The first seminar on ethnic communities in the U.S. was held in Havana in November, 1981. [10] Selected proceedings of the Second Seminar were published in *The Black Scholar*, January- February 1985 and in *Line of March, a Marxist-Leninist Journal of Rectification*, Fall 1985. The seminar, reports *The Black Scholar*, "involved more than 50 scholars and intellectuals from the U.S . . . . The exchange with Cuban intellectuals and scholars was a further indication that minority communities in the U.S. will not be handcuffed by cold war ideologies in the free pursuit of ideas and information. The energy and vigor of the Cuban culture also attested to the success of its revolution. . ." [11]

Armando Hart, Cuban Minister of Culture and Member of the Political Bureau of the Communist Party of Cuba, delivered the keynote address: "The People's Desire to Have Freedom does not Recognize Boundaries." Minister Hart mentioned "the crucial differences existing between the U.S. society and those of Our America," and, commenting on the ban on U.S. travel to Cuba, thanked the participants "for the assurance of friendship implied by your presence . . ." [12]

The Final Declaration by the Participants repeated traditional Cuban themes of peace and disarmament, nonintervention by the U.S. in Grenada, Nicaragua and El Salvador, opposition to the South Africa regime, and support for Jesse Jackson's Rainbow Coalition. And, a fifth theme was stressed: U.S. immigration policy. The participants declared that

> [w]e are bound together by the fact that economic compulsions continue to rip our peoples from their places of origin and drive them to the U.S. . . . [T]here is hidden unemployment among undocumented workers which make up a significant section of the Latino, Caribbean and Asian communities who are terrorized by the reactionary forces behind the Simpson-Mazzoli bill . . . Finally, in our combined colors and experience, we stand poised to challenge the white identity of America, to confront its sadly mistaken racial fixations and infuse it with the new blood of red, brown, black and yellow peoples, so that it may, perhaps for the first time, represent an honorable link with the rest of humanity." [13]

The seminar was held under the auspices of Havana's Center for the Study of the Americas (DISEU) at Casa de las Americas. [14] Here is a selection of presentations from the conference. [15]

- Theresita Sanchez, DISEU and Cuban-American Committee, Washington, D.C., "Socio-Economic Situation of the Hispanics";

- Enrique Meitin, DISEU, "The Chicanos as a Labor Force in the U.S.";

- Manuel Suzarte, DISEU, "The Chicano Community";

- Rene Gomis, DISEU, "The Political Potential of the Hispanics";

- Robert Bach, Department of Sociology, State University of New York, Binghamton, "Socio-economic Comparisons between Cubans and Mexicans (received $158,000 from Ford in 1984 to study characteristics of Mariel boatlift Cubans in the U.S.[16]);

- Jose Luis Valdez and Maria Rosa Garcia, Center for Teaching and Research in Economics (CIDE), Mexico, "Hispanics in U.S. Elections" (CIDE was granted $300,000 by the Ford Foundation in 1984 to study and publish on migration, U.S.-Mexican border relations, and U.S. foreign policy in Latin America[17]);

- Frank Bonilla, Center for Puerto Rican Studies, New York, "Work, Migration, and Puerto-Ricans in the 80s" (Ford Foundation, a "principal supporter of the Center since its founding," in 1984 gave the Center $177,474 for documentation of the Puerto Rican experience in the U.S.[18]);

- Pedro Rivera, Center for Puerto Rican Studies, New York, (film) "Documentary on Puerto-Rican Community Culture in the U.S." (see Bonilla);

- Rina Benmayor, Center for Puerto Rican Studies, New York, (slide show) "The Experience of Puerto Rican Women in the Garment Industry" (see Bonilla);

- Luis Reyes, ASPIRA of N.Y., Inc., New York, "Minority Dropouts: Systemic Failure in the Inner City Schools" (in 1985, Ford granted ASPIRA of America, along with the League of United Latin American Citizens, $450,000 for the high-school component of a larger Hispanic leadership development program[19]);

- "Miguel Diaz," League of United Latin American Citizens (LULAC), Washington, D.C., spoke at the closing session.

When Senator Alan Simpson, primary sponsor of immigration reform legislation, said in 1983 that illegal immigration is the most dangerous threat to our national integrity and security since the Civil War, LULAC General Counsel Ruben Bonilla characterized Simpson's remarks as "an outright lie and a piece of propaganda designed to heighten emotions and scare the American public." LULAC President Tony Bonilla demanded that Simpson apologize: "I challenge him to find one immigrant who entered the country illegally and who is engaged in subversive activity ... These immigrants are not leftists or socialists ... These are not people who came to don leftist uniforms or [speak] shed communist slogans.'' Added Ruben Bonilla, ''He is hypocritical in using this double-fisted approach to immigration, slamming his reform bill in the face of Americans while deceiving the public with this big propaganda push that is typical of right-wing America.''[20] LULAC's next President, Mario Obledo, criticized U.S. foreign policy while on a trip to Cuba.

The papers presented by the Cuban scholars are not readily available in the U.S.

Appendix Four
Ford Foundation Funding of Anti-Reform Organizations

Year	LA RAZA	MALDEF	LULAC	NIRCForum	Year Total
1968	$630,000	$2,200,000	$0	$0	$2,830,000
1969	$21,595	$0	$0	$0	$21,595
1970	$1,953,700	$0	$0	$0	$1,953,700
1971	$150,000	$0	$0	$0	$150,000
1972	$800,000	$0	$0	$0	$800,000
1973	$485,000	$415,000	$0	$0	$900,000
1974	$425,000	$825,000	$0	$0	$1,250,000
1975	$339,996	$0	$0	$0	$339,996
1976	$271,984	$750,000	$0	$0	$1,021,984
1977	$200,000	$0	$0	$0	$200,000
1978	$300,000	$887,200	$0	$0	$1,187,200
1979	$0	$0	$0	$0	$0
1980	$232,500	$742,425	$0	$0	$974,925
1981	$240,000	$391,660	$15,200	$0	$646,860
1982	$375,000	$900,000	$0	$0	$1,275,000
1983	$162,732	$822,350	$0	$152,110	$1,137,192
1984	$500,000	$1,400,000	$0	$142,290	$2,042,290
1985	$0	$1,256,000	$0	$55,600	$1,311,600

Year	LA RAZA	MALDEF	LULAC	NIRCForum	Year Total
1986	$25,000	$1,300,000	$0	$84,000	$1,409,000
1987	$110,000	$630,000	$0	$517,030	$1,257,030
1988	$830,000	$1,350,000	$0	$235,000	$2,415,000
1989	$452,000	$295,000	$134,000	$435,000	$1,316,000
1990	$262,000	$1,575,000	$145,000	$0	$1,982,000
1991	$1,250,000	$792,000	$330,000	$460,000	$2,832,000
1992	$109,300	$1,545,000	$0	$175,000	$1,829,300
GRAND TOTAL	$10,125,807	$18,076,635	$624,200	$2,256,030	$31,082,672

LA RAZA—National Council of La Raza
MALDEF—Mexican-American Legal Defense and Educational Fund
LULAC—League of United Latin-American Citizens
NIRCForum—National Immigration, Refugee and Citizenship Forum

SOURCE: *Ford Foundation Annual Reports 1968–92*

Endnotes

CHAPTER ONE:
AMERICANS DECIDE ON IMMIGRATION REFORM

1. "Court's ruling on Illegal Aliens," *The New York Times*, June 17, 1982, p. B18.

2. William S. Bernard, "Immigration: History of U.S. Policy," *Harvard Encyclopedia of American Ethnic Groups*, Stephen Thernstom, editor. (Cambridge: Belknap Press, 1980), p. 495.

3. Ibid., p. 495.

4. William B. Johnston, *Workforce 2000* (Indianapolis: Hudson Institute, 1987) p. 92.

5. Gene Koretz, "How the Hispanic Boom Will Hit the Work Force," *Business Week*, February 20, 1989, p. 21.

6. Constance Holden, "Debate Warming Up on Legal Migration Policy," *Science* (Vol. 24, 15 July 1988), p. 288.

7. *Workforce 2000*, p. 102.

8. Senate Report No. 99-132, *Immigration Reform and Control Act of 1985* (Report, together with Minority Views of the Committee on the Judiciary, United States Senate), August 28, 1985. This is the governing Senate Report on what became the

Immigration Reform and Control Act of 1986. Contains an excellent rationale for reform and provides the best summary of Congressional history.

9. "Border Agents," *Stephenville Empire-Tribune*, June 17, 1977, p. 1.

10. "Carter Says Aliens Need Amnesty Plan," *Fort Worth Star Telegram*, April 17, 1977, p. 1.

11. Arthur F. Corwin, "A Human Rights Dilemma: Carter and 'Undocumented' Mexicans" in *Immigrants—and Immigrants: Perspectives on Mexican Labor Migration to the United States,* edited by Arthur F. Corwin (Westport, CT: Greenwood Press, 1978), p. 322.

12. "Opinion-TRB from Washington," *San Francisco Examiner and Chronicle*, July 24, 1977, p. 2B. For more information on European guest worker programs, see Jane Kramer, *Unsettling Europe* (NY: Random House, 1980) particularly chapter 2. Kramer is sympathetic towards Third World immigrants but cannot hide the dire consequences their influx has had on European society.

13. Corwin, p. 330.

14. *Final Report of the Select Commission on Immigration and Refugee Policy* (Joint Hearings Before the Subcommittee on Immigration and Refugee Policy of the Senate Committee on the Judiciary and Subcommittee on Immigration, Refugees and International Law of the House Committee on the Judiciary, Ninety-Seventh Congress, First Session. . .), May 5, 6, 7, 1981.

15. Ibid., pp. 24-25.

16. Michael Teitelbaum, "Right Versus Right: Immigration and Refugee Policy in the United States," *Foreign Affairs*, Fall 1980, pp. 32-33.

17. *Final Report of the Select Commission on Immigration and Refugee Policy* (Joint Hearings Before the Subcommittee on Immigration and Refugee Policy of the Senate Committee on the Judiciary and Subcommittee on Immigration, Refugees and International Law of the House Committee on the Judiciary, Ninety-Seventh Congress, First Session. . .), May 5, 6, 7, 1981, pp. 149-160.

18. Ibid., pp. 606-630.

19. Ibid., pp. 251-272.

20. Ibid., pp. 631-644.

21. Id. Pandya later contributed a 1983 piece on immigration reform to the Marxist-Leninist newspaper, *Guardian* (New York), June 8, 1983, p. 3. After working for the ACLU's Salvadoran Asylum Project, in 1988 Pandya was employed at Rick Swartz' National Immigration Forum.

22. Richard D. Lamm and Gary Imhoff, *The Immigration Time Bomb: The Fragmenting of America* (New York: E.P. Dutton, 1985), pp. 201-202. Even immigration expansionists, such as neoconservative Rita Simon, must concede that, ". . .most Americans say they would like to decrease the number of immigrants and refugees permitted to enter the United States." Rita J. Simon, "Immigration and American Attitudes," A.E.I. *Public Opinion*, July-August, 1987, p. 47.

CHAPTER TWO: THE FORD FOUNDATION ENTERS THE FRAY

1. Statement of Michael G. Hapold, Legislative Representative, INS Council, American Federation of Government Employees before House Subcommittee on Immigration, March 12, 1975.

2. *Ford Foundation Annual Report: 1983*, p. 46, $33,600; p. 50, $320,000; *Ford Foundation Annual Report: 1984*, p. 53, $270,000; p. 40, $1,365,000; *Ford Foundation Annual Report: 1985*, p. 51, $240,000; *Ford Foundation Annual Report: 1986*, $1,300,000; *Ford Foundation Annual Report: 1987*, p. 14, $135,000; p. 46, $200,-000, p. 50, $295,000. *Ford Foundation Report: 1988*, p. 89, $1,350,000.

3. *Who's Who in America* (Wilmette: MacMillan, 1986), 44th edition, 1986-1987, Volume 2, page 2277.

4. "The Ford Foundation thus would welcome the increased involvement of other funders—public and private—in work in the refugee and migration field, and Foundation staff are available for discussions with other funders about possible collaborative ventures." "Refugees and Migrants: Problems and Program Responses, A working paper from the Ford Foundation," August, 1983, pp. 64.

5. 1986 Payments, $167,691,000; 1986 Assets, $4,758,862,000, *Estimates of Philanthropic Giving in 1986 and the Trends They Show*, 32nd Annual Issue, American Association of Fund-Raising Counsel, Inc. Trust for Philanthropy.

6. Franklin Thomas, "President's Review," *Ford Foundation Annual Report*: 1984, p. xii. 7. *Ford Foundation Annual Report*: 1983, p. 19.

8. "Thomas, Franklin A(ugustine)," *Current Biography*, p. 416.

9. *Hispanics: Challenges and Opportunities*, A working paper from the Ford Foundation, June, 1984, p. 48.

10. Blanca Facundo, *Responsiveness of U.S. Foundations to Hispanic Needs and Concerns*, Latino Institute, Chicago, 1980.

11. *A Study of Foundation Awards to Hispanic-Oriented Organizations in the U.S.*, Stanford Center for Chicano Research, 1984.

12. Michael Teitelbaum, "Right Versus Right: Immigration and Refugee Policy in the United States," *Foreign Affairs*, Fall 1980, p. 43.

13. Richard D. Lamm and Gary Imhoff, *The Immigration Time Bomb* (New York: E.P. Dutton, 1985), pp. 203-204.

14. Michael Teitelbaum, "Right Versus Right: Immigration and Refugee Policy in the United States," *Foreign Affairs*, Fall 1980, p. 32.

15. *Refugees and Migrants: Problems and Program Responses*, A working paper from the Ford Foundation, August, 1983, pp. 3-4.

16. Around 1981, ". . .a number of the most outstanding and respected authorities in several of the very fields in which [Ford Foundation President Franklin Thomas'] program would concentrate had been ejected, among them Sol Chafkin in community development, Siobhan Oppenheimer-Nicolau in Hispanic and native American affairs, and Michael Teitelbaum in refugee and immigration policies." Waldemar A. Neilsen, "The Prototypes: Ford and Rockefeller," *The Golden Donors*, p. 78.

17. *Refugees and Migrants: Problems and Program Responses*, A working paper from the Ford Foundation, August, 1983.

18. Franklin A. Thomas, "The New Migration," Commencement Address, Cooper Union, New York City, May 23, 1984, Ford Foundation.

19. James D. Cockcroft, *Outlaws in the Promised Land: Mexican Immigrant Workers and America's Future* (NY: Grove Press, 1986), p. 221.

20. Calavita, "Employee Sanctions Legislation", p. 80.

21. Committee on Chicano Rights, *A Chicano Perspective*, cited in Cockcroft, *Outlaws in the Promised Land*, p. 230.

22. *Hispanic Monitor*, February, 1984.

23. Cockcroft, p. 233.

24. Ibid.

25. John E. Huerta, "From Reform to Restriction: The History of the Select Commission on Immigration and Refugee Policy," *The Report of the U.S. Select Commission on Immigration and Refugee Policy: A Critical Analysis*, Center for U.S.-Mexican Studies, University of California, San Diego, Research Report Series No. 32, September 15, 1983.

26. National Lawyers Guild *Guild Notes*, October, 1975. p. 4.

27. Linda Wong, Memorandum to Interested Individuals and Organizations, re *Preliminary Analysis of Roybal's 1985 Immigration Bill and the Consequences*, January 9, 1985.

28. Mario T. Garcia, *Mexican Americans: Leadership, Ideology & Identity, 1930-1960* (New Haven, CT: Yale University Press, 1989), pp. 206, 213.

29. Wong, *Preliminary Analysis*.

30. "Hispanics foresee backlash, ease opposition to immigration bills," *Christian Science Monitor*, April 2, 1985.

31. Mexican-American Legal Defense and Educational Fund, *Annual Report: 1981*, p. 11.

32. John E. Huerta, "Immigration Policy and Employer Sanctions," 44 *University of Pittsburgh Law Review* 507, 1983.

33. Sidney Weintraub and Stanley R. Ross, *The Illegal Alien from Mexico*, Mexico-U.S. Border Program, University of Texas, p. 37.

34. Vilma R. Martinez, "Immigration: Entering Through the Back Door," 15 *Columbia Human Rights Law Review* pp. 1, 2-3, Fall, 1983.

35. *Ford Foundation Annual Report: 1985*, p. 70 and S. Steven Powell, *Covert Cadre: Inside the Institute for Policy Studies* (Ottawa, IL: Green Hill, 1987, p. 407.

36. Vilma Martinez, p. 8 "Immigration: Entering Through the Back Door." 15 Columbia Human Rights Law Review, p. 8, Fall 1983.

37. Sbicca Defense Team, "New Court Order in Sbicca," National Lawyers Guild National Immigration Project *Immigration Newsletter*, November, 1978 - February, 1979.

38. Flier, "Renewing the Promise of Freedom, Justice and Equality; 1986 ACLU's Issues Conference . . . . English Only Movement: Resurgence of Racism, Linda Wong. . .ACLU Board member."

39. Central America Refugee Center, Los Angeles, July, 1987, letterhead stationery.

40. Linda Wong, "The Simpson-Mazzoli Bill, No Justice for Immigrants," National Lawyers Guild National Immigration Project *Immigration Newsletter*, March-April, 1982.

41. Linda Wong, Memorandum to Interested Individuals and Organizations, re *Preliminary Analysis of Roybal's 1985 Immigration Bill and the Consequences*, January 9, 1985.

42. Linda Wong, "A Postscript on Simpson-Mazzoli: What Next?," National Lawyers Guild National Immigration Project *Immigration Newsletter*, January-February, 1984.

CHAPTER THREE: THE RADICALIZATION OF THE IMMIGRATION DEBATE

1. Sasha G. Lewis, *Slave Trade Today* (Boston: Beacon Press, 1979), p. 124.

2. *Illegal Aliens: Information on Selected Country's Employment Prohibition Laws*, General Accounting Office, Washington, D.C., GGD-86-17BR, October 28, 1985.

3. *Illegal Aliens: Parts, 1, 2, 3* (Hearings before Subcommittee No. 1, House Committee on the Judiciary, Ninety-Second Congress, First Session), October 22, 23, 1971, January 21, 1972.

4. Armando Gutierrez, "Hispanics and the Sunbelt," *Dissent*, Fall 1980, pp. 496-497.

5. Peter Skerry, "In the Shadow of Immigration Policy," *The Public Interest*, Summer 1987, pp. 138-139.

6. *Information Digest*, November 2, 1984, p. 312.

7. Gilbert Cardenas and Estevan Flores, "Political Economy of International Labor Migration," in *Immigration and Public Policy: Human Rights for Undocumented Workers and Their Families*, Chicano Studies Center, UCLA, 1978.

8. Gilbert Cardenas, "United States Immigration Policy Toward Mexico: An Historical Perspective," 2 *Chicano Law Review* 66, Summer 1975.

9. "Immigration Workshop," National Lawyers Guild National Immigration Project *Immigration Newsletter*, September, 1973. In 1968, Ramona Ripston was, with Henry DiSuvero, Co-Director of the National Emergency Civil Liberties Committee: *Congressional Record*, September 23, 1975, p. 29920.

10. William H. Steiner, "Police Enforcement of Immigration Laws," National Lawyers Guild National Immigration Project *Immigration Newsletter*, November, 1978-February, 1979.

11. Peter A. Schey and William H. Steiner, "Police Enforcement of Immigration Laws," National Lawyers Guild National Immigration Project *Immigration Newsletter*, March-April, 1979.

12. Rodolfo Acuna, *Occupied America: A History of Chicanos*, second edition (Cambridge: Harper and Row, 1981), pp. 168-169.

13. Vilma Martinez, "Immigration: Entering Through the Back Door," 15 *Columbia Human Rights Law Review* 1, Fall 1983.

14. Karen O'Connor and Lee Epstein, "A Legal Voice for the Chicano Community: The Activities of the Mexican-American Legal Defense and Educational Fund, 1968-1982," 65 *Social Science Quarterly,* June, 1984, p. 2.

15. National Lawyers Guild National Immigration Project *Immigration Newsletter*, March-April, 1987, p. 18, July-August, 1982, p. 4; *Guardian* (New York), May 12, 1982, p. 3.

16. "INS makes a bad Simpson-Rodino law worse," *Guardian* (New York), January 21, 1987, p. 5. Also, "March! Rally! Protest! Join Us In L.A., August 30, 1986, Rally for Immigrant and Refugee Rights . . . . Speakers . . . . Antonio Rodriguez, L.A. Center for Law and Justice . . . . Be There in Struggle. . ." This rally called for a stop to the Simpson-Rodino bill, an end to U.S. "intervention" in Central America, repudiation of the foreign debt in Latin America, and was endorsed by "Antonia Hernandez, Dr., MALDEF."

17. Dick J. Reavis, *Without Documents* (New York: Condor, 1978) p. 141.

18. "Antonia Hernandez Not Afraid to Say She Loves U.S.," *The Los Angeles Times*, August 5, 1985.

19. National Lawyers Guild National Immigration Project *Immigration Newsletter*, January-February, 1978; National Lawyers Guild National Immigration Project *Immigration Newsletter*, July-August, 1979.

20. "Gates Reveals Police Data on Plaintiffs in Illegal-Spying Suits," *The Los Angeles Times*, November 28, 1983.

21. Flier, "MALDEF Thirteenth Annual Los Angeles Award Dinner," December 8, 1987.

22. Mailing, "CARECEN Fourth Annual Dinner," Los Angeles, January, 1988.

23. Antonio Rodriguez, "The Struggle Against the Immigration Control Act," 8 *Chicano Law Review* 1, 1985.

24. Bill Blum, "Frank Wilkinson and the Defense of Freedom," National Committee Against Repressive Legislation, Los Angeles, ca. 1986.

25. *Information Digest*, September 27, 1985, pp. 263-264.

26. Antonio Rodriguez, "The Struggle Against the Immigration Control Act," 8 *Chicano Law Review* 1, 1985.

27. Flier, "The Conference on Immigrant and Refugee Advocacy, c/o MALDEF . . .Los Angeles," March 11-13, 1983.

28. Linda Wong, "A Postscript on Simpson-Mazzoli: What Next?," National Lawyers Guild National Immigration Project *Immigration Newsletter*, January-February, 1984.

29. National Lawyers Guild National Immigration Project *Immigration Newsletter*, January-February, 1980, p. 20.

30. *Hispanics: Challenges and Opportunities*, Ford Foundation Working Paper, 1984, p. 7.

31. Ibid

32. Ibid, p. 47.

33. Ibid, p. 57.

34. Ibid, pp. 6-7.

35. Ibid, p. 45.

36. Ibid, p. 5.

CHAPTER FOUR: HAITIANS, CUBANS AND IRANIANS

1. "Committee tells INS to seal border," *Guardian* (New York), January 10, 1979, p. 7.

2. *Report of the Attorney General to the Congress of the United States on the Administration of the Foreign Agents Registration Act of 1938*, 1966, 1967, 1968.

3. National Emergency Civil Liberties Committee, *The Bill of Rights Journal*, Volume XVI, December, 1985; Center for Constitutional Rights *Docket Report: 1986-1987*, p. 77.

4. *Haitian Refugee Center v. Civiletti*, 503 F. Supp. 442 (S.D. Fla., 1980).

5. "Mobilizations Against the Klan," National Lawyers Guild National Immigration Project *Immigration Newsletter*, November-December, 1977, p. 12.

6. National Clearinghouse for Legal Services, Inc. *Directory of the National Support Centers*, p. 25.

7. "Judge urged to pay lawyers $221,000 for Haitian case," *The Miami Herald*, April 27, 1983.

8. "Haitian Boat People: Flotsam in an American Sea of Plenty," *The Washington Post*, April 19, 1980, p. A9.

9. "More Haitians Come Ashore," *The Washington Post*, April 15, 1980, p. A5.

10. "Cuba Suddenly Permits Mass Emigration to the U.S.," *The Washington Post*, April 24, 1980.

11. Ladislav Bittman, *The KGB and Soviet Disinformation: An Insider's View* (Washington: Pergamon-Brassey's, 1985), p. 165.

12. *The Role of Cuba in International Terrorism and Subversion* (Hearings before the Subcommittee on Security and Terrorism of the Committee of the Judi-

ciary, United States Senate, Ninety-Seventh Congress, Second Session. . .), 1982, p. 35

13. Alex Larzelerl, *The 1980 Cuban Boatlift: Castro's Ploy—America's Dilemma* (Wash. DC: National Defense University, 1988), pp. 221-222.

14. Dan James, "How Castro's spies seek to destabilize U.S.," *Human Events*, October 31, 1981.

15. "Cuba Sends in 'Refugees'," *San Francisco Chronicle*, April 4, 1983, reprinted from *The New York Times*.

16. *The Cuban Government's Involvement in Facilitating International Drug Traffic* (Joint Hearing before the Subcommittee on Security and Terrorism of the Committee on the Judiciary. . .United States Senate, Ninety-Eighth Congress, First Session. . .), Miami, Florida, April 30, 1983.

17. "Fidel suspected of using Haitians," *The Miami News*, February 23, 1982.

18. "Cuba Aided Doomed Haitians," *The New York Times*, November 22, 1981.

19. "Peasant Massacre Casts Regime into New Crisis," *Guardian* (New York), August 12, 1987.

20. U.S. Department of State, Cuban-Haitian Task Force, *A Report of the Cuban-Haitian Task Force*, November 1, 1980, p. 55.

21. Larzelerl, p. 435.

22. Ibid, pp. 229-230.

23. "International Conference Passes Bill of Rights for Undocumented," National Lawyers Guild National Immigration Project *Immigration Newsletter*, May-June, 1980.

24. "Miami Violence Abates, but Blacks Simmer," *The Washington Post*, May 20, 1980.

25. "Haitians, Cubans and the New Refugee Act," National Lawyers Guild National Immigration Project *Immigration Newsletter*, May- June 1980.

26. "Blacks rise up against Miami injustice," *Guardian* (New York), May 28, 1980, p. 6.

27. Aryeh Neier, "Refugee Gulags," *The Nation*, December 12, 1981.

28. Robert L. Bernstein, "Haitians as Hostages," *The New York Times*, January 13, 1982.

29. "Jailed Haitian refugees rebel," *Guardian* (New York), September 16, 1981, p. 4.

30. "Suit by 6 Haitian Aliens Tests U.S. Detention Policy," *The New York Times*, December 4, 1981, p. B6.

31. "3 Haitians in Brooklyn Still Fight for Asylum," *The New York Times*, February 28, 1982.

32. "Justice Dept. Eases Rules for Releasing Haitians," *The Washington Post*, June 15, 1982.

33. Harriet Rabb, " 'Deceitful New Gambit' in Haitian Refugee Policy," Letter to the Editor, *The New York Times*, June 25, 1982.

34. "INS releases 4 Haitians in New York," *The Washington Post*, October 23, 1982.

35. "Lawyers Frustrate U.S. Immigration Policy," *The Washington Post*, October 19, 1981, p. A1.

36. "Springing the Haitians," *The American Lawyer*, September, 1982, p. 35.

37. NECLC: National Emergency Civil Liberties Committee, *The Bill of Rights Journal*, Volume XVI, December, 1985; ACPFB: Laurie Wiseberg, ed., *North American Human Rights Directory* (Washington: Human Rights Internet, 1980), p. 52; National Lawyers Guild National Immigration Project *Immigration Newsletter*, June 1975.

38. Ira Gollobin, "The Bill of Rights and the Foreign Born," National Lawyers Guild National Immigration Project *Immigration Newsletter*, June 1975, October 1975.

39. "Springing the Haitians," *The American Lawyer*, September, 1982, pp. 35-40.

40. "Jackson calls Haitians victims of racist policy," *The Greenville (SC) News*, January 1, 1982.

41. "Haitians' attorneys call discrimination ruling a landmark," *The Miami News*, April 14, 1983.

42. "Judge urged to pay lawyers $221,000 for Haitian case," *The Miami Herald*, April 27, 1983.

43. Howard W. French "Few Haitians Test U.S. Sea Barricade," *The New York Times,* January 21, 1993, p.A6.

44. "Let Them Drown," *The Progressive*, July 1992, p. 8.

45. Clara Germani, "Battling for Boat People" *Christian Science Monitor*, Sept. 17, 1992, p. 13.

46. National Lawyers Guild National Immigration Project *Immigration Newsletter*, September-December, 1984, p. 18.

47. Arthur C. Helton, "The Haitian Pro Bono Representation Effort," National Lawyers Guild National Immigration Project *Immigration Newsletter*, July-August, 1983.

48. National Clearinghouse for Legal Services, Inc. *Directory of the National Support Centers*, p. 25.

49. "Emergency Southeast Conference on Immigration," Human Rights Internet *Reporter*, January-February, 1982, p. 610.

50. Flier, "Emergency Southeast Conference on Immigration Rights and Political Asylum, December 4-6, 1981, Miami. . ."

51. "Miami conference seeks justice for Haitians," *Guardian* (New York), December 23, 1981, p. 8.

52. Human Rights Internet *Reporter*, September-October, 1978, p. 24 (see also, January, 1979, p. 19).

53. National Lawyers Guild National Immigration Project *Immigration Newsletter*, November, 1978-February, 1979.

54. Lawyers Committee for Human Rights, Helsinki Watch, *Mother of Exiles: Refugees Imprisoned in America* (New York: Lawyers Committee, 1986).

55. Arthur C. Helton, "Imprisonment of Refugees in the United States," in ibid., pp. 68-69.

56. Ibid., p. 75.

57. *Interpreter Releases*, February 17, 1987, pp. 207-208.

58. "Broken Watch," *The New Republic*, August 22, 1988, p. 8.

59. "Communism and the Left," *The Nation*, February 27, 1982, p. 231.

60. Ibid., p. 234.

61. *Who's Who in America* (Wilmette: MacMillan, 1986), 44th edition, 1986-1987.

62. Committee for Public Justice, Nation Institute, *Justice Watch*, Fall 1986.

63. Sidney Hook, "The Scoundrel in the Looking Glass," in *Philosophy and Public Policy* (Carbondale: Southern Illinois University Press, 1980) pp. 218-237.

64. Joshua Muravchik, "Think Tank of the Left," *The New York Times Magazine*, April 26, 1981, p. 36.

65. See, generally, S. Steven Powell, *Covert Cadre: Inside the Institute for Policy Studies* (Ottawa, IL: Green Hill, 1987).

66. Aryeh Neier, "Spiking the I.P.S., An Open Letter to the Times Magazine," *The Nation*, May 30, 1981, pp. 660-662.

67. "Seminar on Ideological Exclusion of Aliens: 'Coalition for a Free Trade in Ideas,' " Human Rights Internet *Reporter*, March- June 1984, p. 572: "Meanwhile a coalition of major U.S. organizations on 'Free Trade in Ideas' is being formed and will be launching a major campaign at a September 8, 1984 conference in Washington, D.C."

68. American Civil Liberties Union, Fund For Free Expression, *Free Trade in Ideas: A Conference*, September 8, 1984.

69. *Ford Foundation Annual Report: 1984*, p. 39.

70. *1976 Policy Guide of the American Civil Liberties Union*, p. 269.

71. "Failure: The Reagan Administration's Human Rights Policy in 1983," on Watch Committees, Lawyers Committee, in Human Rights Internet *Reporter*, December 1983-February, 1984, p. 412.

72. "Visas denied to speakers for Peace Council conference," *Guardian* (New York), October 26, 1983.

73. *The CIA and the Media* (Hearings Before the Subcommittee on Oversight of the Permanent Select Committee on Intelligence, House of Representatives, Ninety-Fifth Congress, First and Second Sessions) (Washington: U.S. Government Printing Office, 1976), pp. 548, 560, etc.

74. S. Steven Powell, *Covert Cadre: Inside the Institute for Policy Studies* (Ottawa, IL: Green Hill Publishers, Inc., 1987), p. 271.

75. Center for National Security Studies, American Civil Liberties Union, *Free Trade In Ideas: A Constitutional Imperative*, May, 1984.

76. Immigration Project of the National Lawyers Guild, *Immigration Law and Defense*, Second Edition (New York: Clark Boardman, 1986), Release #8, 10/86, pp. 2-22, 2-19.

77. *Ford Foundation Annual Report: 1987*, $31,500 for refugee and migrant resettlement in Mexico and Central America, p. 17; etc.

78. *Ford Foundation Annual Report: 1987*, p. 46.

79. *Ford Foundation Annual Report: 1987*, *Ford Foundation Annual Report: 1986*, *Ford Foundation Annual Report: 1985*, *Ford Foundation Annual Report: 1984*, etc.

80. Ibid.

81. *Ford Foundation Annual Report: 1986*, p. 46; *Ford Foundation Annual Report: 1984*, p. 38.

82. *Ford Foundation Annual Report: 1987*, p. 46; *Ford Foundation Annual Report: 1986*, p. 46; *Ford Foundation Annual Report: 1985*, p. 39; *Ford Foundation Annual Report: 1984*, pp. 40-41, etc.

83. *Ford Foundation Annual Report: 1986*, p. 46.

84. *Ford Foundation Annual Report: 1987*, pp. 36, 46.

85. *Ford Foundation Annual Report: 1986*, p. 48; *Ford Foundation Annual Report: 1984*, p. 36; *Ford Foundation Annual Report: 1983*, pp. 33-34; etc.

86. National Lawyers Guild National Immigration Project *Immigration Newsletter*, March-April, 1987, p. 18.

87. National Lawyers Guild National Immigration Project *Brief Bank Index*: Supplement II—1986 (Boston: National Immigration Project 1986), p. 18.

88. National Clearinghouse for Legal Services, Inc. *Directory of the National Support Centers*, p. 25.

89. *Directory of Central America Organizations*, Third Edition (Austin, TX: Central America Resource Center, 1987), pp. 24.

90. 1636 W. 8th St., #215, Los Angeles, CA 90017, *Directory of Central America Organizations*, Third Edition (Austin, TX: Central America Resource Center, 1987), pp. 29-30.

91. *Ford Foundation Annual Report: 1987*, pp. 39, 46; *Ford Foundation Annual Report: 1984*, pp. 38, 39.

92. National Lawyers Guild Central America Task Force in conjunction with the Center for Constitutional Rights, *The Illegality of U.S. Intervention: Central America and Caribbean Litigation* (New York: National Lawyers Guild, 1984), p. 15.

93. Sandra Pettit, "Orantes-Hernandez v. Meese," National Lawyers Guild *Los Angeles Chapter News*, Vol. 2, No. 1, January 1986 [sic, should be 1987].

94. "U.S. on trial," *In These Times*, February 18-24, 1987, pp. 12-13.

95. "Judge blasts administration, rules intimidation of refugees unlawful," *Guardian* (New York), May 11, 1988, p. 7.

96. "Sweeping Victory in *Orantes*," National Lawyers Guild National Immigration Project *Immigration Newsletter*, November- December, 1987, p. 1.

97. Sandra Pettit, "Application of the United States Refugee Law to Central American Refugees in the United States, " National Lawyers Guild National Immigration Project *Immigration Newsletter* September-October, 1987, p. 3.

98. *Information Digest*, October 16, 1987, p. 205.

99. "Deporting the Iranian Students—With Liberty and Justice for All?," *Los Angeles Times*, December 2, 1979.

100. *The Washington Post*, April 13, 1980.

CHAPTER FIVE: ACADEMIC AND INDEPENDENT SCHOLARS

1. Wayne Cornelius, "Solution to the Immigration Problem: Make the Illegals Legal," *San Diego Union*, May 25, 1980.

2. *Ford Foundation Annual Report: 1985*, p. 65; Ford Foundation, *Letter*, April, 1985; *Ford Foundation Annual Report: 1987*, p. 74.

3. Wayne Cornelius, *Overview of Activities, 1980-1983; Plans and Assessment of Needs, 1983-1986*, Center for U.S.-Mexican Studies, University of California, San Diego.

4. Leo R. Chavez, "Immigration Reform: What do Hispanics Want?," Los Angeles *Herald Examiner*, October 24, 1983.

5. The Federation for American Immigration Reform (FAIR) 1983 poll of Hispanic and Black opinion on immigration issues "was conducted cooperatively by Democratic pollster Peter D. Hart and Republican pollster V. Lance Tarrance." Respondents were not asked their views on "reform," which could imply merely legalizing a huge flow, but were asked about more specific issues: 66 percent of Hispanic citizens favored penalties and fines for employers who hire illegal aliens, 66 percent thought that "illegal aliens hurt the job situation for American workers by taking jobs Americans might take, 63 percent favored "major increases in spending to enable the Border Patrol to stop illegal aliens from entering the U.S." Richard D. Lamm and Gary Imhoff, *The Immigration Time Bomb* (New York: E.P. Dutton, 1985), p. 203. Such results are consistent with nearly every other major poll.

6. Flier, "Down with the Simpson-Rodino Act! We're all illegals! Here we are; here we'll stay; we will not go!," by the "So. Cal. ad-hoc Committee for the 'Breakdown the Border' Conference," San Diego, 1987.

7. Joseph N. Lopez, "What Hispanics *Really* Want," Letter to Editor, Los Angeles *Herald Examiner*, November 2, 1983.

8. Bert N. Corona, "Chicano Scholars and Public Issues in the United States in the Eighties," in Mario T. Garcia, et. al, *History, Culture and Society: Chicano Studies in the 1980s* (Ypsilanti: Bilingual Press, 1983), p. 14.

9. Jorge Bustamante, "Structural and Ideological Conditions of the Mexican Undocumented Immigration to the United States," 19 *American Behavioral Scientist* 364-376 (January-February, 1976).

10. Jorge Bustamante and James D. Cockcroft, "One More Time: The 'Undocumented'," *Radical America* (November-December, 1981).

11. James D. Cockcroft, "Mexican Migration, Crisis and the Internationalization of Labor Struggle," in *The New Nomads: From Immigrant Labor to Transnational Working Class* (San Francisco: Synthesis Press, 1982), p. 61; originally published as *Contemporary Marxism*, No. 5.

12. Ibid., p. 60.

13. James D. Cockcroft, *Outlaws in the Promised Land: Mexican Immigrant Workers and America's Future* (New York: Grove Press, 1986), p. 11.

14. Ibid., p. 269.

15. "Stepped-up U.S. campaign against undocumented workers alleged," *San Diego Tribune*, January 28, 1982.

16. Flier, "Breakdown the Border: A call for a conference at the Mexican-U.S. border on the U.S. domination of Mexico and the latest stepped up repression against Latinos," by "Breakdown the Border Conference Committee," 1987.

17. "Outcasts, Downcasts, Slaves, Illegals and Rebels: It's Right to Rebel!," *Revolutionary Worker*, April 13, 1987, p. 8.

18. "Jorge Bustamante: U.S. and Mexico Must Seek Bilateral Solutions to Immigration Issues," *Woodlands Forum*, November, 1986.

19. Mexican expert on border assails new U.S. rules," *The San Diego Union*, November 16, 1986.

20. *Ford Foundation Annual Report: 1983*, p. 69; *Ford Foundation Annual Report: 1985*, p. 70.

21. "Immigration Law is Failing to Cut Flow from Mexico," *The New York Times*, June 24, 1988, p. A1. Also see his standard opinion piece: Wayne Cornelius, "Mexican migrants keep heading north and staying," *The Oregonian*, July 5, 1988, p. A2.

22. "Alien-bill debate: Reform proposal flawed, immigration experts say," *San Jose Mercury*, January 9, 1983.

23. Ford Foundation Annual Report: 1985, p. 50.

24. Flier, "Breakdown the Border: A call for a conference at the Mexican-U.S. border on the U.S. domination if Mexico and the latest stepped up repression against Latinos," by "Breakdown the Border Conference Committee," 1987.

25. Mexican American Legal Defense and Educational Fund (MALDEF) *Annual Report: 1984-1985*, p. 24.

26. "Dialogue with Mexico," Ford Foundation, *Letter*, December, 1986, pp. 6-7.

27. Peter Smith, "Uneasy Neighbors: Mexico and the United States," *Current History*, March, 1987.

28. Bilateral Commission on the Future of United States-Mexican Relations, *Agenda and Commissioned Papers for the Workshop; 29 August 1987; Confidential—Not for Distribution*.

29. "Advocates for Human Rights," Ford Foundation *Letter*, April, 1986.

30. *Who's Who in America* (Wilmette: MacMillan, 1986), 44th edition, 1986-1987, Vol 2, p. 2277.

31. National Lawyers Guild National Immigration Project *Immigration Newsletter*, March-April, 1977, p. 5.

32. "Immigration Law Project Set Up at Columbia University," Human Rights Internet *Reporter*, January-February, 1981, p. 419.

33. Aryeh Neier is on the Board of the Lawyers Committee for International Human Rights, and is Vice Chair of Americas Watch and of Helsinki Watch. *Who's Who in America* (Wilmette: MacMillan, 1986), 44th edition, 1986-1987.

34. "Center for the Study of Human Rights, Columbia University," Human Rights Internet *Reporter*, September-November, 1982, p. 18.

35. Julian Simon, "Bring on the Wretched Refuse," *The Wall Street Journal*, Jan. 26, 1990.

36. Julian Simon, *The Ultimate Resource*, (Princeton, NJ: Princeton Univ. Press, 1981), p. 210.

37. Simon Kuznets, *Modern Economic Growth: Rate, Structure and Speed* (New Haven, CT: Yale Univ. Press, 1966), pp. 67-68.

38. "The More the Merrier: An Interview with Julian Simon", *Forbes*, April 2, 1990, p. 80. See also Julian Simon, *The Economic Consequences of Immigration* (Wash., DC: Cato Institute, 1990).

39. Ibid.

40. Vernon M. Briggs, Jr. "Immigration Policy: Political or Economic?" *Challenge*, Sept.-Oct. 1991, p. 17. For a fuller presentation of Briggs' views see his book *Mass Immigration and the National Interest* (M.E. Sharpe, 1992).

41. Ibid, p. 18.

42. Michael E. Porter, *The Competitive Advantage of Nations* (New York: The Free Press, 1990), p. 643.

43. Julian Simon, "Science Does Not Show That There is Overpopulation in the U.S.—Or Elsewhere." in *Population: A Clash of Prophets* edited by Edward Pohlman (NY: New American Library, 1973), p. 55.

44. Ibid, p. 57.

45. Ben J. Wattenberg and Karl Zinsmeister, "The Case for More Immigration" *Commentary*, April, 1990, p. 21. Zinsmeister is also at the American Enterprise Institute, as an Adjunct Fellow.

46. Ben J. Wattenberg, *The Birth Dearth: What Happens When People in Free Countries Don't Have Enough Babies?* (NY: Pharos Books, 1987), p. 21.

47. Ibid, p. 82.

48. Wattenberg and Zinsmeister, p. 24.

49. Julian Simon, "Bring On the Wretched Refuse."

50. Quoted in Richard Lacayo "Give Me Your Rich, Your Lucky. . ." *Time*, Oct. 14, 1991, p. 27.

51. "Congressional Briefing: House Votes, S 358. Immigration" *Insight on the News*, November 19, 1990. p. 28.

52. Briggs, p. 17.

53. Richard Miniter, letter, *Commentary*, September 1990, p. 7.

54. Wattenberg and Zinsmeister, p. 23.

55. Ibid, p. 25.

56. James D. Cockcroft, *Outlaws in the Promised Land*, p. 214.

57. "The Open Door—With Tickets," *National Review*, October 1, 1990, p. 16.

58. Peter Brimelow, "Rethinking American Immigration Policy" *National Review*, June 22, 1992, pp. 45-46.

59. Ibid, pp. 45-46.

CHAPTER SIX: MEXICAN AMERICAN LEGAL DEFENSE AND EDUCATIONAL FUND

1. *Los Angeles Times* (Nuestro Tiempo Section) August 31, 1989, p.1.

2. Mario T. Garcia, *Mexican Americans: Leadership, Ideology & Identity 1930-1960* (New Haven, CT: Yale University Press, 1989), p. 30. Chapter 2 is a history of LULAC.

3. Ibid, p. 35.

4. Ibid, p. 48.

5. Annette Oliveira, *MALDEF: Diez Anos*, Mexican American Legal Defense and Educational Fund, 1979, p. 10. This "official" history of MALDEF is the primary source for this chapter. Only exact quotes from the document and material from other sources will be noted.

6. Ibid, p. 14.

7. Karen O'Connor and Lee Epstein, "A Legal Voice for the Chicano Community: The Activities of the Mexican American Legal Defense and Educational Fund," *Social Science Quarterly* June 1984, p. 249.

8. F. Chris Garcia and Rudolph O. de la Garza, *The Chicano Political Experience: Three Perspectives* (North Scituate, MA: Duxbury Press, 1976) p. 169.

9. Matt S. Meier, "Gonzalez, Henry Barbosa" *Mexican American Biographies: A Historical Dictionary 1836-1987* (NY: Greenwood Press, 1987) p. 94.

10. Garcia and Garza, p. 170.

11. O'Connor and Epstein, p. 249.

12. Ibid, p. 250.

13. Meier, "Martinez, Vilma Sorocco" p. 134-135.

14. Oliveira, p. 31.

15. Ibid.

16. *MALDEF 1978: Annual Report*, p. 4.

17. Oliveira, p. 21.

18. Guadalupe San Miguel, Jr., "Conflict and Controversy in the Evolution of Bilingual Education in the United States—An Interpretation," *The Mexican American Experience: An Interdisciplinary Anthology* edited by Rodolfo O. De La Garza, et al. (Austin, TX: University of Texas Press, 1985), p. 269-270.

19. Office for Civil Rights, *Task Force Findings Specifying Remedies Available for Eliminating Past Educational Practices Ruled Unlawful under* Lau v. Nichols (Wash. DC: Dept. of Health, Education and Welfare, Office of Civil Rights, 1975).

20. San Miguel, p. 273.

21. McWilliams, p. 266.

22. Tom Bethel, "Why Johnny Can't Speak English," *Harper's*, February, 1979, p. 28.

23. "MALDEF Consultant Calls for Alien Voting," *Border Watch*, August 1992, p. 5.

24. Thomas J. DiLorenzo, *Patterns of Corporate Philanthropy*, (Wash. DC: Capital Research Center, 1990), p. 250.

25. "Target for Smear: The Border Patrol" *Border Watch*, August, 1992, p. 2.

26. DiLorenzo, pp. 250-51, 254-55.

27. "Corporations Reply to Our Member's Questions" *Border Watch*, Sept. 1992, p. 2.

28. "Exxon Cuts Support for Pro-Alien Groups," *Border Watch,* October, 1992.

CHAPTER SEVEN: THE NATIONAL LAWYERS GUILD

1. Tomas Borge, as reported by defector Alberto Suhr, "Sandinista foes press for resistance support," *Washington Times*, December 4, 1986.

2. Ann Fagan Ginger and Eugene M. Tobin, editors, *The National Lawyers Guild: From Roosevelt through Reagan*, (Philadelphia: Temple University Press, 1988), p. xx.

3. Ibid., pp. 79-80, 351.

4. *The CIA and the Media* (Hearings Before the Subcommittee on Oversight of the Permanent Select Committee on Intelligence, House of Representatives, Ninety-Fifth Congress, First and Second Sessions) (Washington: U.S. Government Printing Office, 1976), pp. 614, 547.

5. Ann Fagan Ginger and Eugene M. Tobin, editors, *The National Lawyers Guild: From Roosevelt through Reagan*, (Philadelphia: Temple University Press, 1988), p. 81.

6. "The National Lawyers Guild celebrates fifty years of activism and resistance," Guardian (New York), May 20, 1987, p. 10.

7. Barbara Hadley, Executive Director, National Lawyers Guild, Letter to the Editor, *Washington Times*, March 13, 1987.

8. "Lawyers Guild Gaining Respect In Its 50th Year," *The Los Angeles Daily Journal*, January 29, 1987.

9. "Lawyers Guild Marks 50 Years In the Fight for Justice," *Frontline*, June 8, 1987.

10. " 'The law should be an instrument for people's protection, not their oppression,' Haywood Burns," *People's Daily World*, May 21, 1987.

11. National Lawyers Guild National Immigration Project *Immigration Newsletter*, March-April, 1987, p. 2.

12. Sue Susman and Claudia Slovinsky, advertisement: "The Bill of Rights: We must defend and extend it for those with us and those at our shores," National Emergency Civil Liberties Committee, *The Bill of Rights Journal*, Volume XVI, December, 1983, p. 51.

13. Susan Susman of New York City was on the Steering Committee through the National Lawyers Guild National Immigration Project *Immigration Newsletter*, January-February, 1982; Claudia Slovinsky of New York City joined the Steering Committee as of the March-April, 1982 *Immigration Newsletter* and remains as of 1988.

14. National Lawyers Guild National Immigration Project *Immigration Newsletter*, November, 1972, p. 1.

15. "National Office Proposed to Begin a Major Offensive Against INS," National Lawyers Guild National Immigration Project *Immigration Newsletter*, March, 1974.

16. "NLG Convention Opposes Carter Plan," National Lawyers Guild National Immigration Project *Immigration Newsletter*, July-Aug., 1977.

17. "Immigration Project Moves to Boston," National Lawyers Guild National Immigration Project *Immigration Newsletter*, Summer, 1980.

18. National Lawyers Guild National Immigration Project *Immigration Newsletter*, May-June, 1979, p. 3.

19. "An Alien's Advocate," *The Washington Post Magazine*, April 16, 1983, p. 16.

20. Michael Maggio, "Shifting Sands of U.S. Immigration Policy Trap Salvadoran Refugees," *Los Angeles Times*, July 13, 1980.

21. Bob Hilliard, "U.S. groups visit El Salvador: Immigration attorneys asked to aid refugees," National Lawyers Guild National Immigration Project *Immigration Newsletter*. p. 1.

22. "Manzo: Turmoil Continues," National Lawyers Guild National Immigration Project *Immigration Newsletter*, Jan.-Feb., 1977.

23. "Manzo Victory: All Charges Dropped," National Lawyers Guild National Immigration Project *Immigration Newsletter*, Mar.- Apr., 1977.

24. Id.

25. "Deal Attempt on Manzo 4," CASA *Sin Fronteras*, March, 1977, p. 2.

26. "Salvador refugees: shipped from US back to civil war at 'home,' " *Christian Science Monitor*, January, 1982.

27. *S. 2252: Alien Adjustment and Employment Act of 1977, Part 2* (Hearings Before the Committee on the Judiciary, United States Senate, Ninety-Fifth Congress, Second Session. . .), September 1 and 2, 1978, pp. 37-38.

28. Ibid., p. 236.

29. Ibid., p. 31.

30. "International Conference Passes Bill of Rights for Undocumented," National Lawyers Guild National Immigration Project *Immigration Newsletter*, May-June, 1980.

31. Gary MacEoin, "A Brief History of the Sanctuary Movement," in Gary MacEoin, editor, *Sanctuary: A Resource Guide* (New York: Harper and Row, 1985), p. 15.

32. Renny Golden and Michael McConnell, *Sanctuary: The New Underground Railroad* (MaryKnoll: Orbis, 1986), p. 10.

33. Robert Tomsho, *The American Sanctuary Movement* (Austin: Texas Monthly Press, 1987), pp. 18, 21.

34. National Lawyers Guild National Immigration Project *Immigration Newsletter*, November, 1978-February, 1979, p. 2.

35. "Salvadorean Refugee Defense," National Lawyers Guild National Immigration Project *Immigration Newsletter*, September-October, 1981.

36. Gary MacEoin, "A Brief History of the Sanctuary Movement," in Gary MacEoin, editor, *A Resource Guide* (New York: Harper and Row, 1985), p. 19.

37. Gary MacEoin, editor, *Sanctuary: A Resource Guide* (New York: Harper and Row, 1985), p. 215.

38. Robert Tomsho, *The American Sanctuary Movement* (Austin: Texas Monthly Press, 1987), p. 30.

39. Gary MacEoin, *Revolution Next Door: Latin America in the 1970s* (New York: Holt, Rinehart and Winston, 1971), pp. 219-222.

40. Gary MacEoin, "The Constitutional and Legal Aspects of the Refugee Crisis," in Gary MacEoin, editor, *Sanctuary: A Resource Guide* (New York: Harper and Row, 1985), p. 118.

41. "Salvadoran Refugees Focus of Immigration Work," *Guild Notes*, March-April, 1982, p. 12.

42. *Soviet Active Measures* (Hearings before the Permanent Select Committee on Intelligence, House of Representatives, Ninety- Seventh Congress, Second Session), July 13, 14, 1982 , p. 52.

43. "Refugees from El Salvador present U.S. with problem," *Arizona Republic*, March 21, 1982.

44. Robert Tomsho, *The American Sanctuary Movement* (Austin: Texas Monthly Press, 1987), pp. 13, 18, 21, 24, 26, 31.

45. Church World Service Immigration and Refugee Program (NCC), Inter-Religious Task Force on El Salvador and Central America (NCC), Lutheran Immigration and Refugee Service, American Friends Service Committee, *Seeking Safe Haven: A Congregational Guide to Helping Central American Refugees in the United States*.

46. Listed under migrants and refugees, $50,000 for a "demonstration project to improve social services in inner-city neighborhoods," Ford Foundation *Letter*, February 1, 1985.

47. "For the last five years, Church World Service (CWS) and the Lutheran Immigration and Refugee Service (LIRS) have provided substantial amounts of critically needed financial and administrative support for these local projects." Patrick A. Taran and Lauren Pressman McMahon, "Central American Refugees in the U.S.: A Profile Prepared for the International Council of Voluntary Agencies. . .September 11-14, 1986."

48. National Lawyers Guild National Immigration Project *Immigration Newsletter*, July-August, 1987, p. 13.

49. "New Director at El Rescate," *El Rescate* newsletter, May, 1987.

50. *Ford Foundation Annual Report: 1985*, p. 42.

51. "Delivering Pleas From Salvadoran War Zone," *The Los Angeles Times*, December 17, 1987.

52. "Operation Babylift," National Lawyers Guild National Immigration Project *Immigration Newsletter*, August-September, 1976, p. 1.

53. Center for Constitutional Rights *Docket Report: 1974-1975*, cited in *Congressional Record*, September 10, 1975, p. 28534.

54. "Operation Babylift," National Lawyers Guild National Immigration Project *Immigration Newsletter*, August-September, 1976.

55. Center for Constitutional Rights *Docket Report: 1974-1975*, cited in *Congressional Record*, September 10, 1975, p. 28534; Center for Constitutional Rights *Docket Report: 1975-1976*, cited in *Congressional Record*, June 9, 1976. p. 17307.

56. Center for Constitutional Rights *Docket Report: 1974-1975.*

57. *Ford Foundation Annual Report: 1984*, p. 38.

58. National Clearinghouse for Legal Services, Inc. *Directory of the National Support Centers*, p. 25.

59. National Lawyers Guild National Immigration Project *Immigration Newsletter*, July-August, 1985, etc.

60. *Ford Foundation Annual Report: 1985*, pp. 37-39. Deborah Anker's $50,000 grant from the Ford Foundation was written up in the *Harvard Law Record.*

61. National Lawyers Guild National Immigration Project *Immigration Newsletter*, March-April, 1987, p. 19.

62. *Ford Foundation Annual Report: 1987*, p. 46, $225,000; *Ford Foundation Annual Report: 1985*, p. 41, $265,000; *Ford Foundation Annual Report: 1983*, p. 35, $255,000.

63. National Lawyers Guild National Immigration Project *Immigration Newsletter*, March-April, 1982, p. 3.

64. *Ford Foundation Annual Report: 1987*, p. 46.

65. "Skills Seminar on Political Asylum," National Lawyers Guild National Immigration Project *Immigration Newsletter*, September- October, 1982, p. 15.

66. *Ford Foundation Annual Report: 1987*, p. 46; *Ford Foundation Annual Report: 1986*, p. 46; *Ford Foundation Annual Report: 1985*, p. 39; *Ford Foundation Annual Report: 1984*, pp. 40-41, etc.

67. American Civil Liberties Union Washington Office, 122 Maryland Ave., N.E., Washington D.C., "Biographical Information: Wade J. Henderson, Esq.," ca. 1987, no date.

68. *Ford Foundation Annual Report: 1987, Ford Foundation Annual Report: 1986, Ford Foundation Annual Report: 1985, Ford Foundation Annual Report: 1984*, etc.

69. National Lawyers Guild National Immigration Project *Immigration Newsletter*, March-April, 1986, p. 1.

70. National Lawyers Guild National Immigration Project *Immigration Newsletter*, January-February, 1981, etc.

71. *Ford Foundation Annual Report: 1987*, p. 46, $75,000; *Ford Foundation Annual Report: 1985*, p. 40, $250,000.

72. Sandra Pettit, "Orantes-Hernandez v. Meese," National Lawyers Guild *Los Angeles Chapter News*, Vol. 2, No. 1, January 1986 [sic, should be 1987].

73. National Emergency Civil Liberties Committee, *The Bill of Rights Journal*, Volume XVI, December, 1983.

74. *Ford Foundation Annual Report: 1987*, pp. 14, 46; *Ford Foundation Annual Report: 1985* p. 38; *Ford Foundation Annual Report: 1984*, p. 39.

75. Section 1007(a)(5) of the Legal Services Corporation Act of 1974 (42 U.S.C. Section 2996(f)(a)(5)); also, see Sections 1007(b)(6)-(7) of the Act.

76. For example, "The 1980 Appropriations Act for the Department State, Justice and Commerce, the Judiciary and Related Agencies (PL 96-68) provided that none of the money appropriated for the Legal Services Corporation '. . .may be used to carry out any activities for or on behalf of any individual who is known to be an alien in the United States in violation of the Immigration and Nationality Act or any other law, convention or treaty of the United States relating to immigration, exclusions, deportation or expulsion of aliens.' " National Lawyers Guild National Immigration Project *Immigration Newsletter*, September-October, 1982, pp. 5-6.

77. When the Legal Services Corporation, heavily infiltrated by the National Lawyers Guild, faced exceptional scrutiny from the new Reagan Administration, a "survival campaign" was devised. Part of that strategy was for support centers (such as National Center for Immigrants' Rights forming the new N.C.I.R., Inc.) and local Legal Services offices to each form private "mirror" corporations. The mirror corporation, on paper, avoids federal funds and the related prohibitions on political activity. See James T. Bennett and Thomas J. DiLorenzo, "Poverty, Politics and Jurisprudence: Illegalities at the Legal Services Corporation," *Destroying Democracy: How Government Funds Partisan Politics* (Washington: CATO Institute, 1985), pp. 321-324. See also *Legal Services Corporation: The Robber Barons of the Poor?* (Washington: Washington Legal Foundation, 1985) for a detailed account of egregious political abuse of public funds.

78. *Ford Foundation Annual Report: 1984*, p. 38.

79. Carlos Holguin and Peter Schey, "Challenging INS Detention of Minors," *National Lawyers Guild National Immigration Project Immigration Newsletter*, September-October, 1985.

CHAPTER EIGHT: AMERICAN CIVIL LIBERTIES UNION

1. Alexander Hamilton, Federalist #23, December 18, 1787, *Selected Writings and Speeches of Alexander Hamilton*, edited by Morton J. Frisch (Wash. DC: American Enterprise Institute, 1984), p. 134.

2. William A. Donohue, *The Politics of the American Civil Liberties Union* (New Brunswick: Transaction Books, 1985), p. 171.

3. Ibid, p. 193.

4. Ibid, p. 205.

5. National Charities Information Bureau, Inc., New York, #509, June 16, 1983: "American Civil Liberties Union Foundation and American Civil Liberties Union."

6. *Who's Who in America* (Wilmette: MacMillan, 1986), 44th edition, 1986-1987, Vol. 2, p. 2277.

7. *Ford Foundation Annual Report: 1983*, p. 35. Note that Harriet Rabb and Susan Susman of the Columbia Immigration Law Clinic, and Stephen Shapiro of the New York Civil Liberties Union were plaintiffs' counsel in a 1982 immigration case, *Vigile et al. v. Sava*, seeking parole of detained Haitian illegals, "*Vigile et al. v. Sava* . . .," National Lawyers Guild National Immigration Project *Immigration Newsletter*, March-April, 1982, p. 13. Rabb was also a director of the Lawyers Committee for Civil Rights Under Law, 1978-1986, the parent body to the Alien Rights Law Project.

8. "Aiding the World's Homeless," Ford Foundation *Letter*, December 1, 1983; *Ford Foundation Annual Report: 1984*, p. 39.

9. National Lawyers Guild National Immigration Project *Immigration Newsletter*, March-April, 1977, p. 5.

10. American Civil Liberties Union Washington Office, 122 Maryland Ave., N.E., Washington D.C., "Biographical Information: Wade J. Henderson, Esq.," ca. 1987, no date.

11. National Clearinghouse for Legal Services, Inc. *Directory of the National Support Centers*, p. 25.

12. National Lawyers Guild National Immigration Project *Immigration Newsletter*, June-July, 1985, p. 4.

13. William A. Donohue, *The Politics of the American Civil Liberties Union* (New Brunswick: Transaction Books, 1985), p. 208.

14. ACLU National Immigration and Alien Rights Project, Center for National Security Studies, *Salvadorans in the United States: The Case for Extended Voluntary Departure*, April 1984, inside front cover, copyright page.

15. "Storm over the U.S. plan to stem alien tide," United Press International, in *The Fresno Bee*, November 29, 1981.

16. "...The Sanctuary Movement is Justified...The Government Isn't," ACLU *Civil Liberties*, Spring, 1985, p. 1; "Government Indicts Sanctuary Workers: ACLU Participates in Defense," *ACLU State Lobbyist*, June, 1985, p. 3.

17. Norman Dorsen, ed. *Our Endangered Rights: The ACLU Report on Civil Liberties Today*, (New York: Pantheon, 1984), pp. 160-178.

18. Sec. 274A(l) of the Immigration and Nationality Act, as amended by the Immigration Reform and Control Act of 1986 (P.L. 99-603).

19. Lucas Guttentag, American Civil Liberties Union, Memorandum to "Interested Persons . . . . Re: Discrimination Questionnaire. . .March 9, 1987."

20. Jim Harrington, Texas Civil Liberties Union Foundation, Memorandum to "People Doing Immigration Work. . .Re: IRCA (and Other Immigration) Problems . . .November 19, 1987."

21. "Helping immigrants stay in the USA," national American Civil Liberties Union, *Civil Liberties*, Spring-Summer, 1988, pp. 20, 2.

22. Mark S. Campisano, "Civil Liberties: Beyond the Amrodotes" *The Wall Street Journal*, October 20, 1988, p. A24. The author once clerked for Supreme Court Justice William Brennan; his judgement is based on a detailed analysis of the ACLU's case load in selected years.

23. Ibid.

24. Norman Dorsen, ed., *Our Endangered Rights: The ACLU Report on Civil Liberties Today*, (New York: Pantheon, 1984), pp. 160-178.

CHAPTER NINE: OTHER "OPEN BORDER" GROUPS

1. Mike Ervin, "Arthur Kinoy (interview)," *The Progressive*, October, 1992, p. 32.

2. "Coalition on Immigration and Refugee Policy Considered," National Lawyers Guild National Immigration Project *Immigration Newsletter*, January-February, 1981, p. 7.

3. "Dear Colleague" letter, "Re: Meeting of Public Coalition on Immigration and Refugee Policy. February 2, 1981. . .," dated January 21, 1981.

4. National Lawyers Guild National Immigration Project *Immigration Newsletter*, January-February, 1981, p. 2.

5. *Who's Who in America* (Wilmette: MacMillan, 1986), 44th edition, 1986-1987, Vol. 2, p. 2277.

6. *Ford Foundation Annual Report: 1984*, p. 13.

7. National Forum on Immigration and Refugee Policy, *Forum*, Vol. I, No. 1, February 4, 1982.

8. *Ford Foundation Annual Report: 1982*, p. 21.

9. *Ford Foundation Annual Report: 1987*, pp. 14, 46; *Ford Foundation Annual Report: 1985,* p. 38; *Ford Foundation Annual Report: 1984*, p. 39.

10. *Ford Foundation Annual Report: 1985,* p. 38

11. Rick Swartz, Letter to Editor, "Forum not part of coalition," *The Miami News*, September 16, 1983.

12. National Forum on Immigration and Refugee Policy, *Forum*, Vol. I, No. 1, February 4, 1982, p. 4.

13. Senator Alan Simpson: "I do not think it has been very helpful, at least it is not to me. There have been references to Nazi Germany. Those things are not helpful in this debate." *Asylum Adjudication* (Hearings Before the Subcommittee on Immi-

gration and Refugee Policy of the Committee on the Judiciary, U.S. Senate, Ninety-Seventh Congress, First Session, on How Do We Determine Who Is Entitled To Asylum In The United States And Who Is Not?, October 14 and 16, 1981), p. 106.

14. Coalition information from "Local coalitions respond to IRCA," National Immigration Forum *Advisor*, Vol. 1, No. 1, September 17, 1987, p. 3; "IRCA: Rights and Responsibilities," Ford Foundation *Letter*, December, 1987, p. 5.

15. "Texas group seeks delay of new immigration law," West Palm Beach *Evening Times*, April 2, 1987; "Texans seek delay of immigration reform law, changes in INS rules," *Miami News*, April 2, 1987; "Task force decries immigration reform," *Austin American-Statesman*, April 2, 1987.

16. "Rally backs rights for undocumented workers," *People's Daily World*, May 17, 1988.

17. "INS rules spark outcry," *Unity*, organ of "U.S. League for Revolutionary Struggle (Marxist-Leninist)," March 30, 1987.

18. National Lawyers Guild National Immigration Project *Immigration Newsletter*, March-April, 1982, p. 3.

19. Warren Leiden, "Select Commission on Immigration and Refugee Policy: Final Report and Recommendations Issued," National Lawyers Guild National Immigration Project *Immigration Newsletter*, March-April, 1981.

20. National Clearinghouse for Legal Services, Inc. *Directory of the National Support Centers*, p. 25.

21. National Lawyers Guild National Immigration Project *Immigration Newsletter*, July-August, 1987, p. 13.

22. "On this and the following pages are. . .persons in all endeavors who have contributed through the Bill of Rights Journal to the work of the National Emergency Civil Liberties Committee." *The Bill of Rights Journal*, December, 1969, p. 40.

23. "International Conference Passes Bill of Rights for Undocumented," National Lawyers Guild National Immigration Project *Immigration Newsletter*, May-June, 1980.

24. The American Committee for the Protection of the Foreign Born (ACPFB), in its earlier incarnation as the Councils for the Protection of the Foreign Born, was, from its beginning in 1923, closely identified with radical leftist politics. The

ACPFB had two purposes: to agitate among and recruit from the foreign-born, and to protect Party members from deportation. In the days of the Popular Front, the ACPFB attracted an impressive array of liberal support, but in the 1950s was exposed again and again as under the strong influence of the Communist Party USA. Francis X. Gannon, *Biographical Dictionary of the American Left* (Boston: Western Islands, 1973).

25. *AILA Monthly Mailing*, July-August, 1987, p. 1018.

26. Id.

27. Carolyn Patty Blum is Co-Director of the National Lawyers Guild's Central American Refugee Defense Fund. She acknowledges the Ford Foundation's support for her legal research on political asylum. Carolyn P. Blum, "The Ninth Circuit and the Protection of Asylum Seekers Since the Passage of the Refugee Act of 1980," 23 *San Diego Law Review* 327 (1986).

28. Analysis of "AILA Organizational Chart (With Committees)," 1987.

29. Warren R. Leiden, American Immigration Lawyers Association, Memorandum to Interested Attorneys, Accredited Representatives, QDE Counselors, "Plaintiffs Sought for Legalization Litigation," May 15, 1987.

30. *AILA Monthly Mailing*, July-August, 1987, p. 1019.

31. "ACLU/NCA's Political Asylum Project Provides Vital Assistance to Salvadorans," *ACLU State Lobbyist*, June, 1985, p. 5.

32. "AILA Marshals Members to Oppose 'Immigration Judge' Removal from Asylum Regulations," *AILA Monthly Mailing*, November, 1987, p. 1176.

33. Arthur C. Helton, "Alien Exclusion," *The Nation*, May 28, 1988, pp. 737-38.

34. Also a member of the National Emergency Civil Liberties Committee, a hard-left group associated with the Communist Party USA, "Professor Boudion," NECLC *The Bill of Rights Journal*, Dec. 1979, p. 13. and "Springing the Haitians," Sept. 1982, p. 39.

35. A member of the National Lawyers Guild" Mobilization Against the Klan," *Immigration Newsletter*, November-December 1977, p. 12.

36. Attorney's fees were awarded in the total amount of $221,000; *Miami Herald*, April 27, 1983. Kurzban got $104,640; Swartz $39,570; Weisz, $12,515;

Barker, $3,480. Schey's award of $61,667 ran into dispute when he proposed donating it to his new center.

37. "Lawyers Frustrate U.S. Immigration Policy," *The Washington Post*, October 19, 1981, p. A1.

38. Arthur C. Helton, "The Haitian Pro Bono Representation Effort," *Immigration Newsletter*, July-August, 1983.

39. Arthur Kinoy, *Rights on Trial* (Cambridge: Harvard University Press, 1983).

40. Ibid., pp. 263-264

41. See, Kinoy, *Rights on Trial*, pp. 226-233; and, William M. Kunstler, *Deep in My Heart* (New York: William Morrow, 1971), pp. 235-245.

42. "Radical Lawyers Adopt New Life-Style," *The New York Times*, August 2, 1971.

43. Nancy Zaroulis and Gerald Sullivan, *Who Spoke Up? American Protest Against the War in Vietnam 1963-1975* (NY: Holt, Rinehart and Winston, 1984), p. 231, 233-235.

44. S. Steven Powell, *Covert Cadre* (Ottawa, IL: Green Hill, 1987), p. 51.

45. Arthur Kinoy, *Conspiracy on Appeal* (New York: Center for Constitutional Rights, 1971).

46. Arthur Kinoy, *Rights on Trial* (Cambridge: Harvard University Press, 1983), pp. 114-115.

47. Arthur Kinoy, "The Role of the Radical Lawyer and Teacher of Law," in *Law Against the People* (New York: Vintage Books, 1971), pp. 285-286.

48. Ibid., p. 290.

49. Arthur Kinoy, "The Crisis in American Legal Education," in *Radical Lawyers: Their Role in the Movement and the Courts* (New York: Avon, 1981), p. 279.

50. Jonathan Black, "Lawyers of the Left: A Crisis of Identity," *Village Voice*, May 1, 1969. For another early press report, see, "Untraditional Law Group Assisting Anti-Establishment Forces," *The New York Times*, August 17, 1969, p. 67.

51. "Foreword," 5 *Columbia Human Rights Law Review* 262 (Fall, 1973).

52. *Congressional Record*, May 14, 1975, p. 14430.

53. *Congressional Record*, June 2, 1975, p. 16574.

54. *Congressional Record*, May 13, 1975, p. 14159.

55. *Congressional Record*, May 14, 1975, p. 14429.

56. "Defense of the Rights of Immigrant Workers: A Class Question," *Political Affairs: Theoretical Journal of the Communist Party, USA*, December 1979, p. 3.

57. Arizona farmworkers form new union, *Daily World,* June 3, 1980.

58. "Special Report: Reversing the Migrant Trek," Ford Foundation *Letter*, December 1, 1985, p. 3.

59. "Harvest of Dignity," *Denver Post Magazine*, May 6, 1984, p. 21.

60. Guadalupe L. Sanchez and Jesus Romo, *Organizing Mexican Undocumented Farm Workers on Both Sides of the Border*, Program in U.S.-Mexican Studies, University of California, San Diego, Working Papers in U.S.-Mexican Studies, No. 27, 1981. Also, see Gary Delgado, "Organizing Undocumented Workers," *Social Policy*, Spring 1983, pp. 26-29.

61. James D. Cockcroft, *Outlaws in the Promised Land: Mexican Immigrant Workers and America's Future* (New York: Grove Press, 1986), p. 195.

62. Ibid., p. 204.

63. "International Conference Passes Bill of Rights for Undocumented," National Lawyers Guild National Immigration Project *Immigration Newsletter*, May-June, 1980.

64. Ibid, pp. 293-324 (Cora Weiss), p. 11 (Peter Weiss).

65. S. Steven Powell, *Covert Cadre* (Ottawa, IL: Green Hill, 1987), pp. 15, 369, 407 (Samuel Rubin Foundation).

CHAPTER TEN: ALIENS, THE ALIENATED, AND "THE ULTIMATE DOMINO"

1. James D. Cockcroft, *Outlaws in the Promised Land* (NY: Grove Press, 1986), p. 240.

2. Nathan Glazer, *The Social Basis of American Communism* (New York: Harcourt, Brace & World, 1961), p. 38.

3. Ibid., p. 62.

4. Paul Buhle, *Marxism in the U.S.A.: From 1870 to the Present Day* (London: Verso, 1987), p. 129.

5. Jeane J. Kirkpatrick, "The American '80s, Disaster or Triumph?," *Commentary*, September, 1990. p. 14.

6. Sean Piccoli, "No Fall of Marxism in the Ivory Tower," *Insight on the News*, October 8, 1990, p. 46.

7. Daniel Singer, "The New Holy Alliance," *The Nation*, November 5, 1990, p. 522.

8. Frank J. Donner, *The Age of Surveillance: The Aims and Methods of America's Political Intelligence System* (New York: Vintage Books, 1981), p. 414.

9. Ibid., p. 119.

10. "Basic Facts on Agricultural Workers," *Political Affairs: Theoretical Journal of the Communist Party USA*, March, 1981, pp. 32-33.

11. *Political Affairs*, July-August, 1983.

12. Rosalio Munoz, "The Simpson-Rodino Law: An Assault on the Working Class," *Political Affairs*, June 1987, p. 12.

13. Scott McConnell, "Resurrecting the New Left," *Commentary*, October, 1987, p. 38.

14. Paul Buhle, "Reflections on American Radicalism, Past and Future," *Against the Current*, September-October, 1987, pp. 16-17.

15. Paul Hollander, *Political Pilgrims: Travels of Western Intellectuals to the Soviet Union, China and Cuba* (New York: Harper and Row, 1981), p. 35.

16. Peter Collier and David Horowitz, "Another 'Low, Dishonest Decade' on the Left," *Commentary*, January, 1987, p. 24.

17. Joel Bernstein, producer, "Underground Railroad," Sixty Minutes, CBS Television Network, broadcast December 12, 1982.

18. "Defending Political Refugees," National Lawyers Guild National Immigration Project *Immigration Newsletter*, August, 1975.

19. The information in this section comes from: National Lawyers Guild Central America Task Force in conjunction with the Center for Constitutional Rights, *The Illegality of U.S. Intervention: Central America and Caribbean Litigation* (New York: National Lawyers Guild, 1984), quotation from p. 4.

20. "Hispanics: Challenges and Opportunities, A working paper from the Ford Foundation," June, 1984, pp. 56-57.

21. "Citizenship for Hispanics," Ford Foundation *Letter*, April 1, 1985, p. 5.

22. *Ford Foundation Annual Report*, 1983, 1984, 1985, 1986. 1987, 1988, 1989.

23. "Hispanics say their votes to count," *The Atlanta Journal and Constitution*, October 30, 1983; "Minorities Being Pressed to Play Mainstream Politics: Hispanic Leaders Massing Forces for the Democrats," *The Washington Post*, April 4, 1983.

24. Thomas Weyr, *Hispanic U.S.A.* (New York: Harper and Row, 1988), p. 128.

25. Ibid., p. 59.

26. "A Changing Black Electorate," Ford Foundation *Letter*, April, 1987, p. 2.

27. American Council for Nationalities Service: *Ford Foundation Annual Report: 1986*, p. 15, $550,000; *Ford Foundation Annual Report: 1984*, p. 65, $450,-000; *Ford Foundation Annual Report: 1983*, pp. 61-62, $227,000.

28. Merged with the American Council for Nationalities Service. See *Ford Foundation Annual Report: 1986*, pp. 68-69.

29. *Ford Foundation Annual Report: 1986*, pp. 36, 46.

30. Robert Rubin, "The Empowerment of the Refugee Community," *World Refugee Survey: 1986 in Review,* U.S. Committee for Refugees.

31. Sheila D. Collins, *The Rainbow Challenge: The Jackson Campaign and the Future of U.S. Politics* (New York: Monthly Review, 1986), pp. 107, 116.

32. "Chicano Leaders for Jackson," New York *Daily World*, January 11, 1984.

33. "Guild gathering marks 50 years of fighting," *Guardian* (New York), June 10, 1987, p. 9.

34. Los Angeles *Weekly*, April 1-7, 1988, p. 22.

35. "Several L.A. Religious Leaders Pull Out of King Rally," *The Los Angeles Times*, April 8, 1988.

36. Letters, *Guardian,* (New York), July 20, 1988, pp. 22-23, and "Elections 1988." *Unity,* June 20, 1988, p. 4.

37. "The DNC, the November Elections, and Beyond," *Unity*, August 8, 1988, p. 12.

38. "The Balance Sheet After The Democratic Convention," *Frontline*, August 1, 1988, p. 15.

39. "What was won," *Unity*, August 8, 1988, p. 5.

40. Cockcroft, p. 240.

41. Ibid, p. 243.

42. Ibid, p. 246.

43. Aaron Wildavsky and Carolyn Webber, *A History of Taxation and Expenditure in the Western World* (NY: Simon and Schuster, 1986), pp. 561-562.

44. Quoted in "Civil Rights Movement?" *Border Watch*, Oct. 1992.

45. "Alien Voting Proposed for Washington D.C.," *Border Watch*, June 1992.

46. Estevan Flores, *Post-Bracero Undocumented Mexican Immigration to the United States and Political Recomposition*, University of Texas at Austin, 1982, pp. 190, 192 (unambiguous in full context).

47. Jack Anderson, "Soviet bloc uses Mexico as listening post," *The Oregonian*, April 1, 1988.

48. *Soviet Covert Action* (Hearings before the Subcommittee on Oversight of the Permanent Select Committee on Intelligence, U.S. House of Representatives, Ninety-Sixth Congress, Second Session, February 6, 19, 1980), p. 81.

49. "Union Fund Formed to Support Undocumented Mexican Workers," American Friends Service Committee, Sobre Asuntos Migratorios y Fronterizos (English Version), *Boletin: No. 17*, May-June, 1981, p.24.

50. Cockcroft, p. 217.

51. Lester D. Langley, *MexAmerica: Two Countries, One Future* (NY; Crown Publishers, 1988), p. 207.

52. Ibid, pp. 275-76.

53. Antonio Rodriguez, "Latinos Snub Jackson—Is it Racism?," *Los Angeles Times*, July 15, 1988.

54. "Mexico Looks for Friends Among Family," *The Wall Street Journal*, Jan. 4, 1988.

55. Samuel Francis, "Immigration Pressures," *The Washington Times*, May 12, 1992, p. F1.

56. "Latino Activists: Many Immigrants Among L.A. Looters," *Border Watch*, July 1992, p. 1.

57. "Youth Gangs," *CQ Researcher*, October 11, 1991.

58. "Hispanic Extremists Aim for Power" *Border Watch*, October 1992, p. 2.

59. "Mexican-American Group Seeks Power" *Border Watch*, July 1992, p. 4.

60. Mike Davis "In L.A., Burning All Illusions," *The Nation*, June 1, 1992, pp. 744-745.

61. Francis, p. F4.

62. Debbie Nathan, "Mexico Watches the War," *The Progressive,* March 1991, p. 13.

APPENDIX ONE
PROFILE OF A FORD FOUNDATION TRUSTEE

1. Peter Collier and David Horowitz, *The Fords: an American Epic* (New York, Simon & Schuster, 1987), p. 397.

2. *Who's Who in America* (Wilmette: MacMillan, 1986), 44th edition, 1986-1987, Vol. 2, page 2277.

3. Id.

APPENDIX THREE
THE ANTI-AMERICAN WORLDVIEW

1. National Lawyers Guild Central America Task Force in conjunction with the Center for Constitutional Rights, *The Illegality of U.S. Intervention: Central America and Caribbean Litigation* (New York: National Lawyers Guild, 1984), p. 15.

2. Ford grant: *Ford Foundation Annual Report: 1985*, p. 41.

3. "CARDF Conference on Refugee Defense Work," *HRI Reporter*, May-August, 1985, p. 568.

4. John Barron, *KGB Today* (New York: Berkley Books, 1985), p. 237; first published 1983 by Reader's Digest Books. Susan Sontag, much to the ire of Aryeh Neier of Ford's "Helsinki Watch," said one could learn more about Soviet bloc human rights abuses from the *Reader's Digest* than from the New York intelligentsia: "Communism and the Left," *The Nation*, February 27, 1982, p. 231.

5. Paul Hollander, *Political Pilgrims: Travels of Western Intellectuals to the Soviet Union, China and Cuba* (New York: Harper Colophon, 1981), pp. 228, 475. In 1971, the City University Teachers Union assailed a course taught in conjunction with the Center for Cuban studies, because the Center excluded from the course former Cuban citizens.

6. *Ford Foundation Annual Report: 1985*, p. 67.

7. *Ford Foundation Annual Report: 1983*, p. 60.

8. The Ford Foundation contributed $256,000 to link the University of Havana with Johns Hopkins University's school in Washington, D.C., in the "first such exchange since the 1959 Cuban revolution," *Ford Foundation Annual Report: 1984*, pp. 65-71. "Defector bares Cuban spy recruiting," *The Washington Times*, September 24, 1987.

9. "Papers from the Second Seminar on U.S. Minority Communities, Held in Havana, Cuba," *Line of March: A Marxist- Leninist Journal of Rectification*, #18, Fall, 1985. "Featuring Seminar Proceedings on U.S. Minorities Held in Havana, Cuba," *The Black Scholar*, January-February, 1985.

10. Armando Hart-Davalos, "Keynote Address: The People's Desire to Have Freedom Does Not Recognize Boundaries," *The Black Scholar*, January-February, 1985. p. 6.

11. "Racism and the Bully Pulpit," *The Black Scholar*, January- February, 1985, inside front cover.

12. Armando Hart-Davalos, "Keynote Address: The People's Desire to Have Freedom Does Not Recognize Boundaries," *The Black Scholar*, January-February, 1985. p. 8.

13. "Final Declaration by participants in the Second Seminar on U.S. minority communities," *Line of March: A Marxist-Leninist Journal of Rectification*, #18, Fall, 1985. Id., *The Black Scholar*, January-February, 1985.

14. Armando Hart-Davalos, "Keynote Address: The People's Desire to Have Freedom Does Not Recognize Boundaries," *The Black Scholar*, January-February, 1985. p. 6.

15. "Authors and Papers Presented at Seminar II," *The Black Scholar,* January-February, 1985. pp. 47-48.

16. *Ford Foundation Annual Report: 1984*, p. 65, 66-68.

17. *Ford Foundation Annual Report: 1984*, pp. 71-72.

18. *Ford Foundation Annual Report: 1985*, p. 50.

19. *Ford Foundation Annual Report: 1985*, pp. 49-50.

20. "LULAC: Senator 'Lies' About Alien Threat; Leaders demand apology 'owed to all Hispanics,' " *San Antonio News*, June 6, 1983.